The Place of Ethics in Science Education

Also Available from Bloomsbury

Mastering Primary Science, Amanda McCrory and Kenna Worthington
Enhancing Learning with Effective Practical Science 11–16,
   edited by Ian Abrahams and Michael J. Reiss
MasterClass in Science Education, Keith S. Taber
Sustainability Education, Stephen Scoffham and Steve Rawlinson
Reflective Teaching in Primary Schools, 6th edition, Andrew Pollard and
   Dominic Wyse with Ayshea Craig, Caroline Daly, Sarah Seleznyov,
   Sinead Harmey, Louise Hayward, Steve Higgins and Amanda McCrory
Reflective Teaching in Secondary Schools, 6th edition, Andrew Pollard
   and Caroline Daly with Katharine Burn, Steve Higgins, Aileen Kennedy,
   Margaret Mulholland, Jo Fraser-Pearce, Mary Richardson, Dominic Wyse
   and John Yandell

The Place of Ethics in Science Education

Implications for Practice

Amanda McCrory and Michael J. Reiss

BLOOMSBURY ACADEMIC
LONDON • NEW YORK • OXFORD • NEW DELHI • SYDNEY

BLOOMSBURY ACADEMIC
Bloomsbury Publishing Plc
50 Bedford Square, London, WC1B 3DP, UK
1385 Broadway, New York, NY 10018, USA
29 Earlsfort Terrace, Dublin 2, Ireland

BLOOMSBURY, BLOOMSBURY ACADEMIC and the Diana logo
are trademarks of Bloomsbury Publishing Plc

First published in Great Britain 2023

Copyright © Amanda McCrory and Michael J. Reiss, 2023

Amanda McCrory and Michael J. Reiss have asserted their right under the Copyright, Designs and Patents Act, 1988, to be identified as Authors of this work.

Cover design by Jade Barnett
Cover photo by USGS/Unsplash

All rights reserved. No part of this publication may be reproduced or transmitted in any form or by any means, electronic or mechanical, including photocopying, recording, or any information storage or retrieval system, without prior permission in writing from the publishers.

Bloomsbury Publishing Plc does not have any control over, or responsibility for, any third-party websites referred to or in this book. All internet addresses given in this book were correct at the time of going to press. The author and publisher regret any inconvenience caused if addresses have changed or sites have ceased to exist, but can accept no responsibility for any such changes.

A catalogue record for this book is available from the British Library.

A catalog record for this book is available from the Library of Congress.

ISBN: HB: 978-1-3502-5513-5
       PB: 978-1-3502-5514-2
       ePDF: 978-1-3502-5515-9
       eBook: 978-1-3502-5516-6

Typeset by Integra Software Services Pvt. Ltd.

To find out more about our authors and books visit www.bloomsbury.com and sign up for our newsletters.

To Helena Lax and Ginny Page

Contents

List of figures　　viii
List of tables　　x
Preface　　xi
Foreword, *Troy D. Sadler*　　xii

1　Introduction　　1
2　What is science?　　9
3　What is ethics?　　25
4　What is science education?　　41
5　What is ethics education?　　57
6　Should ethics be considered where science is taught?　　71
7　Ethics in school science – its role in socio-scientific issues　　85
8　Ethics in school science – the role of argumentation　　107
9　Ethics and informal science education　　127
10　Conclusion: The only way is ethics!　　149

References　　156
Index　　176

Figures

1.1 An oil palm plantation; such plantations threaten biodiversity. Including material about the ethics of crop production can help in teaching about plant growth   2

2.1 A painting from some 17,000 years ago in El Pindal, Spain. Does this reveal scientific thought?   11

2.2 The Family Resemblance Wheel of Erduran and Dagher (2014). Science is seen as a cognitive-epistemic system that sits within a social-institutional system   16

4.1 Girls carrying water in India   48

4.2 Indicators of progression in ethical reasoning in science   55

6.1 DeWitt Clinton Park School Garden, New York, 1904   77

6.2 Dolly – the first mammal to be cloned   82

7.1 An image of a pug   94

7.2 PARRISE model depicting the relationship between civic involvement in scientific research and innovation through activities in schools. This process is called Socio-Scientific Inquiry Based Learning (SSIBL)   98

8.1 One child's response to a puppet's questions about whether or not she should cheat in a maths exam   117

8.2 A child's concept map linking the words 'cell', 'chromosomes', 'DNA', 'genes' and 'nucleus'   120

8.3 A child's concept map identifying the consequences of the Chernobyl disaster	121
9.1 The 'Mammals with pouches' cases in the Mammals Gallery at the Natural History Museum, London	129
9.2 An innocuous pair of sugar tongs from about 1775 – but intimately connected to the slave trade	130
9.3 The appalling conditions in which slaves were transported across the Atlantic in the eighteenth and nineteenth centuries led to massive loss of life	131
9.4 The Spiral of Discovery (Brunton and Thornton, 2010)	133
9.5 Polar bear at a zoo sometime between 1909 and 1932	138
9.6 A protest against Covid-19 vaccines, in Islington, London, on 18 September 2021	146

Tables

4.1 Different visions for science education and their implications for school science — 44

7.1 Framework for the determination of MTPT when reasoning about socio-scientific issues in the primary school — 104

8.1 Children's responses to the puppet and reasons for their thinking — 118

9.1 Using the Spiral of Discovery. Based on Brunton and Thornton (2010) — 134

9.2 Normative terms that can be used to elicit ethical thinking with younger children when engaging with Forest School. Based on Kenyon et al. (2019) — 134

Preface

Science education, particularly school science education, has long had an uneasy relationship with ethics, being unsure whether to embrace ethics or leave it to others. In this book we begin by asking the fundamental question, 'Should ethics be taught in science?', and argue that while the methods of science and of ethics are very different, ethics plays a key role in how science is undertaken and used. Accordingly, it has a central place in science education, whether we are talking of school science education, for students of all ages, or the informal science education that takes place in through the internet, books, magazines, TV and radio or in places such as science museums, botanic gardens and zoos. Our book is targeted at all science educators, in schools and elsewhere. We therefore presume a basic knowledge of science – that which one would expect a teacher of science in a primary or elementary school to have – but we make no assumption that the reader has any knowledge of ethics beyond the background understandings of morality that virtually all of us have. Our hope is that this book will enable all readers to be much clearer as to the place that ethics has in science education. It provides a rich array of examples as to how science education, both in school and out of school, and for all ages, can be enhanced through including teaching about ethics and examines the potential of ethics in science to enhance learners' ability to develop their skills of argumentation and to understand socio-scientific issues more richly.

Foreword

Troy D. Sadler, University of North Carolina at Chapel Hill

As a college student at the University of Miami, I studied biology and became fascinated by the processes of life. I had always liked science and considered myself to be a *science person*, but it was not until I had opportunities to deeply explore science ideas and principles at the university level that I really fell in love with biology. I was amazed by the intricacies of biological processes and how scientists and their teams came to understand and explain these processes. From basic cellular processes like respiration to events that unfold over a geological time scale like the evolution of flowering plants, I was fascinated.

During my junior year at the university, I took a work-study position in a population genetics lab. For about three months, I spent ten hours a week doing little more than washing lab dishes. The lab used *Daphnia*, commonly referred to as water fleas, as a model organism for studying micro-evolutionary processes, and that meant keeping tens of thousands of tiny aquatic critters swimming happily in hundreds of beakers. It also meant growing a special algal blend that the *Daphnia* found tasty and harvesting this blend on a near daily basis. Studying these organisms resulted in a profusion of dirty lab glassware, and as the lab's work-study student, it was my job to churn through the piles of dirty beakers, graduated cylinders, petri dishes and glass jars. I remember distinctly one Saturday morning being the only person working in the lab, washing beakers no doubt, when the Principal Investigator, Dr Spitze, came in and asked me to turn off the faucet and accompany him to the lab space where molecular work was done. Dr Spitze spent the next hour or so showing me how to set up and run electrophoresis gels as a means of detecting different forms of enzymes, also known as allozymes, that could be used strategically to determine different clonal lines of the *Daphnia*. This is a relatively simple procedure, but it can be a really useful tool to identify specific *Daphnia* lines in a whole range of genetic and micro-selection experiments. For me, I was amazed and excited – I was finally doing real science. Looking back at this experience now, there was not anything particularly innovative about running electrophoresis gels, but it marked a transition for me and became a point when I transitioned from a student with a biology major to someone who would actively pursue a science career. I continued working in the lab and took on additional responsibilities, and after about two years I headed off to another university to begin a doctoral programme in molecular biology.

My tenure in the molecular biology Ph.D. programme did not last long. I was still enamoured with biology and liked the idea of doing research, but I did not enjoy my time in the programme and immediately started asking myself questions about whether lab research was the right direction for me. I had a compelling sense that something was missing for me. Yes, I was a science person, but I was not satisfied just doing science myself. I felt that I should be doing more than just training to be a scientist and found myself thinking about what else I could do with science.

Through a fortuitous series of events, I became aware of an immediate opening for a middle school science teacher in my hometown. I had never really thought about becoming a teacher; had not taken any education courses during my undergraduate career and had no understanding of the challenges that face teachers on a daily basis. But I certainly recognized several of my own teachers as important mentors and saw the work they did as significant and impactful. I wondered about whether teaching science might address the feelings that I had about something missing for me as I worked in the doctoral programme. With the benefit of ignorance (i.e. not knowing how challenging teaching actually is) and the fact that I was young and without much in the way of significant life responsibilities, I accepted an offer to teach middle school science. The school was a small private school that had just opened. The school leaders were desperate for teachers willing to work for low pay and were not concerned about experience or certification, so I was a perfect fit. Looking back, it is easy to see that this situation was rife with potential problems, but in the moment, it seemed like a good opportunity. I quit graduate school, loaded everything I owned in my car and headed back to my hometown to try out a new career pathway as a science teacher.

At some point during my road trip to get to my new job, I stopped off at a fast-food place to grab a bite to eat. The dining area was packed, but I found one of the few open tables and started to eat my meal. Within a few minutes, a man with a tray of food turned the corner into the dining area clearly looking for a spot to sit, and by this time every table was occupied. I watched as the man asked a guy, who was sitting alone with an open spot at his table, if he could sit down and share the table. The seated guy responded aggressively, denied the request and cursed at the man just looking for a spot to eat his lunch. The episode was shocking and uncomfortable – I felt bad for the man who just received this verbal assault and angry with the other guy so unwilling to be kind. But this was not just an episode of unkindness. In the moment, it felt obvious that racism was a significant driver – I should note that this transpired in the Southeastern United States where race and racism have been a part of the fabric of the region since Europeans settled there (and took the land from Native Americans and enslaved Africans to provide labour). The man seeking a seat was Black; the belligerent guy who denied the simple request was White, and most of us watching this all take place were also White. The racial dynamics of this moment in which a white man treated a Black man terribly while a White audience sat by and observed were palpable. I caught the attention of the man, who was standing with his tray of food, and motioned for him to join me at my table. It was a small table with fixed chairs secured to the ground, but one of them was unoccupied, and it was easy for me to make room for someone else. He came over and joined me at the table. We introduced ourselves and chatted, and when we had finished eating headed our separate ways.

I left that episode feeling a wide range of emotions and asking myself many questions. I felt good about inviting the man to sit with me but questioned whether I had done enough in response to the situation. Should I have confronted the guy who seemed driven by hate? Should I have done more to help the man who took the brunt of this hate? The event also prompted thinking and questioning at a grander scale. Why is racism such a prevalent force in our society? What can individuals like myself do, not just in responding in the moment to acts of hate, but in more proactive ways in working towards a more just society? I thought a lot about the role of education and how teachers might be part of solutions. Given my background in science and the fact that I was on my way to start a science teaching job, I also considered how science education specifically might be part of the solution. It was in the aftermath of this event and opportunities to reflect on it and how what I had just participated in represented broader problems in our society that I decided becoming a science teacher created an opportunity for me to be a part of the solution to inequity and injustice. At the same time, I realized that I could not achieve these broader aims if teaching science just meant helping students learn canonical facts. A science education that might help to make the world a better place and address injustice would be one that necessarily created spaces for confronting and discussing ethical issues.

When the authors of this text requested that I prepare a foreword for a book on science and ethics, I was immediately interested, and at the same time, not quite sure what I would write. Later, as I had the opportunity to read draft chapters of the book, I started thinking about my own path to teaching and some of the events that helped to shape me into the educator that I am. I was inspired to consider my own responses to questions that frame several of these chapters:

- What is science?
- What is ethics?
- What is science education?
- What is ethics education?
- Should ethics be considered where science is taught?

Consideration of my responses took me back to my days in the *Daphnia* lab, which became my personal foundation for defining science. They took me back to an undergraduate course in bioethics which served as my first formal introduction to ethics, and later to experiences that I had in my doctoral programme taking classes in the philosophy department with titles such as the philosophy of science and moral philosophy. They also reminded me of the day I described in the fast-food restaurant where I came face-to-face with racism; a day that became pivotal in helping me to determine the kind of education and science education that I wanted to be a part of.

About a year after my experience sharing a table in the fast-food place, I confronted the first of several critiques to my ideas about the necessary connections between science teaching and ethics. I spent a year teaching at the private middle school and by the end of the school year had decided that (1) I really liked teaching and could make a career of it and (2) that I needed to learn about how to be a better teacher. I enrolled in a master's degree programme for teacher preparation that would allow me to earn a teaching certificate which was necessary for most teaching positions in the state. One of the first classes that I took was a science teaching methods course, and a central element of the course was a series of micro-teaching assignments. As a part of these assignments, we planned science lessons designed for about 15 minutes and taught them to our peers. For my first micro-teaching lesson, I taught about the genetics associated with different fur colour in black bears and drew connections to the limited sets of genes that contribute to different levels of pigmentation in human skin. I was trying use the lesson as a means of building a scientific argument against racism. Following my lesson, the methods instructor initiated a conversation with the class about what she framed as appropriate boundaries for science teaching. She drew on several of the points raised in Chapter 6 of this book for why ethics should not be included in science teaching. I was fairly disappointed in the response but not convinced that her perspective was the only way to think about the potential for science and ethics in education spaces.

A few years later, I was teaching high school biology and trying to figure out how to balance school-level expectations for what should be taught, state and national content standards, and my own commitments to raising awareness of injustices and trying to support students' ethical reasoning. I was teaching in the Tampa, FL, area and went over to the closest university, which happened to be the University of South Florida, to look into taking a class. I was not looking to get involved in another graduate programme, but I wanted to learn something new and was seeking an intellectual challenge. I ended up meeting Dana Zeidler that day, and he was getting ready to teach a course titled *Moral and Ethical Issues in Science and Science Education* in the next semester. I took the course and thoroughly enjoyed the experience. As a result of taking it, I started down a path towards a PhD in science education. In contrast to my methods instructor who eschewed the intersections of science and ethics, Zeidler highlighted these connections as some of the most important considerations for science educators. In the years that followed while I was still a graduate student and beyond, Dana Zeidler and I have collaborated on a wide range of scholarship that has helped to establish the socio-scientific issues approach to science teaching. Central to this approach is engaging learners in ethical reasoning about societal problems that involve science. Socio-scientific issues represent one aspect of the broader argument being made in this book by McCrory and Reiss to link ethics and science in science education.

It has been a long time since I had my first authentic experiences with science in the *Daphnia* lab, my first attempts at teaching science, and the afternoon which stood as a pivotal moment in my recognition of the ongoing racism within my community. All of these experiences have helped to shape my orientations as a teacher, a scholar and as someone who still considers himself a *science person*. The topics that McCrory and Reiss tackle in this volume and the approach they take certainly resonate with me and the orientations I hold. By the time I reached the concluding chapter in the book, I too was ready to declare that 'The only ways is ethics!' Of course, the authors did not have to go far in convincing me of this conclusion, but they present compelling arguments and a well-reasoned case to get to this point. They do a nice job of drawing on theory and empirical research from multiple fields to weave an interesting narrative that leads to a very critical message for science educators. For science educators like myself, who are already committed to deliberately incorporating ethics in science learning opportunities, the book provides an interesting and engaging support for ideas that help to substantiate why we teach in the first place. For others who may be more sceptical of blurring the boundaries between science and ethics, I think this book will offer a compelling read with the potential to challenge some assumptions that may underlie this stance.

Introduction

Should ethics be taught in science?

How much of a place should there be for ethics in science education? There are a range of opinions. At one pole sit those who think that the function of science education, perhaps especially school science education, is to introduce learners to core scientific knowledge and scientific practices. The most, therefore, that ethics might be expected to do is to serve to help motivate learners. For example, if teaching in a secondary school physics lesson about the generation of electricity, one might include a little bit about the ethical implications of such generation from renewable as opposed to non-renewable resources.

At the other pole are those who think that while a central function of science education is indeed to introduce learners to core scientific knowledge and scientific practices, these are frequently intertwined with ethical questions – as the electricity generation example indicates. Furthermore, it is only a minority of school students who are interested in science for its own sake; most learners want to see the relevance of what they are learning, and they are more likely to find science interesting if it is discussed in context, with ethical issues being explored.

Take, for example, a standard topic like plant growth. Some students find it fascinating, at primary level, to learn about how water, light and warmth are needed for a plant to grow, with secondary students also learning about the need for chlorophyll and carbon dioxide. Other students find it easier to learn about plant growth if it is set in a context, such as the work of crop breeders to maximize crop yields.

But this immediately begins to raise all sorts of ethical issues. Some 38 per cent of the world's land surface is used for food production – though only about one-third of this is used for growing for crops, with the other two-thirds being used for grazing livestock (Food and Agriculture Organization of the United Nations, 2021). One ethical issue is whether we humans have the right to commandeer so much of the Earth's surface for our food. The resultant habitat loss is one of the major factors driving the extinction of wild species. It is estimated that one species goes extinct about every 20 minutes – a rate some 1,000 times or more higher than the 'background' rate – i.e. the rate at which species would naturally go extinct without humans (Turvey & Creese, 2019; World Wide Fund for Nature, 2020).

Students of any age can think, learn and talk about the tension between growing crops for human ends and preserving natural habitats for the benefit of wildlife. Figure 1.1 shows a commercial palm oil crop. Oil palm (*Elaeis guineensis*) is the most important vegetable oil crop in the world, with an annual production of around 75 million metric tonnes (Wageningen University, 2020), so that on average, each of us consumes about 8 kg of palm oil a year. Oil palm is a perennial plant, and palm oil is derived from its fruit. The problem is that palm oil plantations result in major deforestation. It is a tropical crop with the largest producers being Indonesia, Malaysia, Thailand and Nigeria, so the deforestation occurs in species-rich tropical regions.

This isn't the place for a major analysis of the ethical issues raised by crops but to give one further example – should we grow genetically modified crops? Advocates say that such crops can reduce pesticide loss and increase harvests. Those opposed to them maintain that such crops are unnatural and risk damaging the environment or even human health. Some of these disagreements are about science, some about ethics.

Figure 1.1 An oil palm plantation; such plantations threaten biodiversity. Including material about the ethics of crop production can help in teaching about plant growth.
Source: By T. R. Shankar Raman – Own work, CC BY-SA 4.0, https://commons.wikimedia.org/w/index.php?curid=53021219.

Building on the work of others

This book is intended to help teachers of science, often in schools for 5- to 18-year-olds, but also those working with younger children and with those in the informal sector. We see our work as building on the work of others. Levinson and Reiss (2003) edited a book titled *Key Issues in Bioethics: A Guide for Teachers*. However, as its title suggests, this restricted itself to ethical issues in biology; by now it is also somewhat dated. Jones et al. (2010) edited a book titled *Ethics in the Science and Technology Classroom*. This book was the outcome of a funded research project, so has a specific focus. Saxena (2019) authored *Ethics in Science: Pedagogic Issues and Concerns*. This book convincingly argues that high-quality, engaging and effective science teaching, both at school and at undergraduate level, should incorporate ethics and values. Of the various existing books, this is the one closest to ours in that the author is interested in the full school age range and undergraduate teaching too.

Also worth mentioning are three books which, while not intended for teachers, all valuably contribute to the issue of science and ethics. Bazzul (2016) is the author of *Ethics and Science Education: How Subjectivity Matters*. This is a very fine academic book; it examines how biology texts work to constitute subjectivities related to neoliberalism and global capitalism, sex/gender and sexuality, and ethics. Wilmott and Macip (2016) co-authored *Where Science and Ethics Meet: Dilemmas at the Frontiers of Medicine and Biology*. As the title indicates, this restricts itself to biology but its strengths include being particularly readable and impressively up-to-date. Finally, there is the second edition of the excellent textbook written by Bryant and La Velle: *Introduction to Bioethics*, intended for undergraduates in biology and medicine.

Organization of this book

One of us, Amanda McCrory, has expertise in early years and primary education; the other of us, Michael Reiss, has expertise in secondary and informal education. Both of us taught in schools and now work in higher education with specialisms in science education, having spent many years in initial teacher education (from early years through to secondary). While we believe that the inclusion of ethics within science education can enhance the teaching of science, we do not minimize the demands that this places on teachers and communicators of science. Indeed, what we set out to do in this book is to explore the arguments for and against including ethics in the teaching of science, whilst also helping anyone, whether in a formal or informal setting, who wants to include ethics in their science teaching or communication of science.

Our working assumption is that many readers will be hesitant (at least before they finish reading the book!) about the inclusion of ethics in science education. This might be for a range of possible reasons – including concerns that such teaching doesn't fit within science, would mean less time for the teaching and communication of 'real' science, requires specialist expertise in moral philosophy that few science educators possess and risks students doing less well in terminal science assessments. Our view is that none of these concerns is to be lightly dismissed; all are considered carefully in subsequent chapters. At the same time, we argue that teaching about ethics in science education is for learners of all ages and can help science education and science communication to be responsive to current issues which affect us all – whether those are to do with climate change, our use of animals, vaccine safety, Covid-19 or whatever.

In Chapter 2 we ask, 'What is science?' All cultures engage in science and have done so as far back in time as we know; indeed, many scientific 'discoveries' celebrated as being Western were in fact known about elsewhere long before. Science can be characterized as open-minded, universalist, disinterested and communal. The knowledge it produces should be objective. The nature of science (NOS) describes the essence ('nature') of science – what science is all about. Something of a consensus position about NOS exists among science educators, though some science educators argue that it has shortcomings. The term 'pseudoscience' is used by those who align themselves with conventional science to dismiss the worth of work in areas that claim to be scientific but are adjudged not to be. However, philosophers have long argued that it is not easy to demarcate clearly between science and pseudoscience. The advent of the internet and social media has had major consequences for people's understanding of science and involvement in it, and citizen science has been much aided by it.

In Chapter 3 we ask, 'what is ethics?' We begin by pointing out that ethics is a branch of philosophy concerned with what ought to be done; specifically, it is concerned with what is morally right or wrong in a given situation. We consider how the words 'ethics', 'morality' and 'values' are often used interchangeably but can be distinguished. Understanding the differences between them can be useful for understanding the different types of arguments that can be made for or against certain actions. We then go on to discuss whether morality is culturally specific or universal, drawing on the ideas of moral philosophers, who have long examined this question, and more modern thinkers coming from disciplines such as anthropology. The major ethical frameworks of deontology, utilitarianism and virtue ethics are then discussed before we go on to discuss the relationship between them and the role that religion might play in ethics. Theories of justice and oppression as well as the frameworks they provide to consider ethics and behaviour are then highlighted. We also consider inequality as an ethical issue in its own right before moving on to consider intergenerational, environmental and feminist ethics as well as animal rights.

Having asked, 'What is science?' and 'What is ethics?', in Chapter 4 we ask, 'What is science education?' The answer to the question depends on whether one sees science education as a subset of science or as a subset of education. A variety of aims of science education have been proposed (Rudolph, 2023), but they reflect three overarching visions: Vision I focuses on science (understood narrowly) and is principally intended to produce future scientists; Vision II is intended for all students and has a broader focus on scientific literacy; Vision III is a humanized science education that aims at sociopolitical action. These visions for science education can be related to more general arguments about education, including whether it is about providing access to powerful knowledge or enabling human flourishing. Practical work is generally seen as a key aspect of science education, though there are concerns as to how effective it is. There is a place for ethics in the discussion that should accompany practical work, perhaps especially when the practical work is more investigative and is set in context. There needs to be a good match between curriculum, pedagogy and assessment. Comparing the assessment of ethics in school science with its assessment in other subjects suggests ways in which ethics could be assessed better in school science. Assessment of students' understanding of ethics is unlikely to be best achieved when questions are worth only a very small number of marks; students need to be given time and space to show what they know and to develop an ethical argument. Furthermore, we should expect older learners to have progressed in their ethical reasoning in science.

In Chapter 5 we consider what ethics education is. All cultures communicate ethical standards and reinforce the practice of good behaviours to children as they grow up; this is part of socialization. Although cultures vary in the specific values and behaviours that they regard as desirable, all societies have a system of rules concerning the rightness and wrongness of certain behaviours. Ethics education can have a range of aims. In particular, it might be intended to enable learners to improve their understanding, to become more sensitive to ethical issues or to become better people. We argue that each of these has its place in science education. In order for students to become critical consumers of scientific information and be able to identify unethical practices, they need to understand that ethics is an integral part of science and that scientists have a responsibility to be guided by what is right. We then consider moral development and education in schools and elsewhere. We do so via an historical and theoretical lens, discussing the cognitive, behavioural and affective components of the development of morality. We discuss the psychoanalytical, social and developmental theories that have been employed to understand moral development and examine the role that feminist and cultural theories have played in the aims of moral development in schools. We conclude by examining the character education movement and the rise of philosophy for children as a pedagogical tool in schools to engage children of all ages with ethical thinking.

Chapter 6 is a key chapter. In it we ask, 'Should ethics be considered where science is taught?' There are a range of arguments for and against teaching ethics in science. Those who argue that ethics should not be considered where science is taught make several points, in particular: that science and ethics belong to very different domains of knowledge and so are best considered separately; that it's asking too much of teachers of science to cope with ethics too; and that the science curriculum is already full without taking on ethics also. Those who take the contrary position argue that the epistemological distance between science and ethics can be overstated, or is not so crucial, and that other objections seem to presume a cadre of specialist teachers who teach only science, which may be the case in some secondary school systems but is rarely the case in primary schools, and doesn't really apply as an objection in the informal sector. We conclude that there is much of value in including ethics within the teaching or communication of science. However, if school teachers of science are to be expected to include ethics in their teaching, those teachers have the right to be given appropriate support in their initial teacher education and continuing professional development and through the classroom materials that they use with their students. There is also much to be said for schools making provision for individual teachers of science who do not want to include ethics in their teaching not to have to. Finally, there are instances where other ways of teaching ethics in science can work well – for example, co-teaching between subject specialists, hosting visitors with particular expertise and taking students on visits.

If we accept that one of the aims of education is to prepare students for the challenges that modern life brings and engage students in learning that interests them, then, in Chapter 7, we consider what socio-scientific issues are and discuss how and why today, more than ever, teachers face the challenge of preparing students to understand and engage effectively with these. These are issues which not only have a significant bearing on students' current and future lives but which research and the media inform us that young people today are increasingly interested in. We note that youth activism is on the rise around the globe, as witnessed in 2019 with the co-ordinated protest against inaction on climate change led by the then sixteen-year-old Swedish activist Greta Thunberg, and consider why this might be the case and what this means for schools and the aims of science education. In doing so, we discuss the key role that ethics plays in understanding and negotiating socio-scientific issues and consider how it might be beneficial for students to be taught the skills of ethical thinking and decision-making alongside an understanding of the science involved for them really to be able to engage in a meaningful way with these ever-developing issues in science. We do not claim that every socio-scientific issue should be taught in school science, but instead make suggestions of relevancy and pertinence. In the light of this, we discuss the growing trend in schools to include socio-scientific issues in their curricula, facilitated by a desire by teachers to engage and motivate students in learning about real-life authentic science, enhancing students' scientific literacy, reasoning skills and civic voice.

Chapter 8 focuses on the important role that argumentation (the skill of using evidence to justify or refute scientific claims) plays in everyday science. We highlight how *all* teachers of science need to understand the crucial part that argumentation plays in the advancement of science and why students need to understand this too if they are to act as scientists in school science and develop fundamental scientific process skills. The key role that ethical thinking plays in argumentation is then examined, and we argue that learning about ethics is substantially enhanced by discussion and debate in the science classroom. There has been an increased focus on the importance of classroom discourse, specifically the value of talk in school science lessons, highlighting the merits of taking dialogic approaches in learning science for both teachers and students alike. We do not dismiss the challenges this might present, especially for teachers for whom facilitating classroom discussion might not be integrated into their own pedagogical practice for teaching science. Although research in argumentation has tended to focus on the role of language, we offer case studies which take a more multi-modal approach to teaching these skills as an inclusive way for *all* learners of *all* ages to develop critical scientific literacy and build understanding of fundamental scientific concepts. In early years and primary education, we discuss how this can perhaps more easily take a cross-curricular approach but argue that regardless of student age, incorporating argumentation into school science means that scientific enquiry, ethical thinking and scientific literacy take centre stage rather than serving only as a supporting act. The aim is for teachers of science to extend their pedagogical approaches to teaching ethics in school science more effectively.

People no longer learn most of their science in schools, and the informal sector has grown in importance for science communication. In Chapter 9 we consider how the informal sector might include ethics in their communication of science as opportunities for teaching about ethical aspects of science are often passed over in informal settings. At the same time, there are major inequalities in access to science in informal settings. The informal sector sometimes assumes that addressing inequalities requires attendees to change whereas what may be more important is for institutions to change their offering and mindset. The approaches of 'science capital' and 'community cultural wealth' have proved helpful in explaining why some individuals and groups have less of a connection with science and why some disadvantaged individuals and groups succeed in developing strong science identities. Addressing ethics in science in informal settings, using the tools we have discussed in this book, can have a number of benefits to learners, including empowering them and encouraging them to learn more about science.

Chapter 10 brings together our concluding thoughts about the place of ethics in science education. We discuss the rationale for writing this book and our desire to enable science educators not only to see the connections between ethics and science but to provide research-informed case studies which empower them to teach ethics and science in both formal and informal settings. We also highlight how we hope to inspire other science educators and researchers to undertake further research in this field, especially given that it is an under-researched area with younger children. We end by asserting that we see the development of moral sensitivity to science issues as the responsibility of all science educators, and we argue that science educators, whatever the age of their learners, do not need to have had prior training in ethics education in order to include ethics in their science education.

Final thoughts

The methods of science and of ethics are very different but ethics plays a key role in how science is undertaken and used. As a result, ethics has a central place in science education, whether we are talking of school science education or informal science education. We have written this book for all science educators, in schools and elsewhere. Our hope is that this book will enable all readers to be much clearer as to the place that ethics has in science education. We provide a rich array of examples as to how science education, both in school and out of school, and for all ages, can be enhanced through including teaching about ethics.

Please feel able to contact either of us – e-mail is probably best. At present our e-mail addresses are a.mccrory@ucl.ac.uk and m.reiss@ucl.ac.uk, but should they change, just look us up on the internet.

What is science?

Lessons from history

In getting a handle on 'What is science?' one approach is to start from the lessons of history. An advantage of such an approach is that it helps counteract the notion that science suddenly appeared out of nowhere in the 'Scientific Revolution' in Western Europe in the seventeenth century. However, using history as a source of information about science already requires some sort of agreement as to what is meant by 'science', just as one would need some sort of agreement as to what is meant by 'art' before being able to decide whether to include prehistoric art – such as the famous paintings that date from tens of thousands of years ago and that have been found in Europe, in Asia, in India, in Africa, in Australia and elsewhere.

We shall have more to write about what is meant by science in the next section in this chapter on 'Lessons from philosophy'. Here it's enough to start by saying that science is all about obtaining knowledge – indeed, the word 'science' comes from the Latin *scientia* which means 'knowledge'. Immediately, we run up against the point that science is not the only route to knowledge. We shall have more to say about this in the final section in this chapter: 'The nature of truth in mathematics and the social sciences.' Here, it is enough to note that science – certainly when we talk of the 'natural sciences', like biology, chemistry, earth science and physics, rather than the 'social sciences', like economics, sociology and parts of psychology – is generally understood to be knowledge gained by empirical studies of the material world, things like the study of agriculture, the weather, the movement of objects, metals and the life cycles of organisms.

Our records of art go back much earlier than our records of science. This is because good evidence for science relies on writing, and writing only developed within the last 6,000 years – possibly independently in Mesopotamia (about 3250 BCE), Egypt (about 3250 BCE), China (about 1250 BCE) and Mesoamerica (about 650 BCE) (Bazerman, 2008; Regulski, 2016). What we find is that in all cultures, science is written about from soon after the birth of writing. Accordingly, the earliest scientific records date from about 3000 BCE and are found in Egypt and Mesopotamia. These concern astronomy and medicine.

The fact that all cultures, from their earliest recorded history, practised science, just as they practised art and no doubt a range of other disciplines, is important for science education. Given the power of Western, industrialized science nowadays, it can be of great value for teachers of science, whatever the age of their learners, to stress that all cultures engage in science and have done so as far back in time as we know. This is inclusive and can help learners feel pride in their own culture.

It is also the case that many Western scientific 'discoveries' were in fact known about elsewhere long before. For example, William Harvey is almost invariably credited in school science textbooks and elsewhere with the discovery of the circulation of the blood in humans (as published in his 1628 *Exercitatio Anatomica de Motu Cordis et Sanguinis in Animalibus*). In fact, the circulation of the blood in humans was known to the Chinese by the second century BCE at the latest, when it is described in *The Yellow Emperor's Manual of Corporeal Medicine* (Reiss, 1993). Two separate circulations of fluids were envisaged: blood, pumped by the heart, flowed through the vascular system; and *qi*, vital energy, was pumped by the lungs to circulate round the body. The thinking behind this dual circulation system was central to the practice of acupuncture.

The pulmonary circulation of the blood was discovered by Ala ad-Din Abu al-Hasan Ali Ibn Abi-Hazm-al-Qarshi, known as Ibn Nafis (1210–88 CE). He wrote many books in medicine, but his most famous one was *Sharah al Tashreeh al Qanoon (Commentary on anatomy of the Canon of Avicenna)*. This book was forgotten until 1924 when an Egyptian physician, Dr Altatawi, discovered the manuscript in the Prussian state Library in Berlin (Akmal et al., 2010). Here we read:

> Blood from the right chamber of the heart to the left chamber does not come through direct pathway.
>
> The interventicular septum does not have visible or invisible pores.
>
> The lungs are composed of parts, one of which is the bronchi, the second the branches of the arteria venosa and the third the branches of the vena arteriosa, all of them connected by loose porous flesh.
>
> Blood from the right chamber of the heart goes to – vena arteriosa (pulmonary artery) – lungs – arteria venosa (pulmonary vein) – left chamber (here the vital spirit is formed).
>
> His [Avicenna's] statement that the blood that is in the right side nourishes the heart is not true at all, for nourishment of the heart is actually from the blood that goes through the vessels that permeate the body of the heart. *(Akmal et al., 2010, p. 28)*

To give another example, the following scientific and mathematical concepts were all known about, invented or used in China hundreds of years before they were 'discovered' in the West (Temple, 1991): the compass, magnetic remanence and induction, the iron plough, the 'modern' horse harness, the multi-tube seed drill, sunspots, quantitative cartography, solar wind, 'Mercator' map projections, cast iron, the crank handle, deep drilling for natural gas, the suspension bridge, underwater salvage operations, paper, the wheelbarrow, sliding callipers, the fishing reel, the stirrup, porcelain, biological pest control, the umbrella, matches, chess, brandy, whisky, the mechanical clock, printing, paper money, the spinning wheel, endocrinology, diabetes, immunology, medical use of thyroxine, the decimal system, zero, negative numbers, Pascal's [sic] triangle, Newton's [sic] First Law, the seismograph, phosphorescent paint, the kite, the parachute, masts, hermetically sealed laboratories, chemical warfare, the crossbow, gunpowder and the rocket.

A final point before we move onto the philosophy of science: there are hints, before the invention of writing, that suggest some scientific knowledge and enquiry from far further back in time. Figure 2.1 shows a painting from some 17,000 years ago in El Pindal, Spain. Although known locally as *Elefante Enamorado* ('The

Figure 2.1 A painting from some 17,000 years ago in El Pindal, Spain. Does this reveal scientific thought?
Source: https://www.atlasobscura.com/places/el-pindal-cave.

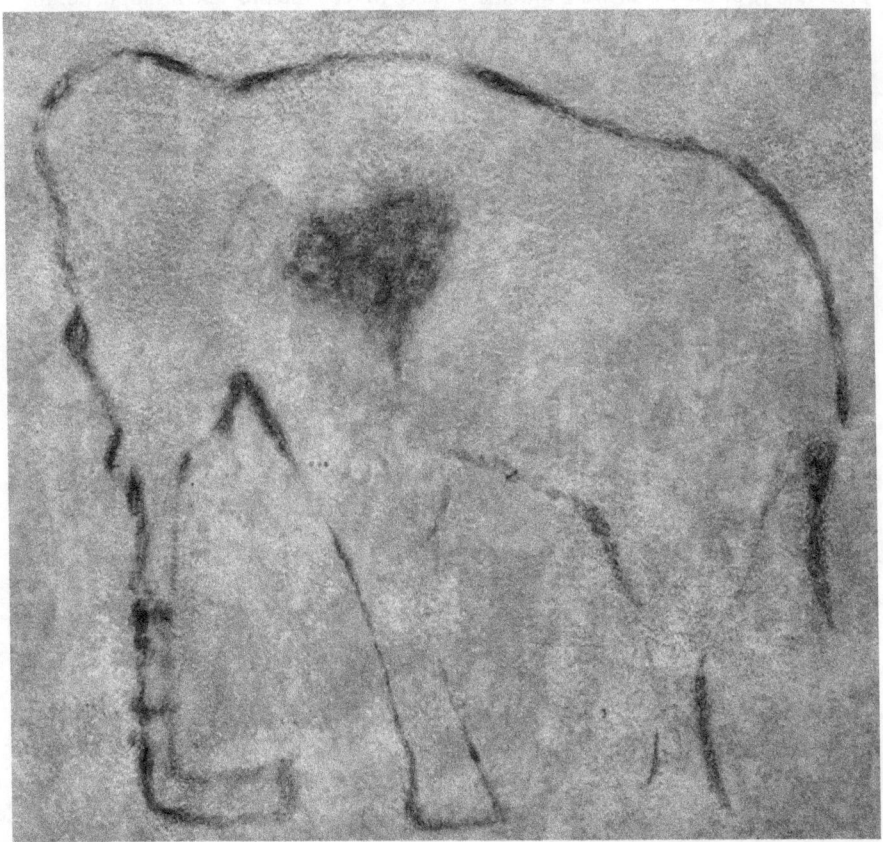

Elephant in Love'), it is thought by archaeologists to show a hunting wound to a woolly mammoth, though whether we can go so far as to assert that 'This hunter was intelligent enough to realise that heart is a vital organ, which should be struck by an arrow to kill the animal and thus to provide food for his survival. Moreover, his abstract thinking was so developed, that it enabled him to select and present the crucial outlines of the anatomical image of heart' (Marinković et al., 2014, p. 104) is perhaps less certain.

Mention can also be made of the science that was presumably known in order to obtain the materials to manufacture certain objects. Some metals – principally gold but also silver, copper, tin and iron (in meteorites) – can be found 'native', i.e. not combined with other elements in ores, and flakes of gold have been found, apparently gathered by humans, in caves that date from 40,000 years ago (Hur, 2019). Certain metals, including copper, can be obtained by heating the rocks in which they occur, a process known as smelting. In a site in what is now Serbia, a sophisticated metal workshop with a furnace and tools, including a copper chisel and a two-headed hammer and axe, have been dated to about 5500 BCE (Anon, 2007). The excavated metal workshop was a room of some 25 square metres, with walls built out of wood coated with clay. The furnace, built on the outside of the room, featured earthen, pipe-like air vents with hundreds of tiny holes in them, presumably to ensure air went into the furnace to feed the fire, and a simple chimney for the removal of smoke.

Lessons from philosophy and sociology

The sociologist Robert Merton characterized science as open-minded, universalist, disinterested and communal (Merton, 1973). For Merton, science is a group activity: even though certain scientists work on their own, all scientists contribute to a single body of knowledge accepted by the community of scientists. There are certain parallels here with art, literature and music. After all, James Joyce, Virginia Woolf and Robert Musil all contributed to the development of modernist literature. But while it makes no sense to try to combine their novels (the very notion is ridiculous), science *is* largely about combining the contributions of many different scientists to produce an overall coherent model of one aspect of reality. In this sense, science is disinterested; in *this* sense it is (or should be) impersonal.

Because science is disinterested, the knowledge it produces should be objective – that is, it should not matter who is producing it, whatever their gender, nationality or ethnicity. Of course, that is an ideal; different scientists have different interests and the science that is undertaken is often the result of economic or other forces, rather than a search for pure knowledge. Nevertheless, scientists should always be prepared to change their views in the light of new evidence or better explanatory theories (Reiss, in press).

Consider, for example, the controversy over whether Covid-19 arose in Chinese food markets or in a Chinese laboratory (Horton, 2021). It is hardly surprising that

China argued furiously against the lab theory, even calling on the US government to launch an enquiry into the possibility that a military laboratory in Maryland was the source. Equally, one doesn't have to have a degree in political science to realize that the positions of many countries on the issue say as much about their relationships with China as anything else. Nevertheless, the presumption of science is that there is an answer out there and that the best way of getting to it, though it may be that the question is never settled for sure, is through the tried-and-tested approaches of science. If we go back a few decades, there was comparable controversy about the origins of HIV, with some suggesting, among other theories, that it resulted from smallpox vaccines. Eventually, it was shown to be a zoonotic pathogen, in other words an organism that had moved from a non-human to a human, causing a new disease. In the case of HIV, the virus came from African primates (Sharp & Hahn, 2011). Here too, there were suggestions that laboratory mistakes were involved (Brown, 1991).

Karl Popper emphasized the importance of falsifiability for science (Popper, 1934/1972). According to Popper, unless you can imagine collecting data that would allow you to refute (i.e. disprove) a theory, hypothesis or statement, the theory, hypothesis or statement isn't scientific. Consider the statement, 'The average man is taller than the average woman'. Is this a scientific statement? The answer might seem to be 'yes' because we can imagine collecting data that would allow us to refute the statement: one would need reasonable sample sizes of men and women, presumably ensuring that they are of comparable ages (the average 4-year-old male is a lot less tall than the average 20-year-old female) and come from much the same place (there are big differences in the heights of people in different parts of the world), at about the same time in history (people are typically taller now than they used to be, thanks to better nutrition and fewer childhood diseases), and then one would need to undertake some statistics on the mean heights of the men and the women. It's clear that testing the statement is not trivial – and we haven't even got onto the fact that while it is pretty straightforward objectively to determine a person's height, it is not so straightforward to assign all adult humans to the category of 'man' or 'woman'. Perhaps we should have stuck to comparing the melting points of lead and copper.

What about the statement, 'The average woman is more intelligent than the average man'? Is this a scientific statement? The answer now is even less clear. Note that we are *not* attempting to provide the answer to the question, 'Is the average woman more intelligent than the average man?' but to the question, 'Is the statement "The average woman is more intelligent than the average man" a scientific statement?' The additional layers of complication that now arise concern agreement as to what is meant by 'intelligent' and the fact that even if we reach agreement on this question, it is much harder to measure intelligence objectively than it is height.

Most scientists are not much interested in philosophy, but Popper is a philosopher of science whose views they generally like, once they know about them. Much school science is Popperian. We devise hypotheses – for instance, that plants require light, warmth and carbon dioxide to grow. We then devise experiments to test these hypotheses – we vary the light levels, the temperature and the carbon dioxide levels in which plants are kept and devise ways of determining their growth in these different conditions. We find that our hypotheses are either refuted or, at least so far, stand.

However, there is more to the philosophy of science than Popper. Thomas Kuhn is most remembered nowadays for his argument that while what we might call the Popperian account of science holds well during periods of *normal science* when a single paradigm holds sway, such as the Ptolemaic model of the structure of the universe (in which the Earth is at its centre) or the Newtonian understanding of motion and gravity, it breaks down when a scientific *crisis* occurs. At the time of such a crisis, a scientific revolution happens during which a new paradigm, such as the Copernican model of the structure of the solar system or Einstein's theory of relativity, begins to replace the previously accepted paradigm. The key point is that the reason why scientists move from believing in one paradigm to believing in another cannot, Kuhn argues, be fully explained by the Popperian account of falsifiability (Kuhn, 1970). In the case of the solar system, it was many years till the Copernican model was as accurate as the earlier Ptolemaic model, yet even while it was less accurate it became widely accepted among scientists for other reasons, such as its mathematical elegance and the possibilities it held out for calendar reform.

Kuhn is sometimes seen as undermining science, by including more of a human element in how it develops, and this is even more the case for the brilliant, but maverick, philosopher of science Paul Feyerabend. His most famous book is *Against Method* (Feyerabend, 1993). There is a clue in the title; Feyerabend was an epistemological anarchist and summarized his views on how scientists work with the phrase 'anything goes'. It should not be thought that Feyerabend rejected science, quite the opposite. What he objected to was the way that science was so often tidied up in its presentation. He argued that what scientists actually do is not stick to 'the scientific method' but use every possible means at their disposal to answer the questions that interest them. Reading Feyerabend can be a refreshing or an unsettling experience, depending on the sort of person one is. The reception of his ideas has not been helped by his tendency to write ironically in places, only to be read literally.

The nature of science

Certain things clearly fall within the field of science – the operation of gravity, the structure of materials and human anatomy, to give three examples. However, what about whether there is life after death, the behaviour of people, decisions about whether we should continue with fossil fuels or go for renewable energy, the appreciation of music and the nature of friendship, for example? Do all of these fall within the field of science? Some people would argue 'yes', and the term 'scientism' is used, somewhat pejoratively, to refer to the view that science can provide sufficient explanations for everything (cf. Boudry & Pigliucci, 2018).

However, most people believe that science is but one form of knowledge and that other forms of knowledge complement science. Whether there is life after death is also a religious or even a philosophical question – or simply unknowable; the behaviour of people requires knowledge of the social sciences (particularly psychology and sociology) rather than only of the natural sciences; whether we should go for fossil fuels or renewable energy is partly a scientific issue but also requires an understanding of economics, risk, politics and the distinctive circumstances of different countries; the appreciation of music and the nature of friendship, while clearly having something to do with our hearing and vision, cannot entirely be reduced to science (Reiss, in press).

The nature of science (NOS) is the phrase that is used to describe the essence ('nature') of science – what science is all about. NOS is therefore about the epistemology of science, science as a way of knowing. It is a phrase that is widely used in science education and while there isn't total agreement as to what it entails, there is widespread agreement. Perhaps the science educator whose name is most associated with work on NOS is Norman Lederman. Lederman died in 2021, after a short and unexpected illness. Back in 1992 he authored a review on students' and teachers' conceptions of NOS (Lederman, 1992). This became one of the most cited science education articles of all time, and Lederman continued to work on NOS, inter alia, throughout his life.

In his attempts to characterize NOS, Lederman made six principal points (Lederman, 2007). First, there is a distinction between observations (descriptive statements about natural phenomena, about which observers can reach consensus with relative ease) and the inferences made from those observations. Second, there is a distinction between scientific laws (statements about the relationships between observable phenomena, such as Newton's Law of Universal Gravitation or Mendel's Laws in genetics) and theories (inferred explanations for observable phenomena). Third, scientific knowledge, though based on empirical observations of natural phenomena, requires human imagination and creativity (for a start, that's where the theories come from). Fourth, scientific knowledge is theory-laden (in that observations and conclusions are affected by the presuppositions held by those who make observations and draw conclusions); scientific knowledge therefore has a degree of subjectivity, rather than being entirely objective. Fifth, science is a human endeavour and is therefore influenced by the human cultures in which it is embedded. Finally, scientific knowledge is always open to revision as a result of improvements in data and theory.

A number of science education authors have proposed different accounts of NOS, though Kampourakis (2016) and McComas (2020) helpfully point out that there is indeed a consensus position among science educators, one that Lederman's (2007) above six points summarize. However, not everyone is happy with the consensus view of NOS. In a highly cited article, Irzik and Nola (2011) argued that it has a number of shortcomings. For a start, it says nothing about the aims of science or about its methodological rules (such as the hypothetico-deductive method of testing). Then, it presents a somewhat monolithic view of science that takes account neither of differences between scientific disciplines (contrast experimental disciplines with those that are largely not, such as astronomy) nor of the history of science, so that science appears timeless. Finally, the consensus view fails to explain how, if science is socially and culturally embedded, it produces knowledge that is valid across cultures and societies.

Irzik and Nola (2011), drawing on Wittgenstein (1958), therefore proposed what they termed 'a family resemblance approach'. Instead of asking, 'what do the various sciences have in common?' we should 'investigate the ways in which each of the sciences are similar or dissimilar, thereby building up from scratch polythetic sets of characteristics [characteristics which occur commonly in members of a group, but none of which is essential for membership of that group or class] for each individual science' (p. 595). The difference may seem a subtle one, but their proposal has been enthusiastically taken up by a number of other science educators.

Michael Matthews (2012) built on Irzik and Nola (2011), arguing that rather than thinking NOS, we should think Features of Science (FOS). Matthews maintains that this would lead to better science teaching. To give just one example, he points out that the ubiquity of models in both the history and current practice of science is widely acknowledged – think of the different models for the structure of the atom, for example, or of models used in teaching to help students understand what happens when liquids evaporate. A good teacher, drawing on FOS, can help students to think about the similarities and differences between models and the reality they attempt to characterize.

Sibel Erduran and Zoubeida Dagher (2014) also built on Irzik and Nola (2011), elaborating, critiquing, extending and applying their approach to science education. They provide a useful visual representation of their ideas (Figure 2.2). Here, science

Figure 2.2 The Family Resemblance Wheel of Erduran and Dagher (2014). Science is seen as a cognitive-epistemic system that sits within a social-institutional system.
Source: Figure 2.1 (p. 28) of Erduran, S. & Dagher, Z. R. (2014). Reconceptualizing the Nature of Science for Science Education: Scientific Knowledge, Practices and Other Family Categories. Dordrecht: Springer.

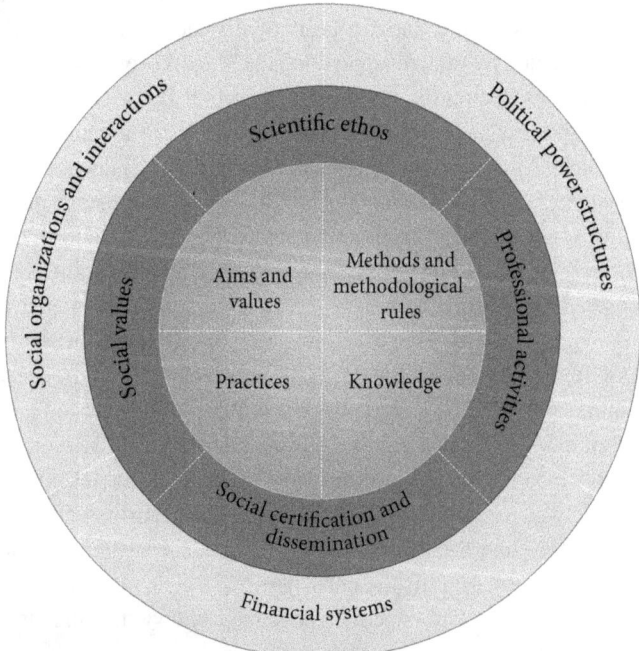

is seen as a cognitive-epistemic system that can be broken down into four quadrants: Aims and values; Methods and methodological rules; Practices and Knowledge. These four quadrants sit within a ring that is also divided into four: Social values; Scientific ethos; Professional activities; and Social certification and dissemination. Finally, beyond this ring is a second, larger ring divided into: Social organizations and interactions; Political power structures and Financial systems.

Whichever view of the NOS you favour, all of them see science as being embedded in human institutions and therefore deeply influenced by human values.

Science versus pseudoscience

The term 'pseudoscience' (literally 'false knowledge') is used by those who align themselves with conventional science to dismiss the worth of work in areas that claim to be scientific but are adjudged not to be. Immediately we run up against a number of problems. For a start, might ascribing the label 'pseudoscience' to an area simply be a means of rubbishing disfavoured views? Consider, for example, the argument of Albert (1986) on the issue as to whether so-called 'scientific creationism' is a pseudoscience. Adopting Popper's criterion of falsifiability as the sine qua non of science, Albert argues:

> By definition, 'scientific' creationism is irrevocably grounded in an appeal to the existence and operation of an obviously omnipotent supernatural being – that is, *a being that by its very nature is capable of virtually anything*. It therefore follows that there is literally no conceivable observation that cannot be reconciled with the virtually limitless actions of such a being. 'Scientific' creationism thus lacks the central defining characteristic of all modern scientific theories. It is absolutely immune to falsification. Literally any problem confronted by 'scientific' creationism as it is applied to the empirical world can be resolved through an appeal to unknown and unknowable supernatural operations.... It is extremely important to emphasize again that 'scientific' creationism is not, as is the case with some legitimately scientific theories, only unfalsifiable *in practice;* it is also unfalsifiable *in principle*. (p. 28)

Let us make it clear that neither of us accepts the arguments of 'scientific creationism'. Indeed, one of us has spent rather more time than he cares to think about over the last forty years reading creationist literature and arguing against it (e.g. Reiss, 2018). However, whatever its shortcomings, one of the interesting features of writings that espouse 'scientific creationism' is precisely how rarely they appeal to 'unknown and unknowable supernatural operations'; what they typically do is argue that mainstream science *supports* creationist conclusions.

More generally, philosophers have long argued that it is not easy to demarcate clearly between science and pseudoscience (Hansson, 2021). In addition to the falsification criterion, other criteria for science have been proposed, including the existence of an ongoing research programme that makes progress. However, we should note that those who work as scientific creationists seem to make progress, in that there are comparable academic arguments to those found in science, some of which are resolved over time as new data accumulate and new theories are developed. A rather different approach is to say that pseudoscience is characterized by a multiplicity of criteria, not all of which need to be met. One such list of criteria is provided by Hansson (2021):

1. *Belief in authority*: It is contended that some person or persons have a special ability to determine what is true or false. Others have to accept their judgements.
2. *Unrepeatable experiments*: Reliance is put on experiments that cannot be repeated by others with the same outcome.
3. *Handpicked examples*: Handpicked examples are used although they are not representative of the general category that the investigation refers to.
4. *Unwillingness to test*: A theory is not tested, although it is possible to test it.
5. *Disregard of refuting information*: Observations or experiments that conflict with a theory are neglected.
6. *Built-in subterfuge*: The testing of a theory is so arranged that the theory can only be confirmed, never disconfirmed, by the outcome.
7. *Explanations are abandoned without replacement*: Tenable explanations are given up without being replaced, so that the new theory leaves much more unexplained than the previous one.

From a pedagogical point of view, there is much to be said for teachers encouraging students to undertake work to decide whether a number of positions are pseudoscientific or not, positions such as belief in astrology, climate change denial, homeopathy, phrenology (not so common now but once very popular – as evidenced by many nineteenth-century novels), scientific creationism, scientific racism and vaccine rejection. Not all of these positions are appropriate for study by students of all ages and care should be taken when using the term 'pseudoscience' as it is value-laden and can be felt to be offensive.

Top scientists are not necessarily immune from supporting erroneous scientific ideas. R. A. Fisher (1890–1962) was a polymath. His name lives on in the F test and Fisher's exact test, and he has been described as 'the single most important figure in 20th century statistics' (Efron, 1998, p. 95). Despite this, towards the end of his life, he became embroiled in a controversy that has not helped his reputation: he argued against the idea that smoking causes lung cancer (Fisher, 1959). Fisher developed four lines of argument:

1) If **A** is associated with **B**, then not only is it possible that **A** causes **B**, but it is also possible that **B** is the cause of **A**. In other words, smoking may cause lung cancer, but it is a logical possibility that lung cancer causes smoking.

2) There may be a genetic predisposition to smoke (and that genetic predisposition is presumably also linked to lung cancer).

3) Smoking is unlikely to cause lung cancer because secular trend [*sic*] and other ecologic data do not support this relation.

4) Smoking does not cause lung cancer because inhalers are less likely to develop lung cancer than are noninhalers. *(Stolley, 1991, p. 419)*

We don't need to go through each of these arguments in detail; to give a flavour, Fisher argued that people smoke as a way of 'getting a little compensation for life's minor ills ... And so, anyone suffering from a chronic inflammation in part of the body (something that does not give rise to conscious pain) is not unlikely to be associated with smoking more frequently, or smoking rather than not smoking' (Fisher, 1958, p. 162). But what is of interest is to ask, how on earth did a scientist and statistician of Fisher's ability manage to end up producing such mediocre arguments and getting his conclusions completely wrong?

In his analysis of this question, the epidemiologist Paul Stolley (1991) advances several possible answers. First, Fisher's personality:

> Fisher's zest for confrontation and polemic was legend; all who knew him comment on this, even his usually uncritical biographer/ daughter. Domestic fits of temper paralleled the intolerance and aggressiveness he demonstrated toward his colleagues ... He hated to admit that he was wrong on any subject. He preached the scientific method and was eloquent on the subject, but had great difficulty following his own strictures. *(p. 422)*

Second, Fisher was a smoker of pipes and cigarettes. Third, and somewhat surprisingly, 'it was recognized by those who worked most closely with him that he was good with data while working on one small set but was not easily able to integrate multiple or large data sets' (p. 423). Fourth, 'He received a lot of public attention for his views on lung cancer and fashioned a talk on the subject which he gave all over the world and which he arranged to have reprinted. It was well received, even by medical audiences' (p. 423). Fifth, he overextended himself. He was not an epidemiologist and was suspicious of arguments that did not rely on randomization. He appeared unwilling to examine the entire body of data available and prematurely drew conclusions. Finally, 'he took a fee from the tobacco industry, although those who know him best doubt that the fee mattered very much. It was probably not large, and he may have stopped taking fees when it was revealed in the *British Medical Journal* letters columns. But we have no hard evidence on any of this' (p. 425).

One cannot really validly accuse Fisher of engaging in pseudoscience, but we have included this material partly because it shows how even a great scientist can get obsessed by an issue and end up on the wrong side of history – for another possible example see the story of Linus Pauling's (the only person ever to win two unshared Nobel Prizes) obsession with the health benefits of large doses of vitamin C

(Thielking, 2015) – and partly because the subsequent history of the controversy over the role of smoking in lung cancer illustrates not so much pseudoscience as fake science.

The overwhelming consensus among medical experts is that cigarette smoking is a major cause of lung cancer and other harms. Perhaps unsurprisingly, given the huge amounts of money involved, the tobacco industry has for decades sought to deny this and to maintain their business model. In the words of a World Health Organization report, 'Thousands of internal tobacco industry documents released through litigation and whistleblowers reveal the most astonishing systematic corporate deceit of all time' (Bates & Rowell, 2004). Publicly, the industry denied for decades, despite knowing the contrary, that smoking causes lung cancer, that nicotine is addictive, that cigarette companies actively target the young and that advertising increases cigarette consumption. The industry buys up scientists 'on a spectacular scale' and, faced with falling demands for cigarettes in many Western countries, moved aggressively into developing countries and Eastern Europe.

Popular science, social media and politics

In 2017, the *Collins Dictionary* named 'fake news' its 'word of the year', usage of the term having increased by 365 per cent over the previous year (Flood, 2017). While it is easy to criticize social media, and the internet more generally, for its effects on people's well-being, there is much that the internet and social media have done that is helpful for science. For example, a US study for the years 2012–18 found that 'Influenza vaccination uptake was highest among those who used the internet for formal health information and communication with a provider (55.1%), and lowest among those internet users who did not use the internet for any type of formal or informal health information and communication (35.6%)' (Khanijahani et al., 2021, p. 76).

Interestingly, social media use is also associated with increased trust in science (Huber et al., 2019). While this may surprise some, social media have the potential to correct misinformation, expand information networks and promote user engagement with content posted by trusted social contacts (Huber et al., 2019). And there's the rub! The way that social media largely works is to put people in contact with one another if they agree about something. If I dislike your views, I can stop you posting to me, and vice versa. The result is lots of islands of relatively like-minded people, an effect exacerbated by the algorithms that drive what one sees on the internet. It's a bit like the shift from the old days where most of us could only watch one or two TV channels to the huge choice there is nowadays. The result is that instead of everyone watching much the same programmes, we splinter. Added to this is a reduction in in-person social interactions – highlighted by the title of a famous US sociology article: 'Bowling alone: America's declining social capital' (Putnam, 1995). Its author showed that although more people in the

United States were bowling than twenty years previously, they were more likely to do so on their own. This exemplified a decline in membership of traditional civic organizations. Putnam argued that this decline in in-person social interactions was associated with an increasing mistrust of government and constituted a threat to democracy. His words may have been prophetic. In a poll conducted for CNN between 3 August and 7 September 2021 by an independent research company, 78 per cent of those who identified as Republicans said that 'Biden did not legitimately win enough votes to win the presidency', compared to 3 per cent of Democrats (CNN, 2021).

The effects of social media on people's understanding of science are varied. Sometimes social media clearly hold back understanding of science, and much else besides, sometimes for political ends, whether national or international. Numerous studies find associations between social media use and beliefs in conspiracy theories and misinformation, though, as always in such correlation studies, the evidence for causality is not so strong (Enders et al., 2021). Furthermore, a careful study of 11,023 unique URLs referring to the origin of Covid-19 appearing in 267,084 Facebook, Twitter, Reddit and 4chan posts between January and March 2020 found that although most (83 per cent) of the stories that reinforced conspiracy theories originated from *alternative* sources (low-credibility outlets, such as Infowars and Breitbart), personal blogs and social media posts, the remaining 17 per cent that originated from *mainstream* sources (high-credibility news outlets, such as the *New York Post* or Fox News [!], scientific websites such as biorxiv.org (a preprint server for biology) and other widely credible sites, such as Wikipedia) resulted in higher numbers of Facebook (60 per cent of the total) and Twitter shares (55 per cent of the total).

There has been a sea change in the provision of information about science in recent decades. When the two of us were growing up in the UK, science news came almost entirely from trusted TV sources such as the BBC, from specialist science correspondents employed by newspapers and from specialist magazines like *New Scientist*. Nowadays, there are far more sources, not all of them trustworthy. In particular, much more of the science 'information' that people receive today will not have gone through the process of scientific peer review that developed from the seventeenth and eighteenth centuries, causing some to declare, and not that recently, that we live in a 'post-truth era' (Keyes, 2004).

But social media can also be harnessed to help people understand and accept mainstream science. In 2009, the human papillomavirus (HPV) vaccine against cervical cancer became part of the Danish childhood vaccination programme to protect Danish girls. The Danish Cancer Society ran a campaign which used Facebook to spread awareness about HPV vaccination (Pederson et al., 2020). In 2015, after a period of massive media coverage questioning the safety of the HPV vaccination, a major decline in HPV vaccination coverage (from about 90 per cent to less than 50 per cent) occurred. In an attempt to regain public trust and increase HPV vaccination rates, a new social media strategy was developed. It focused on 'heart stories', such as personal stories told by women with cervical cancer, combined with 'mind stories', such as facts on vaccine safety and effectiveness. Facebook was used to reach mothers, and other social media platforms, including YouTube and Instagram, were used to reach 15- to 17-year-old girls. One year after the launch of the campaign, twice as many girls were vaccinated and the percentage of parents who trusted the vaccine had increased from 50 per cent to 80 per cent.

Finally, one scientific practice that has been much aided (Silvertown, 2009) by the internet and social media is citizen science, the active participation of the public in scientific research programmes (Hecker et al., 2018). While citizen science has long existed, it has been invigorated by new technologies that connect people easily and efficiently with scientists. To give just one example, the New Zealand Garden Bird Survey started in 2007 and occurs annually over a nine-day period in June and July (Liberatore et al., 2018). It is modelled on similar surveys that have been undertaken in other countries for many years. Volunteer participants observe their garden for one hour of their choosing and record the highest number of individual birds present at one time for each species. For the New Zealand survey, a Facebook group was established on 27 May 2015 as a 'public' group (so all content is freely visible online). In its first year, it became a thriving online community of practice, growing to 1,275 members, who generated nearly 75,000 interactions (posts, comments, likes and shares).

The nature of truth in mathematics and the social sciences

In school, mathematics is often grouped with science – for example, as a STEM (science, technology, engineering and mathematics) subject. But the way that truth is established in mathematics is very different. Consider the equation $(x + 1)^2 = x^2 + 2x + 1$. How do mathematicians know this is true? We can start with what they do *not* do. They do not, as a scientist might, go out into the world and find samples of $x + 1$ and then experimentally, under carefully controlled conditions, multiply them in pairs and determine what results. The very notion is absurd. Although there are some branches of science that to all intents and purposes are applied mathematics – theoretical physics and population genetics, for example – most of science, as we reviewed above, is empirical. It relies on gathering data to test hypotheses and build theories. Mathematics isn't like that.

It's easier to state how mathematical truth is not like scientific truth than to state what it actually is. In fact, quite a range of positions exist in the literature. At first sight, mathematics appears to study abstract entities. As has long been observed, however, if this is the case, how come mathematics is so wonderfully valuable for studying the physical entities that scientists are interested in? In any event, mathematical truths are arrived at by way of proof. We start with $x + 1$, we multiply it by itself and we end up with $x^2 + 2x + 1$. The argument proceeds logically and the reasoning we employ is based on axioms, that is, on certain fundamental (unproven) assumptions. These assumptions, in arithmetic, include things like if $x = y$ and $y = z$, then $x = z$. This isn't as trivial as it may seem; if you and I each tend to win half of the tennis matches we play against each other, and you and another friend of yours each tend to win half of the tennis matches you play, it does not necessarily follow that when I play this other friend of yours at tennis we each tend to win half of the matches.

There are various 'types' of proof in mathematics. One type is known as *reductio ad absurdum* (also known as 'proof by contradiction'). One supposes that something *is* the case in mathematics, for example, that the square root of 2 can be expressed as a ratio of two whole numbers, and then shows that if that something were indeed the case, a logical contradiction would ensue. Since logical contradictions are not possible for mathematical truths, one therefore concludes that the something is *not* the case – in this particular case we therefore conclude that the square root of 2 cannot be expressed as a ratio of two whole numbers, and is therefore said to be 'irrational'.

When it comes to the social sciences – disciplines such as psychology, sociology, economics, anthropology and education – the issues to do with truth differ from those that arise in mathematics. Consider the apparently straightforward question 'What is the optimal number of school students in a class?' (Briggs & Reiss, 2021). As soon as one begins to attempt to answer this question, non-scientific judgements are seen to be involved. For a start, do we decide what is optimum with respect to what the students learn or to their attitudes to the subject (on the grounds that positive attitudes mean that they may be more likely to continue to study the subject once it is no longer mandatory)? There is no objective way of deciding between these two alternatives; we have to make a value judgement.

Assuming we come to a decision as to what our goal for the teaching is, should we consider not just the students in the class but other students? After all, any benefit to the students in one class in a school in having their numbers reduced may mean that another class in the school needs to have more students. If we are talking about decreasing average class size across a large geographical area (such as a country), then correspondingly more teachers will be required overall. If there is a shortage of good teachers – and there nearly always is – it is likely that these additional teachers won't on average be as good as the ones already in post, which further complicates matters. Then there is the reality that teachers prefer smaller classes and are more likely to leave the profession if they have larger classes.

We could go on. Arriving at truth in the social sciences is not only often more complex and more subject to value judgements than in the natural sciences, social scientists are often interested in knowledge that is more affected by local circumstances. The boiling point of water may be virtually the same in London, Cairo and Tokyo (there will be slight differences due to differences in air pressure), but it is not the case that the best teaching methods are necessarily the same.

In the next chapter we go on to look at another type of knowledge, namely ethics.

What is ethics?

Ethics, morality and values

Ethics, morals and values – three words that in everyday life are often used interchangeably, especially the first two, but can also have different meanings depending on the context in which they are used. It is important to have a clear understanding of the meaning of the words but we would not advise becoming preoccupied with the differences between the three and note that 'some languages do not allow for a distinction to be made' (Reiss, 2010, p. 7). Nonetheless, the following distinctions may be useful when thinking about and using these terms.

Morality refers to the thinking that we use to judge what is right and what is wrong. It is this thinking – which has both conscious and unconscious components – that guides our behaviour. Ethics are (or 'is' – the word ethics can be used both as a singular noun and as a plural noun) based on reason and logic; therefore, it can be argued that they are objective, whereas morality is more automatic and includes our emotional responses and so is more subjective. This means that ethics (ideally!) are not dependent on personal opinions or feelings but instead on reasoned and logical arguments. Morality, on the other hand, can be based on personal opinions and feelings. It has an element of subjectivity, because what one person considers to be right or wrong may not be the same as what another person considers, although there will sometimes be shared agreement. At the same time, there are often differences in the ethical conclusions that people reach – though these differences should follow deductively from the reasoning employed.

Ethics is a branch of philosophy concerned with what ought to be done; specifically, ethics considers what is morally right and wrong in any given situation and we make these decisions daily, certainly more often than perhaps we realize. Moral principles therefore help to govern our behaviours. However, deciding what is the right thing to do can sometimes be challenging because although there will be times when the right course of action will be very clear, at other times this may be more problematic. For example, should I buy coffee from a company that does not support fair trade? Should I invest in solar panels for my home given the ongoing issues with climate change?

Is it acceptable to tell my friend I am feeling unwell (even though I'm feeling fine) because I no longer wish to go to something I agreed to attend with them? As we can see from these examples, the considerations of what we might need to contemplate to make a decision are varied. Therefore, ethics is a specific discipline, and considers the way the world ought to be. It does this by critically analysing the reasoning which underpins our moral decisions – our moral life and frameworks which cultivate the values that we hold.

Some philosophers argue that there is a close relationship between ethics and morality whereas others argue that the two concepts are quite distinct. In Kantian ethics, for example, the morality of an action is based on the intention behind the action, with ethical principles being based on a rational understanding of what is morally good or bad. The distinctions between ethics and morality can be useful for us to understand how we make decisions about right and wrong and can also be helpful in resolving ethical dilemmas. When faced with an ethical dilemma, we need to ask ourselves whether the issue at hand is a matter of ethics or morality; indeed, sometimes it is both. If it is a matter of ethics, then we need to reason our way to a solution. If it is a matter of morality, then we need to acknowledge and consider our intuitions and feelings to help determine why we think and feel as we do. Often, the two are entwined.

The distinction between ethics and morality is also useful for understanding the different types of arguments that can be made for or against certain actions. For example, an argument based on ethics might be that something is wrong because it is not in accordance with an ethical principle. An argument based on morality might be that something is wrong because we are offended by it.

Morality usually refers to codes of conduct that are prescribed by religion or society, while ethics are more concerned with the principles that underlie these codes of conduct. Both values, which we now go on to discuss, and morality are shaped by a person's culture, religion and personal experiences and it is important to recognize that not all values are ethical; some sit outside of ethics, as is the case with aesthetic values, for instance. It can be argued that an individual's values are relatively stable and enduring, that they are internalized and motivate a person to act in certain ways.

It is also fair to say that there is sometimes confusion between the concepts of ethics and values; they too are often used interchangeably. But there is a significant difference between the two. As we argued above, ethics are the rules or standards that govern our behaviour, usually based on our sense of right and wrong. Values refer to the beliefs that a person holds about what is important in life, such as family, religion or democracy – so we can talk of family values, religious values and democratic values. There are a few different ways to think about the difference between ethics and values. One way is to think of values as the ends, and ethics as the means. That is, our values are what we want to promote (e.g. a society that prioritizes families, or is based on religion or promotes democracy), while ethics are the guidelines we use to get there. Another way to think about it is that values are what we believe, and ethics are how we behave because of what we believe. That is, our values guide our behaviour. It's also important to note that our ethics and values can conflict with each other. For example, we might value honesty, but we might also feel that it's acceptable to lie in certain circumstances (e.g. to prevent a greater harm). In cases like this, we have to decide what we think is more important in any given situation, which can suggest a hierarchy of values which may vary from individual to individual.

Therefore, we can recognize that while the words ethics, morals and values can be distinguished, they may also be used interchangeably, given that the concepts are closely related. Indeed, although the three words have distinct definitions, trying to distinguish them can be somewhat counterproductive in certain circumstances. It may be enough to bear in mind that as humans we exist as part of a society and the wider world, so that the ethical thinking that guides our behaviour impacts on our own sense of self, and is affected by our morality, the values we hold and the attitudes and behaviours of others around us.

Is morality culturally specific or universal?

There has been much debate surrounding the question of whether morality is culturally specific or universal. Some argue that morality is culturally specific, meaning that what is considered moral in one culture may be considered immoral in another, whereas others argue that there are certain moral principles that are shared across all cultures and that therefore morality is in large part universal. The majority of research on this suggests that morality is, at least to some extent, culturally specific; in other words, it is, at least in part, a cultural construct (Jai & Krettenauer, 2017).

Why is the issue of whether morality is culturally specific or universal important? Put simply, it has implications for how we should judge the actions of others and for how harmoniously we can live. If morality is culturally specific, then we should not judge the actions of others based on our own cultural beliefs. However, if morality is universal, then we can judge the actions of others based on objective shared ethical principles. It is plausible, therefore, that the cultural specificity of morality gives us reason to be more open-minded and to attempt to understand differing moral views; this does not, however, preclude moral judgement. The reality is that people from different cultures hold different moral preferences (think about how cultures differ with regard to how older people should be viewed and cared for, or how we should deal with people once they have died), suggesting that morality is at least partially determined by culture. However, people from different cultures can also often agree on basic moral principles, such as the importance of not harming others, suggesting that there are some universal aspects to morality.

The anthropologist Harvey Whitehouse (2004) argues that morality is not universal, but is instead culturally specific. Whitehouse cites the example of the different moral codes that exist in different cultures, such as the practice of polygamy in some cultures and its prohibition in others. Different cultures have different concepts of what is considered to be morally good or bad. He claims that there are three main types of morality – community-based morality, individualistic morality and hierarchical morality – and that each type is found in different cultures around the world. Whitehouse concludes that morality is not universal and that it is impossible to have one morality that is applicable to all cultures.

Anthropologist Richard Shweder (2000) argues that morality varies significantly across cultures. He found that in the United States morality is largely based on the principles of individual rights and autonomy, while in India morality is largely based on the principles of social order and hierarchy, indicating the influence of culture. Bhabha (2012) argues that it is difficult to make the case for an objective morality if the word 'objective' is being used in a strong sense so that the phrase 'objective morality' would mean a universal or foundational morality that all people, everywhere, understand and accept. The issue arises because individuals and institutions are aware of the existence of conflicting moral values and normative guides to behaviour, but for a range of strategic reasons they want these guides to behaviour to be normalized and consensual. Moral beliefs (which we noted earlier can be a matter of intuition and feeling) can also be the products of discursive interpretations of dialogic deliberation and decision-making; differences in morality are therefore not simply about differences in cultural beliefs and norms. This means that in different settings and cultures, moral beliefs or customs which might on the surface appear very similar might well differ. Morality is not written in stone; it changes over time, even though there may be attempts by governments, laws and religion to stabilize it.

However, some argue that the claim that morality is not universal is based on a false dichotomy – either something is universally moral or not. It has been pointed out that many of the examples Whitehouse uses to support his claim can be seen as examples of universal moral principles, such as the Golden Rule which most cultures have some form of. The Golden Rule states that any of us should treat others as we would like to be treated, which suggests that there are at least some universal moral values. Another argument is that morality can still be objective even when it is culturally specific. Objective moral values can exist independently of our opinions or feelings about them because they are underpinned by ethical frameworks. A third argument is that even if morality is culturally specific, this does not necessarily mean that it is not universal! Universalism is the principle that we should be able to apply moral principles to all people, regardless of their culture. Morality may be thought of as not simply a set of rules that we follow blindly, but as a way of life that helps us to live in harmony with others.

However, there are still some scholars who argue that morality is, at least to some extent, universal. Haidt (2008) has argued that there are six universal moral foundations: care/harm, fairness/cheating, liberty/oppression, loyalty/betrayal, authority/subversion and sanctity/degradation. He argues that ethical reasoning by a single person is usually devoted to finding reasons to support that person's intuitions, but that moral agreements reached between people have a causal force. For Haidt (2008), moral judgement is best understood as a social process, not as a private act of cognition. Even if the specifics of morality are different in different cultures, the underlying principles – such as the importance of compassion and empathy – are the same. More recent research focusing on cooperation in human social life by Curry, Mullins and Whitehouse (2019) argues that morality consists of biological and cultural solutions; their research, which investigated moral behaviours in the ethnographic records of sixty societies, found that there are seven behaviours which are considered morally good in all cultures: 'helping kin, helping your group, reciprocating, being brave, deferring to superiors, dividing disputed resources and respecting prior possession' (Curry et al., 2019, p. 1). These are therefore plausible candidates for universal moral rules.

Moral diversity was widely acknowledged among the Ancient Greek philosophers as it was among mediaeval ethicists such as Thomas Aquinas (das Neves and Mele, 2013), and today it is accepted that among cultures there is diversity in moral perceptions and judgements. People and cultures change over time and space as do their ethical values. Accepting other people's standards of moral behaviour or the values of the majority can lead to moral relativism in which it is held that there are no reliable arbiters as to what is morally right or wrong. In this case, moral judgements are true or false relative to any given moral framework which is, of course, informed by culture. This means that moral relativism can lead to people ignoring their conscience, to moral paralysis and to moral indifference. In spite of this, some ethicists favour moral relativism (Krausz, 1989), while others insist on moral universalism; there is a third group which holds a balanced position between universalism and relativism expressed via a set of agreed ethical values and cultural norms (Gowans, 2012).

In an increasingly connected world, there is a pragmatic reason to seek and promote moral universalism – namely because the ethical issues we face, environmental problems, for example, affect us all. In 1993, in a bid to seek consensus on common ethical values, the Parliament of the World's Religions argued that a better global order would not be possible without a global ethical consensus, recognizing that it is the promotion of shared ethical values which will ultimately help lead to a more humane world.

We therefore conclude that both cultural factors and universal principles play a role in morality, and it is valuable to recognize this. There are certain moral principles that are shared across all cultures, but morality can also vary significantly from culture to culture. As we increasingly live in a globalized society, where people from different cultures need to learn to live together more harmoniously, shared moral frameworks will be required, and hopefully become more widely accepted.

Deontology, consequentionalism, utilitarianism and virtue ethics

Deontology is sometimes known as 'duty', 'obligation' or 'rule' ethics. The theory of deontology states that there are certain duties that we ought to fulfil, regardless of the outcomes. A deontological theory is one that holds that the rightness or wrongness of an action is a function of whether that action conforms to a suitable rule or set of rules, regardless of the outcome of the action. Kantian ethics is a specific type of deontological ethics that was proposed by the German philosopher Immanuel Kant in the late eighteenth century.

The word 'deontology' comes from the Greek word for duty, *deon*, and deontologists see the principles of morality as absolutes. According to deontologists, there are no situations which exist in which another human being's inherent dignity can be ignored; this is because basic dignity always outweighs whatever utility (benefit) could be secured in a given situation. Deontology argues that our duty to obey ethical principles outweighs considerations about increasing the good of others or society as a whole

Consequentialism in ethical philosophy holds that the consequences of one's conduct are the ultimate basis for judging the right or wrongness of one's conduct. For consequentialists, a morally right act is that which will produce the best overall outcome, namely the greatest balance of goods over harms than the alternatives available. Deontological theories have a number of features that distinguish them from consequentialist theories. First, deontological theories are not primarily concerned with the consequences of an action. Instead, they focus on the nature of the action itself. Second, deontological theories typically involve a notion of duty or obligation. That is, they require that we act in accordance with certain rules, even if doing so goes against what we feel is our self-interest. Third, deontological theories often place constraints on what we can do and are therefore sometimes criticized for being too rigid. For example, if one has a duty to tell the truth, then one might end up not telling a lie, even if by not telling a lie, someone ends up being harmed more than would otherwise be the case (a classic thought experiment concerns what one should do if forced by a criminal to reveal the whereabouts of a child from a wealthy family whom the criminal intends to kidnap for financial gain). Finally, deontological theories are often absolutist, meaning they forbid certain actions under any circumstances.

Some critics have argued that deontology is self-defeating, in that it leads to a situation where people are reluctant to make any moral decisions, for fear of doing something that is morally wrong. This can lead to a situation where the only people who are willing to act are those who are confident that they are acting in accordance with the rules, even if their actions might have bad consequences. Deontology also makes it difficult for us to adjudicate between conflicting duties or to rank suboptimal outcomes; this therefore makes it difficult to take a deontological approach to a number of real-life problems. Despite these criticisms, deontological theories remain. One reason for this is that they provide clear moral guideposts, that is, they tell us what we should and shouldn't do, without requiring us to weigh the pros and cons of each situation. Additionally, deontological theories often seem 'fairer' than consequentialist theories in some people's eyes, since they don't allow the ends to justify the means.

The best known example of consequentialism is utilitarianism which is concerned with the greatest happiness for the greatest number. Utilitarianism is the belief that the best course of action is the one that maximizes utility or overall benefit. This theory was first developed by Jeremy Bentham, a philosopher, jurist, economist and legal reformer, in the late 1700s. Bentham equated happiness with pleasure and the absence of pain. For Bentham this was an empirical observation – he argued that people desire pleasure to avoid pain. His scientific attributes led him to believe that the study of ethics could be successfully undertaken in a practical way, carefully measuring the consequences of alternative courses of action before deciding which choice to make. His theories had a great impact and helped lead to extensive social reform. His theory was underpinned by the principle of utility which means considering the usefulness of the results of actions; for Bentham, his principle needed to derive the norm 'the greatest good of the greatest number'. Moral acts maximize pleasure and thus minimize pain – happiness being the supreme ethical value.

Utilitarianism has been criticized for being too simplistic, for not taking into account the complexities of human morality. For example, utilitarians must make a number of assumptions about human nature, including that people are rational and self-interested. It also does not allow us to prioritize our family and friends over strangers which is unrealistic given the societies in which humans live. Another criticism of utilitarianism is that it can lead to unfair discrimination, that it can be used to justify what is sometimes called 'the tyranny of the majority'. This is because utilitarianism can lead to discrimination against minority groups or individuals. Imagine, for example, that decisions about the allocation of land are made by simple majorities and that indigenous people are in a minority. This problem is particularly significant in countries with diverse societies. Diversity brings with it multiple understandings of what might be right to wrong. Audi (2007) puts forward an alternative approach to ethical theory by suggesting that one way we can start to understand what is intrinsically good or of value is if we can see that there is a common theme of contributing to everyone's well-being, reflecting an inclusive approach.

A further criticism of utilitarianism is that it can be used to justify behaviour generally regarded as immoral. For example, a person may justify defrauding a very wealthy person if it results in a greater gain in happiness for them than loss in happiness of the wealthy person. This is because the principle of utility only takes into account the consequences of an action, not the intrinsic value of any individuals affected by the action. For example, a utilitarian might argue that it is acceptable to experiment on and kill a few hundred monkeys for medical research that has a good chance of alleviating the suffering of tens of thousands of people who have a painful disease that also, on average, shortens their life by several years. However, aside from any disagreement about the likelihood of the research indeed leading to such medical benefits, this argument does not consider the intrinsic value of the monkeys' lives. According to the Kantian theory of ethics, one should not treat people as a means to an end, but always as ends in themselves. Those who believe in animal rights maintain that the same logic should apply to non-human animals that can experience pleasures and pains. Despite these criticisms, utilitarianism remains a powerful ethical theory. Its simple framework can be applied to a wide range of real-world situations, and it offers a clear way to make difficult ethical decisions.

A third ethical framework advocates that each of us becomes more virtuous. Why be virtuous? A number of answers can be given. Some people believe that it is simply the right thing to be, while others believe that it will lead to greater happiness (a utilitarian argument). Virtues can be seen as engrained habits that lead to a flourishing life. Virtue ethics is a moral theory that emphasizes the character of the moral agent and the degree to which that agent fulfils his or her duties, rather than the consequences of his or her actions. It was first developed by the ancient Greek philosopher Aristotle. In his *Nicomachean Ethics*, Aristotle argued that the key to a good life is not simply living in accordance with the correct moral rules, but rather developing and exercising good character traits. These character traits, or virtues, include attributes such as courage, wisdom and self-control. Aristotle believed that being virtuous was the key to achieving *eudaimonia*, 'human flourishing'. He believed that people who act virtuously will be happier and more fulfilled than those who do not. Aristotle believed that developing these virtues requires a process of habituation and education. We must repeatedly perform actions that lead to the development of these virtues, in order to make them part of our character. Contemporary ethicists argue that this theory provides us with guidance on how to live good lives. These thinkers point to the fact that virtue ethics emphasizes the importance of developing a good character, which is something that is largely within our control, whatever our circumstances

However, virtue ethics has been criticized for its lack of attention to the consequences of actions. Critics argue that the theory fails to provide clear guidance on how we should act in difficult situations where the outcome is uncertain. Virtue ethics has also been criticized for being too subjective. Others argue that virtue ethics relies too heavily on the character of the individual, and so it may not be applicable to large organizations or groups of people. In conclusion, virtue ethics is a moral theory that emphasizes the character of the moral agent, rather than the consequences of his or her actions, as the key element of ethical thinking. While the theory has been criticized for its lack of attention to the consequences of our actions, it has also been defended by some contemporary thinkers who argue that the theory does provide us with guidance on how to live ethically good lives.

The role of religion in ethics

The importance of religion for ethics is considerable, even in societies that are increasingly secular. There are a number of differing perspectives on this issue, and it is one that is likely to continue to be debated for many years to come. On one side of the debate, there are those who believe that religion plays an important role in ethics, arguing that religious teachings can provide a valuable framework for understanding right and wrong. They also point to the fact that many people do look to their religious beliefs when making ethical decisions. On the other side of the debate, there are those who believe that religion has no place in ethics. They argue that ethical decisions should be made based on reason and logic, not on religious teachings. They would also note that there are many people who do not believe in any religion, and yet they are still able to make ethical decisions. So, what might be the role of religion in ethics?

A divine command system of ethics is based on the belief that there is a God who has revealed certain commands that humans are obligated to obey. Most holy writings (scriptures) are seen as the word of any given religion's divine being and as such a guide to ethics and values. However, the interpretation of those commands is necessarily by humans. In addition, divine commands are often tied to particular religions and are not necessarily universal (think Jewish food laws and the requirements in different religions about prayer). Despite these criticisms, divine command ethics has been influential throughout history, and is still advocated by a vast number of people today. One of the reasons for its continued popularity is that it provides definitive answers to many of the questions of what we ought to do. It also has the advantage of being based on a source of authority that is outside of ourselves, the apparent objectivity of which can be appealing to many people.

Divine command ethics is sometimes contrasted with natural law ethics, which is based on the belief that there are objective moral principles that can be discerned through reason. The key difference between these two systems is that divine command ethics relies on religious faith, while natural law ethics does not. Using reason stems from the argument that it is only through rational scientific enquiry, through seeking objective 'proofs', that we come to know and understand what is correct. During the Enlightenment, there was a drive to understand the world and provide a meaning to life, especially via the growth of scientific ideas. This reason became a powerful tool to support discussions of what is right and wrong independent of the content of the world's scriptures (Knowles and Lander, 2012, p. 15).

There are many reasons why someone might prefer ethics based on reason instead of a divine command system. In particular, reason-based ethics are not reliant on a particular belief system – they can be adopted by anyone, regardless of their religious beliefs (or lack thereof). Of course, reason-based ethics are not perfect. One critique is that they can be overly rationalistic and fail to take into account our emotional needs and desires. Additionally, reason-based ethics can sometimes be difficult to apply in the real world – we may know what the right thing to do is, but actually doing it can be another matter entirely. Still, for many people, reason-based ethics are a preferable alternative to a divine command system. In theory, they provide a flexible and pragmatic approach to morality that can be adopted by anyone, regardless of their beliefs, though, of course, they are likely to be rejected by many religious believers if their conclusions clash with what divine command ethics are understood to require.

Inequity is an ethical issue

Inequity means a lack of justice; as such, it is an ethical issue because it creates disparities in how people (some would include non-humans) are treated and in how they are able to access resources. Inequitable distributions of resources therefore raise ethical issues. This can be seen both within societies, where some groups are marginalized, and between societies, where there are often vast differences in wealth and power. The outcomes of inequity are an ethical issue because they often lead to discrimination. When people are treated differently based on their race, gender or other factors, it often leads to tension and conflict, which we will discuss further in Chapter 7. Additionally, inequity results in some people having less access to resources, for example, health inequalities which can impact their ability to meet their needs (Bradley, 2021).

In principle, there are a number of ways to address inequity. One way is to provide resources to marginalized groups. This can be viewed as one way to help level the playing field and give everyone a more equitable chance. Another approach is to change laws and policies that otherwise perpetuate inequity. Attempting to do this can be challenging and emotionally exhausting, but it is important to continue to fight for justice and for those who are marginalized because for them there is often no choice but to fight. For Friere (1970), inequality is linked to oppression, where the powerful and rich dehumanize the poor. The outcomes of inequality therefore create ethical issues that needs to be addressed. Friere argues that it is only the oppressed who can liberate both themselves and their oppressors by restoring humanity to both groups. But how can this be achieved? We must work to provide education and tools to those who are marginalized so that they can liberate themselves whilst changing the laws and policies that contribute to inequality. Only then can we create a more just and equitable world.

In recent years, there has been a growing recognition of the need to address inequities that exist in science because the marginalized do not get fair access to the products of science, such as foods, medicines, clean water and energy, and this is an ethical issue. There are a number of reasons why inequity in science is an ethical issue. First, science is a public good. This means that it is something that everyone should have access to. Second, science is essential in modern societies for human flourishing (Briggs & Reiss, 2021). If people are denied access to science, they will be unable to live up to their full potential. Third, science is a tool for social change. It can be used to improve the lives of marginalized people.

There are a number of ways to address inequity in science. One way is to increase access to science education. This can be done by providing scholarships and financial aid to marginalized students, by increasing the number of science teachers and science courses in marginalized communities. Another way to address inequity in science is to increase the diversity of scientists. This can be done by increasing the number of women and minorities in science, by increasing the number of scientists from marginalized communities and by supporting science programmes that serve marginalized communities. A further way to address inequity in science is to increase the accessibility of scientific research. This can be done by providing free or low-cost access to scientific journals, by providing funding for research in marginalized communities and by increasing the number of science outreach programmes in marginalized communities. Ultimately, addressing inequity in science is an ethical issue because science is a public good that is essential for human flourishing. By increasing access to science education, increasing the diversity of scientists and increasing the accessibility of scientific research, we can help ensure that everyone has the opportunity to benefit from science.

Feminist approaches to ethics

In recent years, there has been a growing awareness of the need for gender equality in all aspects of life. This includes the workplace, where women have traditionally been underrepresented and undervalued. While there has been some progress made in recent years, there is still a way to go to achieve equality, and there is increasing recognition nowadays that there are not just two genders. One area where gender equality is particularly important is in the field of ethics. As we have already argued, ethics are the principles that guide our behaviour, and they should be applied equally to everyone, regardless of gender. Unfortunately, this is not always the case. One example of this is the way that women are often judged more harshly than men when it comes to their appearance. Studies have shown that women are more likely to be judged on their looks than their male counterparts, and that they are held to a higher standard of attractiveness. This can lead to a number of problems, such as women being passed over for promotions or being treated unfairly in the workplace. Another example of gender inequality in ethics is the way that women are often assumed to be more emotional than men. This stereotype can lead to women being seen as less capable of making rational decisions, and it can also lead to them being ignored or discounted when they do speak up.

Feminist approaches to ethics emphasize the need for women's voices to be heard in moral and ethical decision-making. They challenge the traditional view that ethics is primarily concerned with the rights and wrongs of individual action. Instead, feminists argue that ethics must take into account the social and political context in which moral choices are made. Feminists have also critiqued the ways in which traditional ethical theories have been used to justify discrimination against women. For example, Kant's theory of universal moral law has been used to argue that women are morally inferior to men and therefore should not be given the same rights and opportunities. Similarly, Aristotle's view that the purpose of ethics is to promote human flourishing has been used to argue that women are not capable of achieving the same level of moral excellence as men.

Feminist approaches to ethics offer a different perspective on what is important in moral decision-making. They emphasize the need to consider the impact of our choices on the lives of women and other marginalized groups. In addition, feminists argue that we must take into account the social and political context in which moral choices are made. Furthermore, women are more likely than men to suffer from the negative consequences of moral choices, such as domestic violence or sexual assault. Feminist approaches to ethics therefore provide a valuable perspective on the importance of taking into account the lives of women and other marginalized groups in moral decision-making. By taking into account the social and political context in which moral choices are made, feminist approaches to ethics can help us to make better choices that promote the well-being of all. It is essential that we continue to work towards a world where everyone is treated equally, regardless of their gender. Only then can humans truly claim to be living in a fair and just society.

In science, feminist approaches to ethics are having an increasing influence. For example, it is now acknowledged that much medical research has ignored the possibility that women might have different needs to men and might respond differently to medicines and other treatments than men do, even if they are the same age and mass. Furthermore, it used to be the case that ethical decisions even about matters in which women played a central role, such as nutrition and reproductive health, paid little attention to the views of women. Thankfully, such outdated practices are increasingly changing.

Theories of justice and oppression

The idea of justice is central to ethics. Oppression theories provide a framework for understanding the roles of power and privilege in in justice and the intersectionality of class, race, gender, self and group identity within the context of social practices. Oppression is a structural phenomenon that is a part of the social fabric and the concept of power is central to understanding oppression (Cudd, 2006). A society is an organization of people within a territory governed by a body of principles, institutions and customs. The concept of social structure refers to how a society is organized into distinct groups, based on roles, positions and relations. The concept of a social institution is that it is an organization created and sustained by the society to meet common goals. Social institutions, including economic, political and educational institutions, are found in all societies. They operate through a system of norms and values that establish patterns of behaviour.

Structural oppression is defined as the systematic abuse of power by one social group over another. In Marxist theory, for example, social groups are distinguished by their different relationships to the means of production (Bartkey, 2015). The ruling class is the class of people who owns the means of production as private property. The working class provides the labour to enable production to take place. The ruling class exploits (oppresses) the working class by appropriating the surplus value of their labour. The concept of surplus value refers to the difference between the value produced by workers and the value paid to them in wages.

Other approaches to understanding injustice extend the focus to issues like gender, ethnicity and disability. In each case, institutions and societies can become polarized, with those who have more power – males, those who are white, the mentally and physically able – benefitting at the expense of others. When these inequities become institutionally or societally embedded, we end up not just with sexism, racism and ableism, but with systemic sexism, systemic racism and systemic ableism.

Therefore, power is central to understanding oppression (Palmer et al., 2019). Power is the ability to control the behaviour of others and therefore the ability to get others to do what you want them to do. Power can be used in a positive or negative way, to oppress or to liberate, to control or to empower and can therefore be used to exploit or to protect. Privilege is related to power and can be understood as a special right, advantage or immunity granted or available only to a particular person or group of people. It may be granted by law or custom, inherited or acquired.

Intergenerational ethics

Intergenerational ethics refers to the moral principles that guide our interactions with people of different generations; it considers topics which involve future generations as well as lives not yet in being. These principles help us to think about what is fair and just in our interactions with others, and how we can best meet the needs of all involved. There are a number of different ethical considerations that come into play when thinking about intergenerational interactions. For example, we need to think about the rights of different generations, and how these rights can be balanced with any competing rights. Depending on our ethical view, we might (or might not) also think about the different needs of different generations, and how best to meet these needs (Gardiner, 2006). Additionally, we need to think about the impact of our actions on future generations, and how to make sure that we are acting in their best interests.

When it comes to intergenerational ethics, there is no one-size-fits-all answer. The best way to approach these ethical considerations is to thoughtfully consider the needs of all involved, and to act in a way that is fair and just. One of the key considerations in intergenerational ethics is the question of rights. The interests of different generations need to be taken into account when making decisions that will affect them. For example, the decisions we make today about anthropogenic climate change will potentially have major consequences for future generations (Groves, 2014). When thinking about the rights of different generations, depending on the ethical framework we follow, we might need to make sure that we are not unfairly privileging one generation over another.

Another key consideration in intergenerational ethics is the question of specific needs. Different generations have different needs, and these must be taken into account when making decisions. For example, young people need access to education and to opportunities for economic advancement. Older people are more likely to need access to healthcare and to social support. And there are broader considerations about the decisions we make now which will affect future generations, questions around sustainability being one example of this.

Finally, when we make decisions, we need to think about how our actions may affect the world that future generations will inherit. How can we ensure that we are not causing harm to the environment, as well as to future generations of people? We also need to make sure that we are not creating inequalities that will last for generations. When thinking about the impact of our actions, we therefore need to be mindful of the long-term consequences of these. We need to make sure that we are acting in the best interests of all involved, both today and in the future.

Environmental ethics

Environmental ethics is a branch of philosophy that studies the conceptual foundations of environmental values. In doing so, societal attitudes, actions and policies to protect and sustain biodiversity and ecological systems are studied (Taylor, 2011).

In recent years, the environment has become topical given the drastic changes people are experiencing first hand due to climate change, the loss of biodiversity and other instances of environmental damage. We are constantly being reminded of the importance of protecting our environment. Environmental ethics is the branch of ethics that deals with the moral relationship between humans and the natural environment. It is based on the belief that humans have a responsibility to care for the environment and to use its resources in a sustainable way (Yang, 2006).

There are many different ways to approach environmental ethics. One popular approach is the 'land ethic', which was first proposed by American philosopher and ecologist Aldo Leopold (2017). The land ethic is based on the belief that humans are a part of the natural world and that we have a responsibility to care for the land. This approach has been influential in the development of environmental policies and regulations in the United States. Another approach to environmental ethics is 'weak anthropocentrism', which is the belief that humans are not the only beings with moral worth, but that while we matter more than other species, it is often the case that actions can benefit both us and other species. This approach has been used to justify policies such as the creation of national parks and the protection of endangered species (whose preservation may benefit humans as well as the protected species themselves).

Weak anthropocentrism differs from strong anthropocentrism, which is the view that only human interests ultimately matter. A more radical position than weak anthropocentrism is 'deep ecology'. Deep ecology holds that all living beings (not just sentient ones that can experience pleasures and pains) have inherent worth, regardless of their instrumental value to human beings (Naess, 1973).

Animal rights

Animal rights is the belief that non-human animals should be accorded the same moral worth as humans. Animals therefore are seen to have a right to live free from exploitation and cruelty, just as we do. Animal rights advocates argue that many animals are sentient beings and therefore we should not cause them to suffer. There is a growing body of scientific evidence that supports the view that many animals are not only sentient beings but are more similar to us than many people suppose. For example, a study by Bartal et al. (2011) found that rats show signs of empathy and altruism. The study found that when a rat was placed in a cage with another rat that was in distress, the first rat would try to comfort the other rat. The study also showed that rats will free restrained companions rather than feast on chocolate (one of your authors wonders how he would do in such a test). The researchers concluded that this behaviour was underpinned by empathy. Another study found that chickens demonstrate sophisticated social cognition; they can remember the faces of other chickens and that they preferentially associate with chickens that they have seen before (Mariano, 2017). These studies and others like them show that animals are capable of feeling a range of emotions, and can demonstrate empathy and compassion. This evidence supports the view that such animals should be treated with respect and compassion themselves.

Animal rights advocates argue that it is morally wrong to kill animals for food as there are plant-based alternatives available. They also argue that animals should not be used for entertainment, such as in circuses or zoos, because they are confined to small spaces and cannot express all their natural behaviours. Many animal rights advocates also believe that keeping pets is wrong, however well they are looked after. Finally, animal rights advocates argue that animals should not be used in scientific or medical experiments, whatever the possible benefits, because they often suffer from pain and distress. Animal rights is a complex issue, and there are a variety of opinions on the best way to protect and look after animals. However, the growing body of scientific evidence showing that many animals are sentient beings supports the view that animals should be treated with respect and compassion.

What is science education?

4

It might be thought that the answer to the question, 'What is science education?' follows immediately from the answer to the question that we considered in Chapter 2: 'What is science?' But this isn't necessarily the case; it depends on whether one sees science education as a subset of science or as a subset of education. One's understanding of what the aims of science education should be depends on whether one gives more weight to the overall aims of education, with science education playing a part within that, or to the aims of science, with science education playing a part within that (cf. Mansfield & Reiss, 2020). In this chapter we therefore start by examining what the aims of science education might be, and whether or not ethics has a role to play.

The aims of science education

Science education today operates within a landscape characterized by rapid technological advances within a highly connected and globalized world that is, nevertheless, in certain ways deeply fragmented. Increasing numbers of people in more and more countries are able to communicate in real time across the globe, and an increasing proportion of the world's population has virtually instantaneous access, if they have the necessary financial resources, to information, goods, services and each other via the internet. But it often feels that our cultural evolution is unable to keep pace with this rapid technological change, which manifests, as has long been noted (Beck, 1986/1992), in greater uncertainty about what the future might look like and increased concern at these changes. Such concern is indicated by a rash of dystopian novels such as Margaret Atwood's The MaddAddam Trilogy (published in 2003, 2009 and 2013), Naomi Alderman's *The Power* (in 2017) and Kazuo Ishiguro's *Klara and the Sun* (in 2021), and such films as *Never Let Me Go* (in 2010), *The Hunger Games* series (in 2012, 2013, 2014 and 2015), *Under the Skin* (in 2013), *Snowpiercer* (in 2014), *Ex Machina* (in 2015), *Blade Runner 2049* (in 2017) and

The Matrix Resurrections (in 2021) and such TV series as *Black Widow*, *Human 2.0*, *Westworld* and *Squid Game*.

When one looks at the aims of science education in the current science National Curriculum in England for ages 5–16, one finds the following:

> The national curriculum for science aims to ensure that all pupils:
>
> - develop scientific knowledge and conceptual understanding through the specific disciplines of biology, chemistry and physics
> - develop understanding of the nature, processes and methods of science through different types of science enquiries that help them to answer scientific questions about the world around them
> - are equipped with the scientific knowledge required to understand the uses and implications of science, today and for the future. *(Department for Education, 2015)*

This is a set of aims for science education that draws more from science than from education. The subsequent research review on science by Ofsted (Office for Standards in Education, Children's Services and Skills) helps flesh out in more detail what the official body for inspecting schools sees as good science education (Ofsted is a non-ministerial government department). Indeed, it starts, rather usefully for our purposes, with a section titled 'Aims of Science Education', which, after a short paragraph about the statutory place of science in the curriculum, states the following (references omitted):

> Although the precise purposes of science education have been contested for some time, there is general consensus that it involves pupils learning a body of knowledge relating to the products and practices of science. By learning about the products of science, such as atoms and cells, pupils are able to explain the material world and 'develop a sense of excitement and curiosity about natural phenomena'. By learning about the practices of science, pupils learn how scientific knowledge becomes established through scientific enquiry. By learning this, pupils appreciate the nature and status of scientific knowledge: for example, knowing it is open to revision in the light of new evidence.
>
> As pupils learn science, they also learn about its uses and significance to society and their own lives. This will highlight the significant contribution science has made in the past. For example, by eradicating smallpox and discovering penicillin. But pupils will also learn about the continuing importance of science in solving global challenges such as climate change, food availability, controlling disease and access to water.
>
> Science education also provides the foundation for a range of diverse and valuable careers that are crucial for economic, environmental and social development. *(Ofsted, 2021)*

The first paragraph presents quite a 'pure' vision of science, with little connection to ethics. But it's in the second and third paragraphs that, while they aren't explicitly mentioned, ethical issues come into play. Smallpox was eradicated by means of vaccination, and vaccination raises a whole host of ethical questions. Indeed, even something initially as apparently morally unproblematic as 'controlling disease' can raise ethical issues. Does human health triumph all other considerations? Should we try to exterminate rats just because they can carry human diseases or are even rats worthy of having their interests considered? The last paragraph talks about 'valuable careers that are crucial for economic, environmental and social development' – but is economic development always desirable and, in any case, what is meant by 'environmental development'? We will address questions such as these below and in later chapters.

Visions for science education

Many specific aims for science education have been suggested – from ensuring the supply of future scientists to aiming for social justice. A valuable way of categorizing these is provided by Roberts and Bybee (2014), who build on Roberts's (2007), who identified two contrasting visions for science education – Vision I and Vision II:

> Vision I looks inward at science, to build curriculum from its rich and well-established array of techniques and methods, habits of mind, and well-tested explanations for the events and objects of the natural world. Literacy, in this view, is within science – general familiarity and fluency within the discipline, based on mastering a sampling of the language, products, processes, and traditions of science itself.
>
> Vision II, developed later in the history of school science, begins by looking outside science to build curriculum that illuminates how science permeates and interacts with many areas of human endeavor and life situations. These societal issues and individual life situations usually include political, economic, and ethical considerations. This view is sometimes called science for citizenship, concentrating on matters of more obvious personal and social relevance to students than preparing to grasp more demanding science they might or might not study. The slogan 'science for all' represents a viewpoint that all students need some introduction to citizen science, including such matters as environmental quality, resource use, personal health, and decision making about complex socioscientific issues. *(Roberts & Bybee, 2014, p. 546)*

Increasingly, school science courses try and combine both visions, seeking to produce courses that serve both the *minority* of students who will go on to be scientists and *all* of the students in school. Combining visions is a tough ask, and a lot of the tension experienced in science courses in recent decades around the world can be traced to trying to satisfy these two rather different constituencies.

In Michael Reiss's experience of teaching science to 11- to 18-year-olds, some students clearly preferred Vision I – they were typically the ones hoping to go on and study science in higher education after they left school – whilst others clearly preferred Vision II.

In a way, ethics clearly fits more with Vision II than with Vision I, but there are dangers in this equation. For one thing, ethics becomes associated with lower-level science – note how Roberts and Bybee see Vision II science as 'concentrating on matters of more obvious personal and social relevance to students *than preparing to grasp more demanding science* they might or might not study' (our italics). For another, it might mean that it is concluded that we don't need to teach anything about ethics to those students who are going on to be scientists. That would surely be a mistake for a number of reasons. We need scientists and those working in science-adjacent professions (including doctors and engineers and those working on Artificial Intelligence) to have engaged seriously with ethics in their studies.

You wait for ages for a vision for science education and then three come along, one after another. Sjöström and Eilks (2018) have put forward what they term 'Vision III'. In essence, Vision III is a humanized science education that includes 'critical scientific literacy' and 'socio-political action'. It builds on earlier ideas of such authors as Hodson (1994), Roth and Barton (2004) and Aikenhead (2007). More recently, it has been argued that Vision III 'should include both a broad conception of participation, which makes visible the invisible and informal acts performed by diverse groups to build society, and an alternative notion of emancipation committed to liberation' (Valladares, 2021, p. 557).

Vision III therefore has various elements to it. It builds on Visions I and II in that it requires a good understanding of science (Vision I) and is a science education for all (Vision II). But it goes beyond Visions I and II in that it awakens learners to the effects that science has on others and on the world more generally, and it encourages a moral sensibility so that learners are dissatisfied with injustice and hurt, and strive to use scientific and other knowledge for general good (Guerrero & Torres-Olave, 2021). Table 4.1 provides a summary comparison of these three visions for science education.

Table 4.1 Different visions for science education and their implications for school science.

Vision	School aim	Ultimate aim	Emphasis in science education
I	Induction into science Continue with science	Produce the next generation of scientists	Understand science
II	Scientific literacy for all	Make use of science for everyday life	Ensure science taught is relevant
III	Develop critical scientific literacy	Use science to address injustice	Societal transformation

Powerful knowledge and a science curriculum for human flourishing

As we discussed in Chapter 2, one of the claims about science is that it produces a distinctive type of knowledge – a knowledge that is refutable and amenable to change, a knowledge that is democratic in the sense that it is not (at any rate, should not be) the preserve of a distinct group of people. In his aptly titled book *Bringing Knowledge Back In* (Young, 2008), Michael Young argued that the school curriculum must not restrict itself to everyday practical experience but provide learners with access to the specialist knowledge that they need and which cannot be obtained outside of school, for instance from their homes. This knowledge is powerful when it enables students to understand and think beyond the limits of their own experience. Young's arguments apply to all school subjects, but he was a school chemistry teacher and his arguments are clearly, perhaps especially, applicable to science. At first sight, Young's position seems aligned with Roberts's Vision I or II. However, his position is also an egalitarian one that seeks to challenge educational disadvantage and reduce educational inequalities:

> The school, for all its tendencies to reproduce the inequalities of an unequal society, is the only institution we have that can, at least in principle, provide every student with access to knowledge. The only alternative to schools for all is to accept that the majority will never have the educational opportunities that the minority has always treated as their right. We must respect and value the experience of pupils, but we can never allow them to depend on their experience alone. To do so would leave them (and us) in the position of out Stone Age ancestors, or worse; we would be no different from animals, who have *only* their experience. *(Young, 2014, p. 13)*

In this sense, Young's views about powerful knowledge can support all three visions for science education.

A different way of conceptualizing what the aim of education might be – rather than Young's provision of powerful knowledge – is provided by one of us with John White in *An Aims-based Curriculum* (Reiss & White, 2013). The intention behind that book was to provide a framework for the development of a coherent set of aims for the curriculum, some for implementation at national level, others at the level of each school. The argument begins with the assertion that there should be two principal aims of a school: to enable each learner to lead a life that is personally flourishing; and to enable others to lead personally flourishing lives too. It is then argued that a central aim of a school should therefore be to prepare its students for a life of autonomous, whole-hearted and successful engagement in worthwhile relationships, activities and experiences. This aim involves acquainting students with a wide range of possible options from which to choose. With their development towards autonomous adulthood in mind, schools should provide students with increasing opportunities to decide between the pursuits that best suit them. Young children are likely to need greater guidance from their teachers, just as they do from their parents. Part of the function of schooling, and indeed parenting, is to prepare children for the time when they will need to, and be able to, make decisions more independently (Reiss, 2018).

The argument that schooling should enable human flourishing aligns well with Visions II and III for science education. It also raises questions about what should be the content of school science. Interestingly, here there is a place for Vision I too. One way in which the school science curriculum might do a better job of preparing students for careers in science is to teach more about the sorts of careers that lead from science and about how there are many professions that benefit from a knowledge of science. For example, when teaching about the central nervous system to lower secondary students, one might be teaching about memory. In a curriculum for human flourishing, one might include material on how knowledge about memory is used by nurses who look after patients who have Alzheimer's disease, by cognitive behavioural therapists who work with people who have Obsessive Compulsive Disorder, by dog handlers who train dogs to act in films, not to mention by teachers attempting to help their students to learn and understand, and by students themselves when revising (Reiss & White, 2014).

Finally, in this section, we can note that we are nowadays painfully aware that enabling *human* flourishing is not enough – this would be an anthropocentric perspective. We are living in what is sometimes termed the Anthropocene because of the effects human actions have on all species and on the planet as a whole. We need an education, and a science education in particular, that benefits all, not just humanity (cf. Haraway, 2016).

Pedagogy

Building on the material we have covered in this and preceding chapters, we want now to discuss some of the ways that school science might be taught. A school setting is presumed because informal science education is addressed in Chapter 9. Chapter 5 examines what ethics education might entail and Chapter 6 asks specially whether ethics should be considered where science is taught, so our discussion here does not presume that ethics is an integral part of science education, nor does it provide case studies of how socio-scientific issues and argumentation might be vehicles for the teaching of ethics in science, as those issues are addressed in Chapters 7 and 8, respectively. Rather, here we look at suggestions as to how school science might be taught and examine whether or not there is a place for teaching about ethics.

Practical work

For many primary pupils and secondary students if one asks them what is characteristic of school science, practical work (referred to as lab work in some countries) is the most likely answer they will give. One of us once taught science in a school for

11- to 18-year-olds where a shortage of school laboratories meant that only some of the science lessons were taught in the laboratories, the rest being taught in ordinary classrooms. The students knew that they weren't likely to get much practical work in the ordinary classrooms – though one could enliven a biology lesson on human physiology by measuring reaction times or seeing how exercise (stepping on and off a bench) affected heart rate. However, the same students who would work quietly without any practical work in such a classroom felt deeply cheated if they were expected to spend an entire lesson (all of 35 minutes) in a laboratory without some practical work.

Despite the widespread enthusiasm among pupils and students for practical work in school science, something of a consensus has grown up among science educators that practical work all too often does not lead to much learning of science concepts. In one highly cited study, Abrahams and Millar (2008) collected data on twenty-five 'typical' science lessons involving practical work in English secondary schools. As they concluded:

> The teachers' focus in these lessons was predominantly on developing students' substantive scientific knowledge, rather than on developing understanding of scientific enquiry procedures. Practical work was generally effective in getting students to do what is intended with physical objects, but much less effective in getting them to use the intended scientific ideas to guide their actions and reflect upon the data they collect. (p. 1945)

Of course, practical work can have a number of aims. As well as hoping to enable such conceptual learning, it can arouse and maintain interest, encourage the development of a range of scientific skills (such as careful observation and the manipulation of equipment) and help students to understand how scientific knowledge is built up (Hodson, 1990; Bennett, 2003). Nevertheless, the increasing body of research that indicates how little conceptual learning can take place despite pupils and students enthusiastically engaging in practical work is discouraging. Accordingly, the distinction is now often made between the 'hands-on' doing of science (undertaking the practical activities) and the 'minds-on' thinking that is needed if learning (of conceptual knowledge) is to result. Such thinking is greatly helped by relevant talk, whether with peers or the teacher.

Using the hand-on/minds-on framework, Abrahams and Reiss (2012) found that primary science teachers in England spent a substantially higher percentage of their science lessons talking with pupils about the scientific ideas associated with practical activities than did secondary science teachers (thus facilitating minds-on thinking). On the other hand, students in the secondary lessons spent a substantially higher percentage of their science lessons engaged in manipulating objects and materials (i.e. hands-on activity) than did their primary counterparts.

It is in the teacher-facilitated talk around practical work that ethical thinking is most likely to feature. A simple piece of practical work in primary science about filtration could easily lead into a discussion of the importance of clean water for drinking and then into consideration of inequalities among people in access to such water. A National Geographic article on water inequality, designed for Grades 5–8 pupils, points out that in 2015, 29 per cent of people globally suffered from lack of access to safely managed drinking water, with more than twice that number being at risk for water contamination from improper wastewater management (National Geographic, 2019). That article goes on to consider the impacts of this on health and people's use of time; in sub-Saharan Africa, more than 25 per cent of the population must walk 30 minutes or more to collect water, a burden that falls the world over on women and girls the vast majority of the time (Figure 4.1).

If it is possible for ethics meaningfully to be included within a short piece of practical work in science, this is even more the case where students undertake a more extended investigation. An example of such an extended investigation where ethics is involved is provided by a research project being undertaken by year 9 students at Liverpool Life Sciences UTC (University Technical College) in England. These students are investigating whether mealworms (larvae of the beetle *Tenebrio molitor*) can digest plastic waste, potentially providing a partial solution to one of our planet's greatest environmental challenges. Previous research suggests that these creatures can turn up to half of the plastic they ingest into harmless substances. The intention is to develop a household plastic waste digester box that uses mealworms to break down non-recyclable plastic waste (Liverpool Life Sciences UTC, 2021).

Figure 4.1 Girls carrying water in India.
Source: Wikimedia Commons https://commons.wikimedia.org/wiki/File:Girls_carrying_water_in_India.jpg. *Photograph by Tom Maisey.*

The Liverpool Life Sciences UTC investigation is, at the time of writing, still at a relatively early stage. Davis and Schaeffer (2019) report findings from the conclusion of a two-year interdisciplinary science unit on water, designed for Black children in the United States in a city ('Riverview' – a pseudonym) where water access issues are present, but seldom discussed. Ethnographic data were collected over a two-year period while grade 4/5 pupils undertook their study:

> A guiding question for the year in Ms. Janelle's classroom was, 'How does water support life?' The Water is Life unit was designed to critically engage children with this question through socio-scientific explorations of water and water access. The unit featured dialogue, debate, collaborative group work, documentary screenings, a field trip to a local river, and engagement with a panel of local water activists. Consistent with the place-based focus of the school, teachers Janelle and Bobby foregrounded inquiries of water in Riverview. In recent years, many Riverview residents in the school's surrounding community were affected by mass water shut-offs. The water shut-offs made national news and were investigated as a human rights violation. However, due to the stigmas associated with poor hygiene and being too poor to pay your water bill, those most affected often suffered quietly. *(Davis & Schaeffer, 2019, p. 373)*

In addition to the field trip to the river, pupils undertook six activities on water. They also spent large amounts of times discussing their findings, making posters and engaging in debates, and related these to water issues:

> By design, the unit leveraged traditional science content (e.g., properties of water, water's role in the human body, physiological consequences of lead poisoning), as a means of helping children to make sense of water issues. Although increased knowledge about water's properties was understood as important, teachers wanted students to also gain a deeper understanding of people's lived experiences with water injustices and recognize the need for systemic change. *(p. 373)*

This is a hands-on *and* minds-on way of undertaking practical work, and an example of science education being undertaken in the light of Vision III. As the unit progressed, 'children began to understand water justice as a sociopolitical (and in some cases raced) and ethical issue' (p. 384).

Project work

In the preceding section, we examined the potential for practical work to manifest an ethical dimension. Of course, project work in science that lacks a practical component can also manifest an ethical dimension. Tolppanen et al. (2019) studied a case study of life-cycle assessment (LCA), arguing that it can be a useful way to increase the relevance of science education to students' everyday lives (references omitted):

> Typically, LCA is used to assess the environmental burden and health impact of a product, throughout a products' [sic] life-cycle, from acquisition of raw materials to utilizing waste. In education, LCA can also have a strong emphasis on sustainability in a wider sense, as it can also be used to discuss issues, such as values, human rights, and how psychology, norms, and marketing may affect our consumption. Examining a products' life-cycle is also closely related to circular economy and can help students develop system thinking. Furthermore, LCA is also related to science ethics and moral awareness and is often used to evaluate how ecological a product is – for instance, from the perspective of a carbon or water footprint. *(Tolppanen et al., 2019, p. 3)*

At the same time, Tolppanen et al. point out that LCA is rare in education and, when it does occur, is typically a feature in higher education rather than in school education. Their study was undertaken with grade 9 students (aged 15–16) in Finland, in two classes, each of which received six 45-minute lessons. Students were first shown short videos about the food industry and then asked to discuss the different type of products they use in their everyday lives. They were then divided into groups of two or three students and asked to choose a product and examine its life cycle. The students were also required to interview someone working with the product during its life cycle. The groups were free to choose a topic of their interest from a predetermined list of industries: the plastic industry, cosmetics, the pharmaceutical industry, the paper industry and the textiles industry.

After researching their topic, the students were asked to make presentations in which they:

- Explain the main features of the manufacturing process concerning chemistry;
- Describe the product's life cycle and define where it ends up after use;
- Present evidence about the environmental burden of the manufacturing process and about the consumption of the product;
- Find out what type of specialists are needed for the manufacturing the product;
- Interview a specialist from the industry. *(p. 5)*

Questionnaire analysis showed that the students found the intervention to be socially relevant, as they understood that they were dealing with a topic that was important to the whole world and that the problem was scientifically relevant. Interviews with both students revealed that the students enjoyed the intervention and understood a number of the ethical issues that were raised:

> The products' lifecycles dealt with many environmental issues. For example, we found out how much water a pair of jeans needs and so forth.

> We used to all be somewhat reckless in how we disposed plastic, but in the future, we want to pay more attention to this, because making the presentation really got us thinking (about these issues).

> Human actions can cause direct plastic problems to the environment. Plastic dumbed [*sic*] into oceans and our surroundings can harm animals. For instance, consumed plastic has been found in the stomach of dead birds. Also, water animals, such as fish and turtles have died because they have been trapped in plastic in the water. After use, plastic must be disposed properly and not be left into the nature.
>
> It is better to buy local products, because then you support local companies … clothes produced in far-away countries (especially in Asia and Africa) have 'hidden water,' and the workers may work under bad working conditions and may even use child-labor. Also, the transportation of materials pollutes the environment.

This study illustrates a more general point, namely that teaching ethics within school science requires consideration of the context within which science is used. There is a long history of teachers using contexts to motivate students and to illustrate the applications of science. There is also a body of opinion that says that context-based science education can lead to better learning of science concepts by students. In reality, the evidence for this is limited (Bennett et al., 2007). It seems more likely that some teachers prefer teaching 'pure', abstracted science while others prefer teaching science as it is embedded in its use. We'll return to this issue in Chapter 7 when we consider socio-scientific issues. We now move on to the final part of this chapter where we discuss the importance of assessment.

Assessment

Good curricula are valuable and good pedagogy is essential, but unless there is a good match between curricula, pedagogy and assessment, the learning that a curriculum intends and a teacher desires is less likely to result. Students' performance on science courses has traditionally been assessed at the end of the courses with the emphasis on scientific knowledge and understanding, perhaps with a focus on how such knowledge is built up and how it is applied. However, if ethics is to be an important component of science teaching, then it will need to be assessed too.

When one looks at how ethics is assessed in school science, one generally finds that it features more strongly in biology than in the other sciences. This is hardly surprising – there are ethical issues in much of biology: our use of the natural environment, including sentient animals for farming, scientific research and other purposes; medicine – for example, how to determine who gets transplants when these are in short supply; and modern biotechnologies – for example, the acceptability of genetically modified organisms. Furthermore, some biology courses contain more ethics than do others for the same age range. For example, the current Salters-Nuffield Advanced level biology course (for 16- to 19-year-olds) includes the following requirements in its specification, where it states that student should:

- Be able to discuss the potential ethical issues regarding the use of invertebrates in research.
- Be able to identify and discuss the social and ethical issues related to genetic screening from a range of ethical viewpoints.
- Be able to discuss different ethical positions relating to whether the use of performance-enhancing substances by athletes is acceptable.
- Be able to discuss the moral and ethical issues relating to the use of animals in medical research from two ethical standpoints.
- Understand how the outcomes of genome sequencing projects are being used in the development of personalised medicine and the social, moral and ethical issues this raises.
- Also consider the ethical issues presented by their work in the laboratory, which might include consideration for the ethical use of live subjects, the safe disposal of waste materials, and appropriate consideration for other people involved in their own work or who are working nearby. *(Pearson Edexcel, 2018)*

However, it is noteworthy not only that some science courses make more reference to the assessment of ethics than do others, and that ethics generally features more strongly in biology than in other science courses, but that the coverage of ethics is generally particularly modest for younger age ranges. In England, the current version of the science National Curriculum only refers to ethics in two places, both at Key Stage 4 (for 14- to 16-year-olds):

- Through the content across all three disciplines, students should be taught so that they develop understanding and first-hand experience of appreciating the power and limitations of science and considering ethical issues which may ar.ise
- Students should be helped to understand how, through the ideas of biology, the complex and diverse phenomena of the natural world can be described in terms of a number of key ideas which are of universal application, and which can be illustrated in the separate topics set out below. These ideas include ... the uses of modern biotechnology including gene technology; some of the practical and ethical considerations of modern biotechnology. *(Department for Education, 2015)*

What can we learn from how ethics is assessed in other school subjects? A comparison of the assessment of ethics in school science examinations and the examinations of other subjects revealed some key differences (Nuffield Foundation, 2009). For example, here is an example of the assessment of ethics in religious studies. The question was one of two alternatives on the June 2008 paper to examine the AQA Advanced Level (for 16- to 18-year-olds) Religious Studies Unit 4: An Introduction to Religion and Ethics, and needed answering in 40 minutes:

(a) Explain how the teachings of **one** religion you have studied can be applied to the medical issue of euthanasia. (15 marks)

(b) Explain Kant's theory of the categorical imperative, and assess the view that any law concerning euthanasia should be based on Kant's theory. (25 marks) *(AQA, 2008a, p. 2)*

The mark scheme for part (b) of this question was as follows:

Candidates need to explain the categorical imperative.

Kant perceived that most people behaved well because they felt they ought to, especially if they wanted something back in return. He called this the hypothetical imperative. However, he said that people ought to do things because people 'knew' them to be the right things to do. People worked this out using reason. Kant called this the categorical imperative, and formulated three principles of it; the universal law, treating humans as ends in themselves rather than just means to an end, and living in a Kingdom of Ends.

Maximum Level 3 (6 marks) if no example used.

(10 marks)

Any explanation of the categorical imperative should then be applied to euthanasia, e.g. is it possible to make a universal law regarding euthanasia? Many religions would reject a law allowing euthanasia, although Holland has such a law. The UK criminalizes euthanasia. It can be argued that allowing euthanasia is both treating a person as an end in themselves, and also as a means to an end (cessation of pain for the relatives seeing a loved one die). Allowing euthanasia country-wide does raise issues of the slippery slope and continuation of the human race.

Assess

For
- UK has a law on euthanasia which is in effect a universal law
- It is very important and commendable not to treat people as a means to an end
- The categorical imperative is not based on emotion which can colour any decision-making.

Against
- Religious groups would be alienated if a law permitting euthanasia is passed
- Kant did not mention euthanasia, therefore we do not know what he would have said about it
- Countries should make up their own laws.

Maximum Level 3 (8 marks) if no reference to a law regarding euthanasia.

(15 marks)

(AQA, 2008b, p. 7)

The first point to note is that fully 15 marks are available for part (a) and 25 for part (b), with the whole question intended to take abut 40 minutes. In science examinations, ethics rarely gets more than a couple of marks. It is also noteworthy that, setting aside subject-specific differences in the specificity of the mark scheme (this one is far less detailed than one finds for science subjects), high demands are made of candidates in regard to their understanding of ethical theory and their ability to use it with reference to specific cases (euthanasia here). In science examinations, even for this age range, it is common to see candidates able to get full marks (typically, two out of two) simply for being able to state one possible beneficial consequence and one possible adverse consequence of a course of action (like greater use of nuclear energy or the planting of GM crops). One of the recommendations of the Nuffield report was that 'Assessment of students' understanding of ethics is unlikely to be best achieved when questions are worth only a very small number of marks. Students need to be given time and space to show what they know and to develop an ethical argument' (Nuffield Foundation, 2009, p. 6).

Progression in ethical thinking

The Swiss psychologist Jean Piaget was perhaps the first person carefully to investigate the subject of moral development, i.e. how individuals progress over time in their ethical thinking and actions. In the 1920s he and his collaborators studied the ways in which children viewed the rules of the games they were playing – hopscotch for girls and marbles for boys (Carpendale, 2009). He concluded that morality was a developmental process. To a young child, morality is about obeying rules. So, telling lies is wrong because the child will have been told something like 'Only tell the truth' or 'Do not tell lies'. As children age, and in interactions with others, particularly their peers, they move to a less rule-bound and more autonomous view of morality, in which they begin to make decisions for themselves as to what is morally right and what is morally wrong, based on some sort of judgement (Piaget, 1932).

Piaget's work was extended by Lawrence Kohlberg, who, while also accepting that moral reasoning proceeded in stages, argued that it can continue throughout our lives and that very few of us ever reach its ultimate end point. Kohlberg viewed the moral reasoning and practice of individuals as falling into one of six stages (Kohlberg, 1958). Stage one, as for Piaget, is characterized by the acceptance of moral teaching because of a fear that one will be punished if one goes against what one has been told is right. At the other extreme, stage 6, rarely found in empirical studies, is characterized by abstract principles of moral reasoning in which whether or not an action is morally acceptable is judged against principles of ethical rightness that are established as such not so much because people agree with them but because they result from universal, logical argument.

Piaget's and Kohlberg's work and conclusions have been critiqued, refined and extended (e.g. Gilligan, 1982; Gibbs, 2019). However, the fundamental notion remains of moral development from an unreflective and self-centred position where the individual simply wants to avoid punishment to one in which the needs and wants of others are also considered and acted upon.

The work of Piaget, Kohlberg and their successors in the field of moral development is invaluable, but not straightforward to apply directly to science education. One of us, in a New Zealand project on bioethics education (Reiss, 2010), developed a range of indicators to indicate how a science teacher might want students' ethical thinking to progress (Figure 4.2).

Figure 4.2 Indicators of progression in ethical reasoning in science.
Source: Adapted from Figure 1 of Reiss, M. J. (2010). Ethical thinking. In: Ethics in the Science and Technology Classroom: A New Approach to Teaching and Learning, *Jones, A., McKim, A. & Reiss, M. (Eds.), pp. 7–17. Rotterdam: Sense.*

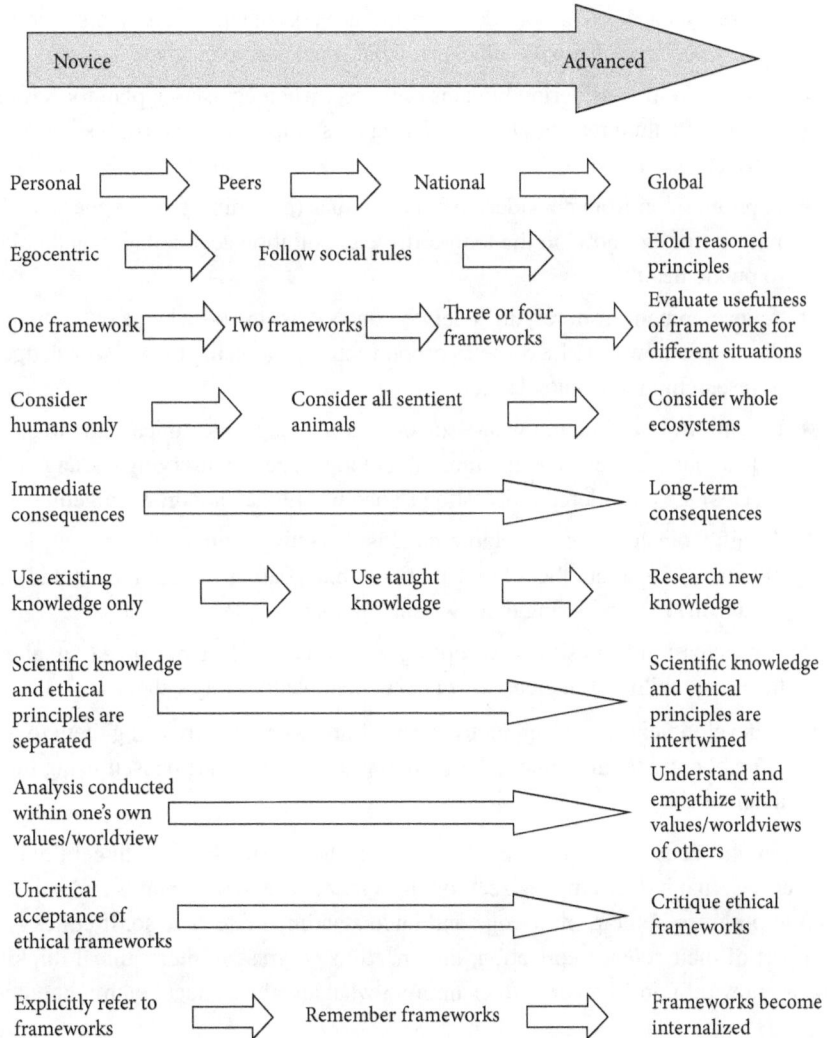

Such movement in Figure 4.2, indicating progression in ethical thinking, would entail such things as the following:

- Moving from viewing an ethical issue (e.g. eating eggs from battery-farmed chickens) in terms of its effects for oneself (e.g. the eggs are the cheapest I can buy) to one's peers (e.g. how do others with whom one eats feel about this?) to others in one's country (e.g. consequences for national employment) to people globally (e.g. effect on world trade).
- A shift from seeing oneself as the moral universe (I can have a pet because I want a pet) to following social rules (e.g. one should not buy a pet in a pub because this is illegal) to holding reasoned principles (e.g. one should not buy a pet when there is a significant chance of animal suffering as a result of congenital disorders, even when such purchase is legal).
- A progression from only being able to use one ethical framework (e.g. utilitarianism) to using several to evaluating the usefulness of the frameworks for different situations (e.g. considering the frameworks of utilitarianism, rights and virtues when considering whether one should pay more to purchase an electric car).
- Moving from considering humans only (e.g. when devising a plan for how to manage a nature reserve) to considering all sentient animals to considering whole ecosystems.
- A progression from considering ethical issues (e.g. mining for copper) solely in terms of the 'now' to the long-term (e.g. pollution accumulation and risks to public health).
- A development from relying solely on one's existing knowledge (e.g. when discussing how to reduce one's carbon footprint) to using taught knowledge to researching new knowledge.
- Moving from a situation where scientific knowledge and ethical principles (e.g. about whether time and money should be spent conserving endangered species) are considered in isolation to one where they are drawn together.
- A shift from considering socio-ethical issues only within one's own set of values (e.g. about the relative merits of meat eating, vegetarianism and veganism) to considering them within other's too.
- A progression from simply accepting standard ethical frameworks (e.g. about the acceptability of nuclear power) to being able to critique them.
- A development from needing to consult frameworks before using them to remembering them to internalizing them, so that one finds oneself using them automatically.

Figure 4.2 does not claim to be the last word for progression in ethical thinking in science. What it does emphasize, though, is that just as school pupils and students need to progress in their knowledge and understanding of science so, if ethics is to be a part of their science education, they need to progress in their ethical thinking too. We now turn, in Chapter 5, to examining what an ethics education might entail.

What is ethics education?

5

A number of aims of ethics education can be envisaged, both generally and within science education. Ethics education might enable learners to improve their understanding of ethical issues, to become more sensitive to ethical issues or to become better people. We argue that each of these has its place within science education. For example, with respect to the human use of animals, ethics education in science might enable learners to better *understand* the capacity of different species to experience pleasures and to suffer; it might enable learners to become *more aware of* issues such as the consequences of animal breeding for the welfare of both farm and companion animals; and it might help learners *make better personal choices* (such as ones to do with diet or fashion) for themselves about their use of animals and animal products and/or *seek to improve* the lot of animals through societal actions and individual action. Ethics education in science education is therefore not limited to facilitating the moral development of students; it also includes the promotion of awareness of and understanding about ethics and ethical practices in science.

It is important for students to know about the regulatory ethical frameworks within which scientists operate, so that they can understand the ethical guidelines to which scientists adhere and appreciate why they are so important. Ethics is an integral part of science and scientists must be guided by what is right or wrong; this helps to ensure that science is done appropriately. By understanding this and the processes involved in thinking ethically about science, students learn to become critical consumers of scientific information and are thus better able to identify unethical practices.

There are a number of ways in which teachers can incorporate ethics into their science lessons which we discuss in more depth using a number of case studies in Chapters 7–9. Here we discuss the approaches which schools can take to developing moral reasoning in their students and the theoretical perspectives which underpin them.

Moral development and education in schools

In every culture, communicating ethical standards and reinforcing the practice of good behaviours in developing children are paramount to the task of socialization. Specific values and behaviours regarded as desirable vary among cultures; however, all societies have a system of rules concerning the rightness and wrongness of certain behaviours. In today's climate, with the perception among some of a widespread breakdown of morality in society and perceived loss of the moral influence of the family and community, the school environment may be a particularly important stable and long-lasting moral experience for some children and so plays, and will continue to play, a key role in children's moral development.

One of the many responsibilities of a school is to develop the values of young people; these should reflect and embody the values of society, while good education also enables the development of criticality in students. Schools must pay attention to the diversity of values in the communities they serve (Beck, 1990). However, there has been much disagreement about the meaning of the terms 'values' and 'moral values'. Halstead and Taylor (2000) note that these terms have been defined as thoughts and behaviours which are considered to be inherently good, such as loyalty and other attitudes or feelings which an individual is proud of, as well as patterns of behaviour that promote well-being in people.

In this book, 'morals' and 'moral values' are understood in terms of the norms of the culture in which young people live. Here, 'moral' is concerned specifically with what is right and wrong, as we discuss in Chapter 3, whilst 'moral values' pertain to the beliefs concerning what is right or wrong or the rules of right conduct (the criteria by which we make value judgements).

The moral development of an individual or group is usually measured in relation to others, for instance, in a social context of some kind. Many psychologists believe *internalization*, when a child's behaviour is increasingly maintained by its own standards of conduct rather than by external restraints, to be the basic process in the development of morality. The development of moral reasoning is a complex, long learning process which incorporates the acquisition of rules that govern behaviour in the social world, the development of a sense of right and wrong, as well as understanding the values that guide and regulate behaviour within a given social system (Maccoby, 1980).

Specifically, Damon (1988) argues that the evaluation of good and bad behaviour, concern for the welfare and rights of others, obligations to social and collective experiences, commitment to honesty, responsibility for acting on one's concerns for others and the judgemental and emotional responses produced when rules and conventions are breached should all be considered when promoting moral development.

The development of morality has three main dimensions: the *cognitive* component, referring to the intellectual understanding of society's rules and the judgements of the outcomes of various actions; the *behavioural* component, i.e. our actual moral conduct and behaviour in a variety of situations which involves ethical behaviour; and the *affective* component which refers to feelings, for example, guilt, shame or pride. The relationship between these three dimensions and their roles in the process of internalization has been the focus of much psychological research.

Historically, cognitive theories have emphasized moral judgements and reasoning, psychoanalytic theories have focused on the affective components of morality and learning theories have examined ethical behaviour. Thus, no one theory of moral development is a comprehensive explanation of how moral knowledge, behaviour and feelings interrelate, although Rest (1979) did attempt to cover these three areas. In real life it is the complex interplay between these three components that determines how one might behave when faced with making a moral decision. So, it is possible for us to behave in a way that most people would judge to be immoral and yet feel no guilt or remorse; conversely, we may be a law-abiding citizen and yet suffer from a guilty conscience.

Approaches to moral development and the theories which underpin them

Psychoanalytic theories

Freud's *Psychoanalytical Theory* (1938) argued that our moral behaviour is controlled by the superego, which comprises our conscience and our ego ideal (i.e. the image we have of the person we would like to be). The conscience is the part of our personality which punishes us when we have committed some perceived wrongdoing, and is thus the source of feelings of guilt. The ego ideal, on the other hand, rewards us when we have behaved in accordance with our basic moral values and is thus the source of feelings of pride. Our conscience can therefore be thought of as the 'punishing' parent whilst our ego-ideal is the 'rewarding' parent. According to Freud, the superego is acquired via a process of identification and this process is complete by the age of five or six.

Freud's theory of moral development must be considered in the context of his stages of personality development in which he argued that children proceed through five psychosexual stages with the phallic stage (third stage) being important as far as moral development is concerned. This is because the Oedipus complex occurs during this stage with the outcome of the acquisition of the superego, via the process of identification. Freud sees the conscience in our superego as a function which observes the ego, gives it orders, judges it and threatens it with punishments, exactly like the parents it has replaced. Therefore, when moral development is no longer dependent on a parent but on internalization, the child's self-esteem is improved by self-reflection whilst demonstrating adult-like behaviour; feelings of guilt are experienced when a child deviates from the ego ideal.

However, Freud's theory of moral development has been heavily criticized. One major criticism (Kohlberg, 1978; Hoffman, 1979) has been that the conscience does not suddenly appear at the age of five or six; rather, moral development is a process which begins in young children and continues into and even throughout adulthood. Freud limits the causes of the child's moral development to the family, which perhaps was a greater influence on the child at the start of the twentieth century, when Freud was first formulating his theories, than it is now. The twenty-first-century child is bombarded with moral influences ranging from their family to peers, teachers, mass media and social media such as Instagram and Twitter.

Psychoanalytic theories have built upon early Freudian concepts and focus on the relationship between child and parents, and the general consequences of living within a family. The development of morality is described in relation to those who conform to society, whilst also taking into account the role of empathy in the development of altruism.

Dunn (2013) undertook naturalistic observations of children with their families to see how they behave. From her observations, Dunn noted the role that the child's emotions play in acquiring a principled morality. She found that preschool children became increasingly distressed when they failed to meet adults' standards, concluding that as adults refer to acceptable standards of behaviour, children learn a great deal from this about moral rules. Young children felt ashamed or anxious after a transgression and also made jokes about rule violations, suggesting that positive, not simply negative, emotions heighten children's understanding of other people's feelings. Dunn concluded that communication of moral rules to young children may reside very much in the non-verbal emotional aspects of their interactions with adults.

Dunn expanded beyond and deviated from Freudian conceptualization to demonstrate that siblings and birth order also influence moral growth. Furthermore, the comprehension of moral rules may develop within peer relationships, with their accompanying emotional processes. There is an emotional urgency and significance to family relationships which may lead children to moral understanding well in advance of their capacity to reason about moral dilemmas. Everyday social interactions provide the child with direct experience of a justified moral and social order. Thus, the lack or presence of siblings and peers provides the child with various experiences of sharing and responsibility, dependent on the role of the child in each particular social setting. Howes (2009) argued that if children, from the age of two months, are given the opportunity for interaction with their peers, then by the age of two years they demonstrate complex patterns of behaviour to maintain friendships and reciprocated affection. Put simply, peer attachment takes preference to attachments with adults.

It was once argued that if teachers wish to take a psychoanalytical approach to moral development, they need to scaffold and provide the boundaries and opportunities for peer interaction to encourage the growth of positive moral behaviour (Edwards, 1987). Thus, for psychoanalytic theory, the basis for internalizing moral conventions derives from the emotional connections and relationships between the child and their parents, siblings and peers; without this close tie, the development of moral traits such as empathy, sympathy and altruism will be seriously hindered. If we consider this via a narrow lens, this makes sense, for there has been much research which supports the argument that children internalize moral conventions from relationships and the modelling which takes place via interaction between social agents (Mammen et al., 2021). However, more recently psychoanalysts have argued that to take a psychoanalytical approach to moral development is a complex and broad undertaking. Authentic teaching and learning must involve the student and teacher in all of their psychodynamic complexity as emotional and ethical beings, which is no easy feat (Clifford, 2009).

Social learning theories

Social learning theory partly arose as an attempt to 'translate' Freud's theories, especially his concept of identification, into terms of learning theory, as well as being an offshoot of behaviourism. Learning theory argues for the importance of observational learning, also known as modelling, and focuses on the role of cognitive factors intervening between stimulus and response. Therefore, social learning is based on behaviourist principles, where specific behaviours are identified for positive reinforcement whilst undesirable behaviours are discouraged by non-reinforcement or punishment.

John B. Watson (1919) had distinct ideas about child development which were based on learning theory. He studied the acquisition of irrational fears through learning as he was very interested in whether infants naturally show fear or whether such fears were learned. One famous study, designed to evidence classical conditioning, showed that once a baby (Little Albert) was deliberately frightened whilst playing with a live white rat (via a loud noise caused by clanging an iron rod), the baby became classically conditioned to experience fear at the sight of a rat. Albert's fear generalized to other stimuli that were similar to the white rat, including a fur coat and a Father Christmas mask. (We can note that the ethics of this research in itself was unethical by modern standards, given it was considered acceptable to frighten a baby in the pursuit of knowledge and Little Albert was not unconditioned after the experiment.)

Bandura (1977) argued that the development of self-control is influenced by the patterns of direct reinforcement encountered, e.g. the disciplinary measures used by adults and the models children observe. Therefore, it is the importance of the child's perception of the model and how the child interprets the model's behaviour that is important in observational learning. For example, research suggests that talking to children is not enough; children need to imitate behaviour. So, 'Do as I say, not as I do' (parent) becomes 'I'll say as you say and do as you do' (child). Moreover, those who educate children need to model the behaviour they hope to inculcate. Aronfreed (1976) emphasized the importance of the child's realization of and relationship to 'significant others' in their moral development.

Insights arising from social learning theories recognize that moral socialization will vary between cultures that reinforce different values. Garbarino and Bronfenbrenner (1976) conceptualized five types of moral judgement and behaviour after examining responses to a variety of moral dilemmas posed to participants of (pre-1989) communist and Western countries. They proposed five orientations which did not follow a developmental sequence but instead focused on a series of environmental systems that would either directly or indirectly affect a child's development, namely self-orientated, authority-orientated, peer-orientated, collective-orientated and objectively orientated motivations in moral reasoning. They concluded that adolescents tend to group their answers around a single orientation, with adolescents in Western societies mainly using authority-orientated answers, whereas those in communist societies tended to give collective-orientated responses.

Thus, if teachers wish to adopt a social learning approach to moral education, it is necessary for them to decide which moral values are to be reinforced and what is the most appropriate strategy to use, whilst maintaining themselves as a positive and significant 'model' of behaviour in their pupils' lives. This is no simple task, especially with the pressures that modern-day teachers face. The difficulty lies in finding a balance between punishing undesirable behaviour and rewarding desirable behaviour with positive reinforcement. Planning and pursuing a programme incorporating positive character virtues is possible, but may be difficult to maintain; thus, it would be wise for the teacher to use this strategy in conjunction with other approaches when actively promoting moral development.

Cognitive developmental theories

Classical research into the development of moral reasoning, focusing on the cognitive component of moral development, was pioneered by Jean Piaget (1932) and built upon by Lawrence Kohlberg (1958). It is Piaget's and Kohlberg's research that is cited most frequently in education and thus has influenced curriculum content.

Piaget's *Theory of Moral Development* (1932) proposes a cognitive developmental theory in which the child's moral concepts evolve in an unvarying sequence from an early stage of *moral realism* to a more mature stage, namely the *morality of reciprocity*, also known as *autonomous morality*. According to Piaget, no one can reach the stage of moral reciprocity without first passing through the stage of moral realism. Only at about the ages of 9–11 years will morality of reciprocity begin to emerge. At this stage children recognize that social rules can be questioned and changed, and can consider the feelings and viewpoints of others in judging situations.

Piaget analysed children's attitudes towards game rules, clumsiness, stealing and lying, and he explored many aspects of children's notions of justice. He argued that the youngest children are motivated by arbitrary, external rules which must not be transgressed because they have been laid down by adults. Children at this level are at a stage of heteronomy; thus, lying or stealing are not seen as procedures established for the smooth functioning of a community, but simply rules which must be obeyed.

Over time, as children experience more cognitive stimulation, a process of cognitive restructuring begins to take place; therefore, heteronomy gradually diminishes in favour of autonomy. At this stage, rules are seen as mutually agreed requirements for group relationships to function.

In particular, Piaget was interested in finding out how much correspondence there is between the consciousness of, or respect for, rules and the practice of them. To investigate this, Piaget observed children of different ages playing marbles, since the rules are learned without the influence of adult reward or punishment. He then asked the children if they could explain the rules – what they are, how they originated and whether or not they could be changed; he wanted to find out whether the children believed that the rules are fixed and external, thus believing in heteronomy, or whether the rules are the outcome of the mutual consent of the players, indicating consciousness of their own autonomy.

Piaget's findings indicated several different mental orientations towards both the consciousness and practice of the rules of marbles. For children up to about the age of two, there is no consciousness of rules regulating the use of marbles; it is purely motor activity. Between the ages of two and six, Piaget's second stage, the child begins to imitate rituals observed. He is conscious of the governing rules of the game, but his practice of the rules is somewhat egocentric for he does not understand the game as a social activity. At this stage, although children are aware that others are playing with them, they are in fact playing their own game for their own gains. Throughout this stage children are undertaking a transition from purely individualistic play to social cooperation and so although rules influence a child's actions, he does not yet have the necessary cognitive structures to apply the rules in any form but imitation.

In the third stage, between the ages of seven and ten, the child develops from the initial egocentric stance to gaining pleasure from agreeing a set of rules under which to compete. The child considers himself submissive to all of the rules that govern his life, even if he has some role in creating them. When playing games, rules are recognized as a regulatory necessity to social activity. Winning only has meaning within the parameters of the agreed set of rules, with differences in opinion compromised, since the desire to cooperate with their peers is powerful. It is during the later ages of this stage that heteronomy finally starts to give way to autonomy, achieved through cognitive maturity and cooperative play; rules become the outcome of mutual consent, rather than enforced laws from authority figures.

From around the age of eleven or twelve, children develop the ability for abstract reasoning. There is a strong desire to cooperate, as in the previous stage, but here the rules provide the structure for cooperation and therefore no detail is left to chance. Piaget argued that the closest correlation between the consciousness and practice of rules occurs at this stage. However, heteronomous submission does not disappear altogether in every person's life, for example, adherence to governmental laws.

What are the consequences of each stage for the practice of moral rules, in particular the child's judgement of right and wrong? Piaget argued that all rules are similar to a young child and so the process of developing respect for moral rules will be identical to that of game rules. Therefore, during this period moral rules are seen as sacred and untouchable; again, the practice of them is egocentric and an imitation of observed behaviour. For a child of this age, rules are taken literally and obeyed by the letter. There is no consideration of extenuating circumstances or intention. Unlike the very young child, the egocentric child feels a sense of obligation towards the rules. When a child accepts a command, such as not to lie, from an adult whom they respect, their moral conscience deepens. The egocentric child's intention is to submit to the moral rules laid down, but these remain external to his conscience rather than internalized rules directing behaviour.

Piaget constructed stories which forced the child to make a judgement about behaviours that deviated from the rules about breaking property, stealing and lying. A child associates clumsiness with adult anger, regardless of how the act of clumsiness occurs, so stories were created which asked the children to consider two types of clumsiness – one the consequences of a well-intentioned act, but resulting in considerable material damage, and the other an ill-intentioned act resulting in little material damage. Piaget also constructed stories which provoked the child to compare selfishly motivated acts of stealing with those that were well intentioned. Both sets of stories aimed to determine whether a child paid more attention to motive or material result. The children were told the stories and asked to consider the guilt of the protagonist in each story.

Piaget found that younger children, up to about the age of eight, judged guilt on the size of the material damage; the larger the amount of damage caused, the naughtier the perpetrator was judged to be. At this stage, intention is not given consideration because the child cannot identify with or relate to others; however, as the child grows older he is more able to relate to others and it is then that the intentions of the person acting are considered. As a result, the average age for judgement on the basis of objective responsibility was found to be seven, with no instances of moral realism (evaluating wrongdoing in terms of consequences and not the intentions of the wrongdoer) in clumsiness after the age of ten, or stealing after seven. Subjective responsibility is as much a product of cooperation as objective responsibility is the product of restraint. When a child is able to take on the role of others and see actions from their perspectives, the child, Piaget argued, is able to reduce heteronomy; thus, egocentrism begins to give way to a true social intercourse.

Piaget also examined how a child judges the content and consequences of a lie. He constructed stories which first included lies resulting in no material consequences. These were designed to assess the 'size' of a lie without the distraction of a consequence. Here, a difference occurred in the children's moral reasoning. Again, younger children judged actions on the basis of the size of the material consequences. From the responses given it was clear that the youngest children thought that the further away from the truth, the larger the lie was. At this stage, this transgression is taken as a much more serious offence than in later development when it is simply considered an exaggerated lie. All of the children agreed that all of the lies told in these stories were meant to deceive, but the seriousness of the lie was judged strictly on the size of the lie told.

There has been much support for Piaget's contention that children develop from one moral stage to another in a fixed and invariant sequence. Research in industrialized Western countries, such as France and Great Britain, has reproduced the essentials of Piaget's findings. For example, Ferguson and Rule (1982) found that regular age trends in moral development are evident across a range of social classes and populations and for both sexes. However, it would seem that findings of cross-cultural studies are less consistent (Havinghurst & Neugarten, 1955), indicating that cultural factors can alter the sequence of Piagetian moral judgements.

Other studies suggest that Piaget underestimated the cognitive capabilities of young children. Chandler, Greenspan and Barenboim (1973) found that even six-year-old children are able to consider intentions when judging the behaviour of others, as long as the situation in which they are presented is a medium which they can understand. In a similar vein, another shortcoming of Piaget's theory has been revealed by the findings of various researchers, including Yuill and Perner (1988). They argued that Piaget's stories included methodological weaknesses, for example, where the intent of the child in the story was confounded with the consequences of his or her behaviour. When stories are presented where good and bad intentions can be evaluated separately from good and bad outcomes, even young primary-aged children are able to use the intentions as the basis for their judgements.

Significantly, Piaget's tasks have also been criticized for being over-simplified. Rest (1986) argued that many more factors, for example, whether the person was provoked and the extent or degree of the consequences, to name but two, need to be considered in understanding moral reasoning rather than only intentions and consequences. In 1979, Rest devised the Defining Issue Test (DIT), subsequently a widely used research instrument, which asks subjects to state what they think are the most important issues when considering moral dilemmas. It presents a selection of statements for rating various aspects of reasoning found in interviews. This research instrument has been found in a large number of studies to have good test-retest reliability and shows individuals sequencing through stages of moral development (Langford, 1995).

Rest's (1986) four-component model of moral reasoning postulates the interaction of four components which contribute to moral decisions and behaviour, namely moral sensitivity, moral judgement, moral motivation and moral character. He suggests that when a child encounters a situation, the child will interpret the situation in terms of what effects the child's actions may have on people's welfare. From this, the child has to determine what the ideal moral course of action, from his perspective, will be. After the child has determined this, the child will then decide on what course of action to take before finally performing the act.

Lawrence Kohlberg (1963) extended, modified and refined Piaget's theory on the basis of his analysis of interviews of 10- to 16-year-old boys who were confronted with a series of moral dilemmas. Kohlberg proposed a six-stage theory of the development of moral judgement. Each stage was based upon not only whether the boys chose an obedient or need-served (one's own interest) act, but also on the reasons and justification for their choices. As with Piaget, Kohlberg argued that the order of the development through the stages is invariant, pointing towards higher stages of development. Furthermore, both Piaget and Kohlberg believed that the cognitive capabilities of individuals determine the stages of their moral development.

However, Kohlberg differed from Piaget by proposing that although the order of the stages is fixed, they do not occur at the same age in all people. Rest (1986) and Walker (1989) both supported the view that children proceed through Kohlberg's stages of moral judgement in a fixed manner. Cross-cultural studies in Israel (Snarey, 1985) and Taiwan (Lei and Cheng, 1984) support the expectation that individuals develop through the sequence of Kohlbergian moral stages in the same manner, regardless of their cultural background. This, however, has been increasingly contested in recent years with some data and findings from research in other cultures not fitting with Kohlbergian stages and thus 'Kohlbergian [and Piagetian] models are increasingly being abandoned in developmental psychology' (Kim and Sankey, 2009, p. 27).

Kohlberg's theory of moral judgements has more current support than Piaget's theories of moral development, but that is not to say that his theory does not have its critics as well. Examples of possible cultural bias have been found, with some arguing that Kohlberg's focus on individual rights and obligations may lead either to underestimates of moral development in other cultures or to the exclusion of some domains of morality that are culturally distinct, such as that in New Guinea which emphasizes community obligations over individual rights (Shweder & Much, 1987).

Damon (1988) further criticized Kohlberg's methodology by arguing that his dilemmas were derived intuitively and were highly unrealistic. Damon has consistently shown that children are capable of moral decisions and actions at an earlier age than Kohlberg concluded. Damon listened to moral debates among children using realistic interview items which he had created. From these interviews, Damon derived a six-step 'positive-justice sequence' which describes children's reasoning about sharing, fairness and distributive justice. He argued that children learn justice through sharing experiences and that play is particularly important to achieve this. Children do not need adult intervention to mediate and get along. They develop from an object orientation to awareness of other children and then ultimately to a reasoned obligation of sharing, to maintain play.

Feminists, arguing that there is a sex bias against females in the theory, have criticized Kohlberg's work. Gilligan (1982) maintained that Kohlberg's scoring scheme was biased against women. She argued that there was a dimension of 'care' which had not been considered by Kohlberg. Women may appear to have lower scores on moral reasoning than men, not because their moral reasoning is poorer, but because they, not infrequently, have a different moral orientation than men. Gilligan argued that boys demonstrate a 'masculine' orientation, including a response that emphasizes logic and the balance between life and property rights, whereas girls demonstrate an interpersonal orientation by focusing on the impact of an action on human relationships.

Others have supported Gilligan's claims; for example, Walker, deVries and Trevethan (1987) found that women were more likely to have a 'caring' orientation while men more often adopted a 'rights' orientation. Damon (1988) noted that it is possible for gender to influence a child's moral orientation, but only if gender makes a difference to the child's social context. Furthermore, Damon argued that a change in the child's social circumstances, for example, a male becoming a 'house husband' could cause a dramatic change in orientation. More recently, Walker (2006) argued that most models of moral development make no claims about gender differences and that there is no empirical support for Gilligan's claim that the Kohlbergian model of moral development downscores the moral thinking of women. For Walker, 'Gender explains a negligible amount of the variability in moral reasoning development' (2006, p. 109).

In contrast to Kohlberg and Piaget, Turiel (1998) proposed that children's thinking is organized from an early age into two domains: morality and social convention. Turiel assessed children's moral development by measuring the judgements that children used to justify their actions and opinions. He found that not only could children distinguish between morality and social convention but they were also able to reason about them in different ways. For example, children found it acceptable to call a teacher by his or her first name if permitted (social convention) but found it unacceptable to hit a teacher even if the action was permitted by the teacher (moral rule). This indicated that children understood that social conventions could be negotiated and changed whereas moral rules are invariant. Turiel found that children as young as four could not only understand the difference between these two domains but understood moral rules as being more binding that social conventions.

There have been criticisms of both Piaget's and Kohlberg's theories for tending to underestimate the influence of parents in the development of moral judgements. Some evidence (Aronfreed, 1976; Edwards, 1987) suggests that consistent experience of reasoning and explanation, and concern with the feelings of others, leads to both more mature moral judgements and greater self-control.

Subsequent research into moral reasoning

Over the past three decades, research on children's moral judgement has changed considerably, providing new theories and methods for analysis. There has been a move away from a global-stage model towards domain-specific models of development. Instead, therefore, of children's social judgements being explained by hierarchical stages, more recent studies suggest that children apply multiple forms of reasoning, for example, moral (fairness, justice, rights), conventional (customs and etiquette) and psychological (autonomy and identity) simultaneously when evaluating transgressions or social dilemmas (Turiel, 1998; Smetana et al., 2006).

Some theories of moral development emphasize the role that relationships play, specifically when moral outcome is influenced by the type (character) of person a child interacts with. These theories draw upon aspects of the previous theories mentioned, having much in common with cognitive developmental theories. They also stress the importance that experience provides for participation in moral life.

The role of caregivers in early relationships is to set rules in a loving and affectionate environment. Therefore, the quality of the parental relationship will, of course, affect the child's moral presence in social situations (Youniss, 1988). The child learns empathy through the closeness of his parental relationships; attachment opens the social world for the child as authority and power relations are introduced.

Doise explored ways in which social interaction promotes further changes in a child's thinking. He argued that to promote ethical behaviour, 'social representations of ideal relationships have to govern interaction patterns' (1990, p. 61). When cooperating with others in a social group which is significant to them, children gain direct experience of learning about what is morally right for that group; therefore, they construct what Doise terms 'cognitive coordinations' which they are not capable of individually. However, once they have experienced this, they are often able to execute these 'cognitive coordinations' alone. Schools are in the perfect position to create the kind of context to promote cognitive progress by encouraging children to participate in democratic procedures and social responsibility. The moral development of children must, of course, also be viewed in context of the family and the community (Wolff and McCall-Smith, 2000).

Cultural theory, which lends itself to social learning theories, suggests that the moral individual conforms to societal norms. Each society endorses its own moral conventions and so differences occur, for example, between so-called Western culture and cultures of so-called developing countries. Whiting and Whiting (1975) observed that children in Western societies were parentally dominated and so given fewer societal responsibilities than their counterparts in what are customarily described as developing countries. Consequently, Western children were more egotistical and less altruistic. Thus, cultural theory emphasizes conformity to dominant social groups and 'internalization of transmitted conventions as its explanation of moral development' (Kutnick, 1992, p. 40). A variety of research has shown that children are able to distinguish between different kinds of infringements and can do so at a, to many, surprisingly early point in their development. Some researchers propose that certain significant aspects of moral understanding are present in young children, at least from the age of four (Nunez & Harris, 1998; Turiel, 2006).

More recent research empirical work suggests that moral reasoning and moral motivation are partially independent dimensions. Nunner-Winkler (2007) argues that moral motivation is linked to the moral judgements that children make because children are motivated by the desire to do what is right in a particular situation. She also asserts that children have a good understanding of moral rules from a very young age whereas 'moral motivation is acquired in a second differential learning process' (2007, p. 399).

Thus, as is evident in other realms of development, such as perception (Gibson, 1979) and cognition (Vygotsky, 1978), children are more competent at earlier ages than previous generations of developmental psychologists ever believed. Approaches to support moral development in the classroom must take into account the multiplicity of approaches available. Kutnick (1992) argued that responsibilities for actions of self and others must be promoted. The teacher must plan for the positive, active engagement of the child in real-life situations as this will inform development through 'conscious realization', where children will become aware of moral principles and then assess their own character and behaviour against these. In order to draw the child out of egocentricity into autonomy, cooperation in relationships is fundamental.

Character education movement

We have considered in some depth theoretical perspectives of ethical education; now we turn to concrete teaching programmes designed to promote moral development. In response to tragedies in the United States, such as the Columbine High School massacre (20 April 1999) and the Virginia Tech massacre (16 April 2007), there has been a resurgence of debate amongst educators, researchers and politicians about character education and its role in public schools (Nucci et al., 2014). Consequently, character education and how best to help school children develop into responsible citizens has become a national priority in schools and with the general public, particularly in the United States, where it focuses specifically on promoting values and appropriate behaviour in classrooms.

Supporters of the character movement have argued that schools should be given a more extensive role in the teaching of societal values. First, by providing good role models in the forms of teachers, and second by directly teaching about fundamental social and moral values such as honesty, loyalty, respect, discipline and hard work. Thus, in 2008 the US Department of Education made funds available to states and districts such as Florida to train teachers in delivering character building lessons.

Researchers in other parts of the world including Canada, England and the United States (Halstead & Taylor, 2000) have raised concerns with regard to promoting values in schools. The challenge is on how to agree on which values are to be taught and promoted, especially in pluralist societies. As Halstead notes, 'It would be a serious mistake to view it as a matter of dreaming up a list of values or opting for a prepackaged set' (2000, p. 8). Schools must ensure that they take into consideration the diverse values of their communities as well as society as a whole.

Philosophy for children

Around the world, philosophy has often been thought of as a subject only for adults. When it is included in schools, it is typically taught to students over the age of fourteen. This approach is in line with Piaget's thinking, discussed above, that before the age of about twelve, children lack the cognitive abilities to engage in the sort of rational discussion that philosophy requires. However, as we also discussed above, this rather dismissive view of the reasoning abilities of younger children has been extensively critiqued. In *Philosophy and the Young Child*, Matthews (1980) provides what Pritchard (2022) refers to as 'a number of delightful illustrations of very young children's philosophical puzzlement':

- TIM (about six years), while busily engaged in licking a pot, asked, 'Papa, how can we be sure that everything is not a dream?' *(p. 1)*
- JORDAN (five years), going to bed at eight one evening, asked, 'If I go to bed at eight and get up at seven in the morning, how do I really know that the little hand of the clock has gone around only once? Do I have to stay up all night to watch it? If I look away even for a short time, maybe the small hand will go around twice.' *(p. 3)*
- One day JOHN EDGAR (four years), who had seen airplanes take off, rise, and gradually disappear into the distance, took his first plane ride. When the plane stopped ascending and the seat-belt sign went out, John Edgar turned to his father and said in a rather relieved, but still puzzled, tone of voice, 'Things don't really get smaller up here.' *(p. 4)*

The Philosophy for Children (P4C) movement (https://p4c.com) exists to teach reasoning and the skills of argumentation (see Chapter 8) to all young people, including those below the age of eleven. Without wanting to oversimplify it, the principles are not difficult to understand. In a spirit of open-minded enquiry, children are encouraged to think about philosophical questions (rather than, for example, scientific, mathematical or artistic ones). Sometimes such questions start with a teacher – classic ones used in P4C include 'What is friendship?' and 'Do animals have feelings?'; sometimes they arise from news stories; and sometimes they are produced by the children themselves – as in the examples of Tim and Jordan above.

The function of the teacher is not to attempt themselves to answer the questions but to facilitate thoughtful discussion among the children, discussion in which the children respect the views of others even if they disagree with them (unless the teacher decides that the views are wholly unacceptable) and learn to listen and then to develop their own views rationally. In the case of ethics in science, a teacher might want to get children to think about such questions as 'Should we allow experiments on animals to try to develop new medicines?', 'Is a well-fed lion in a zoo better off than a lion in the wild?' or 'Should we stop flying on aeroplanes to help tackle global warming?'.

Should ethics be considered where science is taught?

6

Following the discussion in Chapter 4 of what science education is and the discussion in Chapter 5 of what ethics education is, in this chapter we turn to the key issue of whether ethics should be considered where science is taught. Those who argue that ethics should not be considered where science is taught make several points, in particular: that science and ethics belong to very different domains of knowledge and so are best considered separately; that it's asking too much of teachers of science to cope with ethics too; and that the science curriculum is already full without taking on ethics also. Those who take the contrary position argue that the epistemological distance between science and ethics can be overstated, or is not so crucial, and that other objections seem to presume a cadre of specialist teachers who teach only science, which may be the case in some secondary school systems but is rarely the case in primary schools, and doesn't really apply as an objection in the informal sector. We will examine the various arguments on both sides before stating our conclusions and exploring further some of the implications of this if science teaching is to consider ethics.

Arguments against the inclusion of ethics in science

One of the main arguments against the inclusion of ethics in science stems from epistemological considerations. As we have seen in Chapters 2 and 3, science and ethics have very different ways of arriving at their conclusions. Above all, science is empirical; for all that there are a number of different sciences – astronomers, industrial chemists and ecologists, for example, work very differently – it is the case that the principal way in which scientists work is close to how students are taught in most countries' school science lessons. Scientists have theories about the way that the material world operates and these theories enable them to generate hypotheses that can be tested. To make these tests, appropriate data are gathered and analysed as objectively as possible and the findings compared with the predictions of the relevant theory.

Ethicists work very differently. They do make appeals to reality, including aspects of the material world, but fundamentally, ethics is normative not empirical – that is, it is about how things *should be* not how they *are*. It is the Scottish philosopher David Hume (1711–76) who is particularly remembered for arguing that there is a crucial 'gap' between statements about how things are and statements about how they ought to be:

> In every system of morality, which I have hitherto met with, I have always remark'd, that the author proceeds for some time in the ordinary way of reasoning, and establishes the being of a God, or makes observations concerning human affairs; when of a sudden I am surpriz'd to find, that instead of the usual copulations of propositions, *is*, and *is not*, I meet with no proposition that is not connected with an *ought*, or an *ought not*. This change is imperceptible; but is, however, of the last consequence. For as this *ought*, or *ought not*, expresses some new relation or affirmation, 'tis necessary that it shou'd be observ'd and explain'd; and at the same time that a reason should be given, for what seems altogether inconceivable, how this new relation can be a deduction from others, which are entirely different from it. But as authors do not commonly use this precaution, I shall presume to recommend it to the readers; and am persuaded, that this small attention wou'd subvert all the vulgar systems of morality, and let us see, that the distinction of vice and virtue is not founded merely on the relations of objects, nor is perceiv'd by reason. *(Hume, 1739, p. 469)*

In other words, we cannot reason from how things are (the scope of science) to how they should be (the scope of ethics). As Hume put it, "Tis not contrary to reason to prefer the destruction of the whole world to the scratching of my finger' (1739, p. 416). Hume was not, of course, advocating that the world should be destroyed so that he could avoid one of his fingers getting scratched – he was no narcissistic psychopath. His point is that while we (appropriately) feel moral revulsion at the very idea – this revulsion cannot be shown to be 'correct' by any form of reasoning, whether such reasoning appeals to logic or the conclusions of science.

Given this central difference between how scientists and moral philosophers establish knowledge, it can be argued that these two very different ways of building up knowledge are best addressed separately by different groups of subject specialists – with specialist science teachers teaching science and those with expertise in philosophy teaching ethics. Jim Donnelly was an example of a leading science educator who argued on such epistemological grounds against the growing tendency for school science curricula to include ethics (Donnelly, 2002).

A rather different argument as to why ethics should not be included within school science is that many science teachers don't want it to be, so that if such teaching is required, the consequences might be adverse. As one of us wrote some time ago, this argument goes something like as follows:

> Science teachers are generally educated in science, not in moral philosophy. It is therefore unrealistic and unfair to expect them to teach ethics. If such teaching is

required it would/might (a) reduce the time they have available to teach science; (b) lead to lower quality teaching, since science teachers will be teaching outside their sphere of competence; (c) lead to lower levels of professional satisfaction amongst existing science teachers; (d) result in fewer science graduates wanting to enter teaching, thus exacerbating the shortage of science teachers that exists in many (e.g. the UK) but not all (e.g. Germany) countries. *(Reiss, 1999, p. 119)*

Good evidence for widespread lack of enthusiasm among teachers in secondary schools and further education institutions in England and Wales for the teaching of ethics in science first came from a large and influential study published as *Valuable Lessons* (Levinson & Turner, 2001). In that study, data were gathered from heads of biology/science departments, heads of humanities/social science departments and PSHE (Personal, Social and Health Education) coordinators or equivalents. As the authors of the study concluded:

> A large proportion of teachers across the curriculum perceive the teaching of science to be about the delivery of facts, and not about values, opinions or ethics. Almost half of all science teachers interviewed feel that their teaching of science should be 'value free' – that it does not yield issues that have social or ethical implications. Others inferred that considering the ethical and social concerns raised by science might undermine the integrity of the subject overall. One science teacher provided a revealing concern about the teaching of ethics within science classes:

> "When we talk about the ethics of anything you're going to give an opinion rather than something that's fact based. Once you start giving an opinion then you express disagreement. Then they treat the whole of the subject in the same way that they treat your opinion in that they disagree with it personally. So they might end up treating your fact-based stuff in the same manner." *(Levinson & Turner, 2001, p. 7)*

Levinson's and Turner's work is from over twenty years ago. It would be good to revisit it; it is clear that whatever the arguments against the inclusion of ethics in school science, such inclusion has become more common since then. Nevertheless, before we look at the arguments in favour of such inclusion, it is worth examining more recent work that looks at the problems that such inclusion can raise.

A study by Jim Ryder and Indi Banner (2013) investigated how science teachers experienced a major reform to the secondary school science curriculum in England. This reform was intended to enable all 14- to 16-year-olds to become more scientifically literate (whilst also allowing some students to choose to take traditional, academic options and other students to take applied science options). The reform therefore meant that there was more emphasis on the teaching of socio-scientific issues (to which we return in the next chapter) and on the nature of science (which we considered in Chapter 2). What Ryder and Banner found was a great diversity in how science teachers felt about these reforms:

> While some science teachers described the reform as the best thing that had happened to them in their professional lives, other teachers were more

ambivalent, and other teachers felt that the reforms threatened the teaching of science in schools. *(Ryder & Banner, 2013, p. 491)*

Ryder and Banner went on to interpret this variation among science teachers in terms of teacher identity. The teachers they interviewed could be divided into two groups – those for whom being a teacher (whose subject was science) was core to their professional identity and those for whom being a scientist (who taught) was core to their professional identity. The teachers in the second group were less likely to be comfortable with the new curriculum with its greater emphasis on socio-scientific issues, including ethics, and the nature of science:

> Those teachers identifying themselves as 'scientists' tended to focus on the teaching goal of preparing high attaining students for post-compulsory science study, typically though a focus on canonical science knowledge. *(Ryder & Banner, 2013, p. 501)*

A final argument against the inclusion of ethics in science is that this gives a degree of control about ethical issues to those who are responsible for the curriculum, pedagogy and assessment. One can imagine situations where such control might be abused, whether at national, regional or local level. Consider, for example, students who express certain views about the acceptability of in vitro fertilization or genetically modified crops being marked 'wrong', or even experiencing more serious consequences.

Arguments for the inclusion of ethics in science

The arguments in favour of including ethics in science are primarily to do with motivation and helping students see the contexts within which science is undertaken and applied. We will turn to these shortly. However, it is worth starting with epistemological arguments in favour of including ethics in science, despite what we write above.

The chief argument in favour of the teaching of ethics in science that stems from epistemological considerations is an argument about the source and purpose of scientific knowledge. It begins by pointing out that all scientific knowledge is formulated within particular social contexts. At the very least this means that the topics on which scientists work – and so the subject matter of science itself – reflects the interests, motivations and aspirations both of the scientists who carry out such work and of those who fund the work. There is no doubt that the majority, almost certainly the great majority, of the funding provided for scientists around the globe has been and is provided on the presumption that particular applied ends will result. These might be the production of a new medicine, the development of a new crop variety, the manufacture of a new type of battery, the construction of a better anti-tank missile and so on (Reiss, 1999).

It can be argued that ethics is inevitably entwined with science in most cases. Both the scientists and those who fund them hope that production of a new medicine will lead to more lives being saved or to the relief of suffering, that the development of a new crop variety will lead to increased food yields or more nutritious food, that the manufacture of a new type of battery might allow more energy to be stored, thus helping reduce our dependency on fossil fuels, or to that the construction of a better anti-tank missile will enhance a country's ability to defend themselves from invasion. In each of these cases, the science is carried for a purpose. Purposes can be judged normatively, that is, they may be ethically good or bad. Indeed, just beginning to spell out some of the intended or presumed purposes of a particular instance of science alerts us to the possibility that there may be other ways of achieving those purposes or that perhaps the purposes are not ethically unproblematic.

In other words, in the real world, science and ethics are often not as distinct as they can appear in school classrooms. This argument has perhaps been made most often in connection with bioethics (Willmott & Macip, 2016; Bryant & La Velle, 2019; Saxena, 2019) as there are so many issues where biology and ethics seem intertwined.

A distinct epistemological argument for including ethics in science starts from the premise that to do science well is to do it virtuously. With reference to science specifically and scholarship more generally, Schwartz (2022) maintains:

> I believe that learning how to think requires the development of a set of intellectual virtues, virtues that will make people good students, good employees and professionals, and good citizens. And cultivating these virtues is just as important in programs of specialized training as it is in the liberal arts. I use the word 'virtues,' as opposed to, say 'skills,' deliberately, because each of them has an essential moral dimension. *(Schwartz, 2022, p. 63)*

Schwartz then goes on to offer a list of these virtues: Love of truth; Fair-mindedness; Perseverance; Courage; Perspective taking and empathy; Wisdom. Most of these do not require explanation but Schwartz's mention of 'Courage' may surprise some. What he has in mind is that:

> Scientists, scholars, and students need intellectual courage, too. They need it to stand up for what they believe is true, sometimes in the face of mass disagreement from others, including people in authority like their professors or journal editors. And they need it to take intellectual risks, to pursue intellectual paths that might not pan out. *(Schwartz, 2022, p. 65)*

This is hardly the courage of Anne Frank, Nelson Mandela and countless others, but the overall point Schwartz and others (Reiss, 1997; Deane-Drummond, 2008; Willmott & Macip, 2016; Pennock, 2019) make is that bad science is not only incompetent or erroneous science; it is also science that is morally bad.

Closely allied to these epistemological arguments for including ethics in the teaching of science is the argument that including ethics in the teaching of science can help students see the contexts within which science is undertaken and applied. Take a topic like photosynthesis. To a biologist, photosynthesis is absolutely fascinating – it's all about manufacturing sugars like glucose from nothing more than carbon dioxide (present at a concentration in the atmosphere of only 0.4 per cent) and water. This entails the splitting of both water and carbon dioxide despite both of these being very stable compounds – something that plants, algae and certain bacteria do so long as they have even a low level of light (whether sunlight or artificial). Furthermore, the 'machines' that can carry out these demanding chemical reactions can grow themselves. In the case of sexually reproducing flowering plants, all that are needed are what botanists call seeds (embryonic machines), some soil, moisture and light and before long not only do these embryonic machines grow themselves and start to photosynthesize, they also produce seeds in turn so that a new generation of machines can be produced to carry on photosynthesizing. Many plants are so good at doing this that we call them weeds – it is difficult to stop them from reproducing themselves generation after generation; given time, they even help produce the very soil in which they grow.

Unfortunately, most learners, whatever their age, don't find photosynthesis to be absolutely fascinating. In primary schools, the teaching sometimes doesn't get much further than naming the parts of a plant and putting a plant in a dark cupboard and showing that it doesn't grow as much as a plant in daylight (amazing). At secondary level, too much time is often spent doing little more than learning the biochemical reactions of photosynthesis or the structure of leaves.

Many school students (but not all) find that the inclusion of ethics in their science lessons makes the science more interesting, resulting in them becoming more engaged and motivated (Cerini et al., 2003; Chowning et al., 2012; Chowdhury, 2018). In the case of photosynthesis, inclusion of ethics might entail discussing such questions as:

- Should we all be vegans or vegetarians? [Students need to think about what the consequences would be for ourselves, for farm animals and for land use.]
- Should we grow more of our crops in the UK rather than importing them from abroad? [What would be the consequences for our diet, for UK employment, for overseas employment, for food miles, for global climate change?]
- Should we genetically engineer crops to boost yields? [How does such genetic engineering work? What would be the consequences for our use of fertilizers and pesticides? Would the widespread use of genetically engineered crops be good or bad for biodiversity? Why do some people feel so strongly that we should not eat genetically modified crops? Would more detailed labelling of foods help?]

Still sticking with the topic of photosynthesis, there is much to be said for school gardens. School gardens used to be more widespread than they are today (Figure 6.1). While there are reasons that go far beyond ethics in advocating school gardens – students undertake exercise and they may improve their diets in eating the produce from such gardens (Ozer, 2007) – it has been argued that they can play a role in building community food security (Carlsson et al., 2016). Sadly, this may become

Figure 6.1 DeWitt Clinton Park School Garden, New York, 1904.
Source: Wikimedia Commons https://commons.wikimedia.org/wiki/File:DeWitt_Clinton_Park_School_Garden.jpg.

more necessary in the years ahead, even in countries where most people have never had to worry about food security. School gardens can therefore provide a route into discussing such pressing ethical issues as food inequalities and help to make a topic like photosynthesis more engaging for learners.

Where else might the ethics of science be taught?

Of course, even if it is accepted that science education benefits from ethical issues being addressed, this doesn't necessarily mean that those responsible for the teaching of science have to teach ethics. Where else might the ethics of science be taught?

Early years and primary

Let's start by considering the education provided from birth to age five in family and in what in England is called the Early Years Foundation Stage (EYFS). It is sometimes supposed that there isn't much science education that takes place in the first five years of post-birth life, but this isn't the case. Young children learn a tremendous amount about the way the world works and this area is increasingly being explored in both science education (e.g. the *Journal of Emergent Science*, https://www.ase.org.uk/resources/journal-of-emergent-science, that one of us used to edit) and in developmental psychology (e.g. Gopnik et al., 1999; Goswami, 2015).

Even children in their first year of life can be shown to 'know' certain things about the world. Given that children at this age typically cannot speak more than the occasional few words, much of the evidence for what they know relies on the useful observation that they spend longer looking at what they find surprising. Babies as young as three and a half months spend substantially less time staring at an experimental set up that shows a moving short carrot that disappears behind a wall that is taller than the carrot and then re-appears than they spend staring at an experimental set up that shows a moving tall carrot disappearing behind a wall that is shorter than the carrot and then re-appearing (Goswami, 2008). In everyday language, even babies of this age 'know' that part of the tall carrot should have been visible above the wall.

Using this and other techniques, psychologists have established that pre-school children know the following:

- Objects exist continuously in time and in space (so, for example, a rabbit cannot suddenly appear, disappear or change greatly in size or move instantaneously from one place to another).
- Objects need to be supported to avoid falling downwards (so a box falls if the table on which it is standing is withdrawn).
- Changes to inanimate objects are generally the result of causes whereas animals are agents who can move on their own (so it is not surprising when a dog moves without anything coming into contact with it but it is when a meaningless shape does).
- Causes precede effects (so if a marble is to cause a jack-in-the-box to appear it needs to be dropped into the apparatus before the jack-in-the-box appears).
- If an effect has a number of potential causes, the actual cause is likely to be one that covaries with the effect (so by the time they are three years old, children can work out which of a pair of levers on a box causes the light on the lid of the box to come on).
- Causes and effects must be contiguous in time and place.
- By and large, causes and effects are of similar types (so a mechanical effect, such as a change in movement of an object, is more likely to be caused by a mechanical cause, such as its collision with another object, than by a flash of light or the appearance of a smell).
- The behaviour of objects is frequently the result of intentions (so in a computer display that initially shows (i) a large circle and a small circle separated by a tall rectangle, then shows (ii) each circle in turn expanding and contracting twice and then shows (iii) the small circle moving towards the large circle, reaching the tall rectangle, retreating, moving again towards the large circle but this time passing above the rectangle and making contact with the large circle is interpreted by adults and infants alike as a mother (large circle) calling to her child (small circle) who then runs towards her, only to be prevented by a barrier, which causes the child to retreat so as to be able to run towards the

barrier and jump over it and thus reach mother, whereupon mother and child embrace). Even three-month-old babies are sensitive to movement information that is interpreted by adults as specifying social causality.

- Artefacts do not grow but organisms do (so small kettles do not increase in size over time whereas rabbits do).
- Offspring have characteristics that resemble those of their parents (so when four-year-olds are shown a picture of a newborn kangaroo – a shapeless blob – and then told that it was raised with goats they are almost all sure that it grows up to be good at hopping not climbing). *(Abrahams & Reiss, 2012, p. 414)*

This may not yet seem to have much to do with ethics but young children learn about the world about them partly by themselves and partly through their interactions with others, especially their peers and significant adults. These interactions are fuelled by dialogue and play, in which children imagine what characters are doing and often whether what these characters are doing is right or wrong. Consider the last bullet point above; parents almost inevitably talk to their young children using language that indicates what is good and what is not good: 'Look at this poor little kangaroo. It is so small and needs to be helped. Who is going to help it? Look! Here are some nice goats. What lovely goats. The mummy goat is helping the tiny kangaroo. She is keeping it warm. And she is giving it milk to help it grow. What a good goat', etc.

The important point for our purposes is that from birth to age five and in primary school, it is the same adult who helps the child to learn science *and* to learn all other subjects, including ethics. Inevitably and immediately, therefore, links can be made between science and ethics. We shall have much more to say about this in Chapters 7 and 8, but the important point is that around the world, primary school teachers are experts at teaching almost the full range of subjects – though some subjects, e.g. music or certain foreign languages, may also benefit from subject specialists.

Furthermore, there are resources to help primary teachers teach ethics alongside ethics. To give just one example, many textbooks intended for use in primary schools link science and ethics. Gola (2017) examined how environmental ethics is portrayed in science textbooks for primary school pupils in Poland. She pointed out that environmental ethics is central to environmental education:

Many researchers stress the fundamental role of environmental ethics, claiming that it should be one of the most important components of environmental education if it is meant to develop environmentally friendly behaviour ... Understanding the natural world as our common home requires changing attitudes and taking ethical action. It is crucial to connect science with ethics and scientific expertize with the knowledge of ethics. Therefore, stressing the importance of ethics becomes necessary in the teaching of ecology ... *(Gola, 2017, p. 323)*

Gola went on to examine the five science textbooks most frequently used in the fourth grade of elementary schools in Poland (for children aged eleven). Ethics permeated the treatment of the environment in these texts. Children were enjoined to respect nature, to not frighten animals, to not destroy plants, to admire the beauty of plants and so forth. The many benefits that humans obtain from the natural environment were discussed, and attention was paid to how pets should be cared for. Translated quotations from the textbooks about pets include 'Every animal deserves proper care and you need to ensure this is the case for your pet', 'Do not harm your pet and do not tease it even while playing with it' and 'Spend time with your pet so that it does not feel abandoned. Remember that animals need your companionship' (p. 330).

Secondary

Secondary schools differ from primary schools in many important regards but as far as the teaching of ethics in goes, the most important difference is that in most countries, much of the teaching of science in secondary schools is done by specialist science teachers. In countries where ethics is taught on the secondary school curriculum, this means that one logical possibility is for the ethical aspects of science to be taught as part of ethics, by teachers with a specialism in teaching ethics.

The obvious advantage of this is that students benefit from expert teaching in ethics. There is perhaps a partial analogy with where creationism might be addressed in the curriculum. In England, creationism is routinely included in Religious Education (RE). There isn't a National Curriculum for RE but back in 2006 the government department – the Department of Children, Schools and Families (DCSF) – in charge of school education and the Qualifications and Curriculum Authority (QCA) published a non-statutory national framework for RE and associated teaching units that included a unit asking 'How can we answer questions about creation and origins?' (QCA, 2006). The unit focused on creation and the origins of the universe and human life, as well as the relationships between religion and science. A carefully written 23-page guide was produced. For example, in answer to the question, 'Is the universe designed? Who could have designed it?' it is suggested that teachers of 13- to 14-year-olds should:

> Give the pupils opportunities to explore ... a range of different answers to these questions, including answers given by members of different faiths. These answers should include the views of creationists, evolutionists, advocates of intelligent design and philosophers of religion, such as Anselm, Thomas Aquinas, Blaise Pascal and Francis Bacon. *(QCA, 2006, p. 16)*

A year later the DCSF published guidance on how school science might address creationism. This guidance included the following under the heading, 'What is appropriate to teach in science lessons':

> Creationism and intelligent design are not part of the science National
> Curriculum programmes of study and should not be taught as science. However,

Chapter 6 Should ethics be considered where science is taught?

there is a real difference between teaching 'x' and teaching *about* 'x'. Any questions about creationism and intelligent design which arise in science lessons, for example as a result of media coverage, could provide the opportunity to explain or explore why they are not considered to be scientific theories and, in the right context, why evolution is considered to be a scientific theory. *(DCSF, 2007)*

One of the important words in this quotation is 'could'. The guidance is clear that there is no expectation that science teachers *should* teach about creationism. In answer to the question, 'Should time be given to creationism and intelligent design in science lessons?' the guidance states:

Creationism and intelligent design are not scientific theories and do not form part of the science National Curriculum or the GCSE and GCE A level subject criteria. There may be situations in which it is appropriate for science teachers to respond to student comments or enquiries about the claims of creationism or intelligent design. This would be to establish why they are not considered as scientific theories as described above in 'What is appropriate to teach in science lessons'. One way to do this would be to consider the mechanisms by which new scientific knowledge becomes established and why creationism and intelligent design do not meet these requirements. *(DCSF, 2007)*

Nevertheless, there are a number of problems with the suggestion that the ethical aspects of science are taught within the subject of ethics, by teachers with a specialism in that subject. For one thing, formal teaching of ethics as a school subject in its own right, or as a discipline within philosophy, is not that common (Teke, 2021). Some countries do teach philosophy in school, sometimes as a subject with that name and sometimes within subjects like government and civics, but many don't and in some that do it is an optional subject, often reserved for older students, despite the success of the Philosophy for Children movement (The P4C Co-operative, 2022).

However, even if there were sufficient specialist teachers of ethics in secondary schools, with the foundations of moral philosophy being covered in philosophy or Religious Education, there would still be arguments in favour of ethics being taught in science. One argument for this, in addition to the ones already examined in this chapter, is that sometimes it simply makes more sense to cover both the science and the ethics at the same time. Consider, for example, the question of cloning animals like Dolly the sheep (Figure 6.2). Other subjects, such as philosophy or literature (e.g. such books as *Brave New World, Never Let Me Go, The Cloning of Joanna May*) may look at the issue of cloning but one major argument for examining the cloning of non-human animals in school science is that evaluation of the debates surrounding such cloning is helped by an understanding of science. One of the major arguments against cloning is that it is ineffective (there were 277 attempts before Dolly resulted); another is that it results in excessive animal suffering (CIWF, 2022). Arguments in favour of animal cloning include that it can accelerate the production in

Figure 6.2 Dolly – the first mammal to be cloned.
Source: Wikimedia Commons https://commons.wikimedia.org/wiki/File:Dolly_face_closeup.jpg.

farming of the most productive livestock and that it can be used in the conservation of endangered species (BIO, 2010). Evaluation of these arguments requires the sort of knowledge one might expect a specialist biology teacher to have but not necessarily a teacher of school philosophy.

Informal

Education does not only take place in schools. Chapter 9 is dedicated to the informal sector. Here, it is sufficient to point out that the informal sector can present science without including ethical considerations but often chooses to consider both science and ethics. Unsurprisingly, stories about biodiversity and conservation often feature heavily in zoos, botanic gardens, aquaria and nature reserves/national parks. Examples where ethical considerations are absent include certain specialist magazines and certain science centres. However, there are many science magazines, including some of the best known ones with the largest circulation (e.g. *Scientific American*, *New Scientist*), that regularly (albeit not invariably) deal with ethical issues. Articles, for example, on new battery technology, while concentrating on the science, may be situated within a story about the benefits of improved storage of energy from renewable sources (to counter anthropogenic climate change) or the benefits of making batteries that avoid the use of heavy metals, with their associated environmental and humanitarian issues; when it comes to articles on biodiversity or conservation, there is typically explicit reference to our responsibility to other species for their benefit and/or for ours. Science magazines often also deal with ethical issues within the practice of science, such as scientific misconduct and inequities within science.

Values, ethics and controversial issues

There is a final worry about the inclusion of ethics in science that is worth addressing, one that is relevant for both the formal and informal sectors, and that is that in including ethics, those responsible (whether teachers of science in schools, colleges or universities or communicators of science in informal settings) may promulgate their own ethical views or values, thus failing to teach in a balanced manner. For some teachers, their unease at this possibility is a particular reason for preferring not to include ethics in their science teaching.

These concerns can be alleviated by drawing on the lessons learnt about how to teach controversial issues in science. The central feature that makes an issue controversial is that a range of positions are held by different people and that these positions cannot simply be dismissed as extreme (at the risk of alienating some readers, belief in abduction by aliens can be considered extreme and is not a controversial issue that warrants examination in school science). These may be for reasons that have nothing to do with ethics but they can be. Take, for example, the question of euthanasia for humans. This is an issue about which, unsurprisingly, people can feel strongly and where a range of positions are held. A science teacher may be wary – even if lecturing to trainee doctors and nurses at university – of getting into a discussion about the ethics of euthanasia.

There are three standard ways of teaching controversial issues in science (Reiss, 2022). One is the approach of *advocacy*, where the teacher argues for the position they hold. For example, one teacher might assert, 'We do not have the right to help someone end their life, whatever the circumstances.' Another might assert, 'If someone is not going to recover and is suffering, it's the duty of the medical profession to enable them to end their life if that is what they wish.' A problem for the position of advocacy in a school classroom is that a teacher is almost always more powerful and articulate than their students, and this is particularly the case the younger the students are. There is therefore a risk that when a teacher adopts the model of advocacy in the teaching of a controversial issue, students become persuaded by the teacher's point of view, without having carefully thought matters through for themselves.

A second approach is one of *affirmative neutrality*, in which a teacher presents to their students as many sides of a controversy as possible, without indicating their own position. This approach is more balanced than the approach of advocacy, though the teacher may find it difficult to avoid indicating their own views. Additionally, this approach may accord more attention or credence to a position than that position deserves. A further problem is that the lesson may end up being somewhat dry and fail to engage some students. It can also be the case that a teacher with strong views about an issue feels uncomfortable at presenting as many sides of that issue as possible, without indicating their own position.

A third approach is one of *procedural neutrality*, where the teacher acts as a facilitator. Information about the controversial issue and various points of view are elicited from students and from source material. Again, the teacher does not reveal their own position. This approach has a number of advantages, though obtaining suitable source material may require a considerable investment of time by the teacher unless the developers of a course provide suitable curriculum materials for students. Without suitable source materials, this approach runs the risk of failing to elicit a sufficient range of views from the students, in which case the lesson may become unbalanced or require the teacher to intervene in a manner more akin to that of affirmative neutrality or even advocacy.

Conclusion

As you have probably gathered, our view is that there is much of value in including ethics within the teaching or communication of science, and our next three chapters explore how this might be done. Nevertheless, we have a number of caveats. First, if school teachers of science are to be expected to include ethics in their teaching, those teachers have the right to be given appropriate support in their initial teacher education and continuing professional development and through the classroom materials that they use with their students. Second, there is much to be said for schools making provision for individual teachers of science who do not want to include ethics in their teaching not to have to. Third, there are instances where other ways of teaching ethics in science can work well – for example, co-teaching between subject specialists, hosting visitors with particular expertise and taking students on visits. It is better to focus on student entitlement than on what individual science teachers are required to do.

Ethics in school science – its role in socio-scientific issues

7

Science is a human activity, an ongoing endeavour to better understand the natural world and the universe in which we live via observation, experimentation and theoretical explanation. However, as we have already highlighted in Chapters 2 and 4, scientific enterprise is not value-free. Scientists bring their own values, beliefs and biases to their work, operating within various sociocultural contexts which invariably underpin and inform what scientific questions are asked and how they are answered. In doing so, the outcomes of scientific work can, and often do, have significant ethical implications for the human race and the world in which we live. Therefore, as we have already argued in Chapter 6, considering ethical issues in school science helps students to understand the values which shape scientific endeavour and the ways in which scientific knowledge can, and should, be used.

What are socio-scientific issues and wicked problems?

We would predict that for the majority of people, when asked to consider what socio-scientific issues are, issues such as genetic testing and climate change might very well come to mind first and this seems fair given the dominance these subjects are given in the media. However, it is important to note that socio-scientific issues can arise from any area of science. Socio-scientific issues are multi-faceted and controversial in nature; based in science they have the potential to have a significant impact on society, both negatively and positively as we have all too well experienced recently with the impact of the Covid-19 pandemic. They are therefore socially relevant and raise ethical and moral dilemmas (Kahn & Zeidler, 2019). Examples of socio-scientific issues include fish farming, genetic technologies, fracking, space settlements, etc.

A controversial issue is a matter which different individuals and groups interpret and understand in differing ways, where conflicting courses of action are offered (Woolley, 2010). It may be an issue for which society has not found a solution that can be almost universally accepted or one which has sufficient significance that each of the proposed ways in dealing with it is objectionable to some section of the community and thus arouses dissent, opposition or protest. Many researchers (Zeidler et al., 2003; Sadler & Donnelly, 2006) have also highlighted the important role ethical and moral reasoning plays in considering controversial issues for they must involve value judgements, so that the issue cannot be settled by facts, evidence or experiment alone. It must be considered to be important by an appreciable number of people (Wellington & Ireson, 2013). For the purpose of this chapter, we define controversial issues as issues about which there is social disagreement, competition or conflict but are also not easy to define (Outlon, Dillon & Grace, 2004). Socio-scientific issues are therefore controversial, involve values and require ethical thinking and reasoning about a vast range of scientific topics.

Closely linked to this is the concept of a 'wicked problem'. Originally coined by Ritter and Webber (1973), 'wicked problems' are argued to be problems which have an ethical basis – solutions are not simply true or false but instead good or bad. They are problems which are essentially unique and do not have an enumerable set of potential solutions but can be considered a symptom of another problem or indeed lack an inherent logic which signals when they are solved. They are notoriously difficult to solve and often 'plagued by disagreement among stakeholders over their nature and cause' (Kawa et al., 2021, p. 1). Solutions to wicked problems are not immediate, with every attempt being a significant 'one-shot operation' that matters rather than solutions being tested by trial and error. Such problems are never permanently solved but can only, at best, be 're-solved' (Ritter & Webber, 1973); for example, food and water security, cancer, dementia and cyber security are but a few problems which fit the bill (Briggs, 2007). This can give a somewhat depressing and pessimistic impression of the world in which we live and what we as individuals can do about this, especially it seems for children. This should give science educators reason to pause and consider the role they might play in addressing this.

What is the place of ethics in socio-scientific issues and why is this important?

In Chapter 6 we discussed whether or not ethics should be considered where science is taught and concluded that although we recognized that including ethics within an already cognitively demanding subject such as science risks expecting too much of teachers as well as reducing the amount of time to teach an already over-burdened science curriculum, the role ethics plays in the formation of scientific knowledge and its use, as well as the ethical implications that science brings to society are too important to ignore. The history of science teaches us that there has always been a strong relationship between science and society. For instance, Darwin hesitated before publishing his *On the Origin of Species* (1859) as he was apprehensive about the possible backlash from Church and society about his controversial theory. There are more contemporary examples, such as the risks of nuclear power or genetic engineering. Science education, particularly over the last forty years, has been concerned with changing its content and aims in order to widen the scope of science taught:

> Students ought to know that at some historical point new scientific ideas were very controversial ... because once students begin to have some notion that scientific ideas have often resulted from struggle, grey areas become more acceptable. *(Levinson, 2013: 35)*

It is clear then that science is deeply embedded in social and ethical contexts. If we accept that scientific knowledge is formulated within social contexts, then the subject matter of science itself must reflect the interests of the scientists who carry out the work, those who fund them and those who might or might not benefit from them, reflecting the values and considerations of society. Ethics is therefore an important consideration of socio-scientific reasoning and decision-making. The justification of science, and of truth-telling in science (to build true and accurate knowledge about how the world works), is in terms of short- and long-term social consequences. It is impossible for science to arrive at ultimate truths, but what science does do is focus more on what something does as opposed to what something is, functional truths that are thus agreed on by consensus, underpinned by the factual, objective evidence available at any given time. Socio-scientific issues involve moral and ethical dilemmas that lack an objective and universal 'truth'. In order to make informed decisions, science and ethics cannot simply be de compartmentalized for 'they are inseparable in the context of socio-scientific issues' (Sadler, 2011: 3). Thus, the science is undertaken for a purpose, which is always subject to judgement. Judging and debating these purposes alerts us to the consequences of the actions, which after debate may not seem to be as simple as initially thought. These socio-scientific decision-making skills are not born overnight; they need to be developed from a young age and developed throughout a child's education.

Real-life engagement with socio-scientific issues and activism

Socio-scientific issues are frequently reported in the media (to name but a few contemporary examples: climate change, health-protective behaviours such as vaccinations, whether humans should be travelling to Mars, etc.), thus providing a source of information and viewpoints about science and socio-scientific issues for a range of citizens. Contemporary life is dominated by a multitude of media, with a significant number of people gaining information about socio-scientific issues via newspapers, radio, television, the internet and so on. The overall coverage of science is substantial, and if conflict or controversy is involved then this helps a story to qualify as newsworthy. Science and scientists are increasingly visible in the media, and news coverage of certain socio-scientific issues, such as climate change, has increased rapidly over the past two decades. Attention to media coverage, along with various forms of genre-specific entertainment use, has distinctive influences on citizen evaluations, suggesting that the mass media provide an important part of the social context by which citizens judge controversial science.

Therefore, the way in which science is portrayed in the media will, no doubt, have a significant impact on our perceptions, be it positive or negative. A joint study in 2001, by the Office of Science and Technology and the Wellcome Trust, found that 64 per cent of participants agreed with the statement that 'the media sensationalises science' (Technology and the Wellcome Trust, O.O.S.A., 2001). This perception was reinforced in 2006 by a report published by the Social Market Foundation who argued that it is the media's sensationalist treatment of scientific stories that leads to misunderstandings by the public. This onslaught of information is not discriminatory in its approach and the quality of information provided is varied, as we have seen more recently in the response to the Covid-19 pandemic and the reasons given for the reduced take-up of vaccines by various groups, such as a lack of information or absence of trust in the information available (Bullock et al., 2022). With frequent sensationalist reporting of socio-scientific issues in parts of the media it is difficult for adults, let alone children, to fully appreciate the issues at hand. Certainly, these issues are not simply restricted to broadsheet newspapers or adult documentaries but are evident in the various forms of the media that reach all ages, thus appealing to children of primary and secondary school age. Therefore, it is not only adults who discuss the issues, but also young people of both primary and secondary age as they become more and more accustomed to the relevant arguments of these debates. Is it then surprising that these groups wish to learn more about the issues involved?

Young people of today are realizing the power they have to effect social change and are using social media to advocate for this, believing that social media activism is the most effective way not only to have their voices counted and heard but also to effect real change (Fullam, 2017). Throughout history, protests have been used to fight for social justice, but the way these are organized is changing. With the advent of social media and the world becoming much more connected, albeit virtually, we can see that activism among young people is on the rise (Scherman & Rivera, 2021). Social media have given young people a new space in which to share information, ideology, raise awareness and even raise money to support their activism (Macafee & De Simone, 2012). Young people are organizing and mobilizing like never before. This has been seen most recently in the organization of the Parkland protests when students from the Parkland school in Florida walked out of classes in protest against the US guns laws that enabled the massacre on their school campus; this protest was organized via Instagram and Snapchat. This in turn inspired youth activists in the Teens for Equality group to lead a movement in Nashville via Twitter in response to the death of George Floyd.

More globally and pertinent to science education, in 2019 a series of school strikes inspired by a then-16-year-old Greta Thunberg's protests regarding the inaction on climate change were organized to take place before the United Nations Climate Summit. The aim of the movement was to urge adults to take responsibility and stop Climate Change. More than a million young people demonstrated in around 2,200 events worldwide across 125 different countries, most not old enough to vote and all organized via social media – Facebook, Instagram, Twitter and WhatsApp. For young people this is personal, it is about their future.

Greta Thunberg first learned about climate change at the age of eight and was shocked that adults did not appear to be taking the issue seriously. She notes that it was hard not to think about climate change and she worried incessantly about whether or not she was going to have a future, which subsequently affected her mental health. Greta Thunberg is not alone. Substantial levels of climate-related distress are reported globally with children and young people particularly vulnerable (Wu et al., 2020), emphasizing that science and society are not separate entities but rather that 'all aspects of science are inseparable from the society from which they arise' (Sadler, 2004, p. 342).

There has also been an increasing focus on the mental health and well-being of young people in schools with the aim of positively impacting on the development of students' confidence, resilience and knowledge so that they can keep themselves mentally healthy (Glazzard, 2018). Schools constitute the core public service that makes a difference to the lives of their students. It is teachers who see students every day, form key relationships and, along with their families, often know them best. Teachers require an understanding of their students' mental health needs and have a role in intervening where students manifest anxieties or other mental health issues (DoH/Dfe, 2017, Glazzard, 2018). To focus on the mental health and well-being of students is to take seriously a broad conceptualization of the aims of education, one which includes attempting to ensure that students flourish (Reiss & White, 2014). But schools are also places where subjects are taught, to give students access to 'powerful knowledge', which otherwise they would be far less likely to be able to access (Guile et al., 2018; Young, 2018). Relatedly, researchers and others have called for subjects to re-examine the bases of their curricula including their aims, content and pedagogy and to consider each subject's contribution to epistemic literacy. This move has been especially strong in the sciences (Harlen, 2010), in Religious Education (Wintersgill et al., 2017), in history (Chapman & Wilschut, 2015) and in geography (Lambert, 2011) but is increasingly spreading to other subjects (Standish & Sehgal-Cuthbert, 2017).

As we have argued in Chapter 4, an important goal of science education is to foster students' appreciation of the epistemology of science (Lin & Chan, 2018), to help them understand the nature of science and develop greater scientific literacy, to enable them to participate more effectively in civic and cultural affairs, as well as make personal decisions and informed judgements regarding social issues using knowledge and understanding of scientific concepts and processes (Millar et al., 2007; Archer et al., 2015). Therefore, for some time, science educators have been debating about whether there is a need for science education to undergo a 'convergence' with other sectors of education such as environmental and/or health education in order to address these complex issues (Dillon et al., 2016), advocating that science literacy should emphasize social responsibility (Santos, 2009), producing 'activists – people who will fight for what is right, good and just' (Hodson, 1999, p. 789).

One way therefore for educators to address this is to empower students with the ability to engage in socio-scientific issues that might well influence their lives so that they can both now and in the future become reflective citizens who engage in, and are a part of, a democratic society. Given the reality that students are interested in and concerned about these issues, the increasing statutory focus on this in schools as well as the effect that this has on students' mental health, surely as science educators the moral imperative lies with us.

Should socio-scientific issues be taught in school science?

Over the past twenty years a host of educators (e.g. Levinson, 2006; Pope, 2017; Owens, Sadler and Zeidler, 2017; Reiss, 2019) involved in socio-scientific issues education have developed educational methods including ethical frameworks for teaching socio-scientific issues in the classroom. One of the aims of including ethical thinking when considering socio-scientific issues in science curricula is to develop students' skills in moral discourse. This in itself has ramifications for future citizenship, since Zeidler et al. (2009) found that without time in science lessons to discuss ethical issues, students tended not to use their science knowledge and understanding when engaging in arguments about socio-scientific issues.

Teaching socio-scientific issues in school science has both critics and defenders. Historically, there are countless examples which demonstrate how ethical and social issues are an important consideration of science, from the Galileo affair to more contemporary issues such as those that surround nuclear power or genetic engineering. Science education, particularly over the last forty years, has been concerned with changing its content and aims in order to widen the scope of science taught. School science syllabuses have been greatly influenced by the science and technology in society movement, as Reiss (2009) identifies so that now more applied science, e.g. environmental chemistry, is taught in schools. Contemporary school science is now more likely to be embedded in a social and cultural context as is evident from projects such as the Science Capital Teaching Approach (Godec et al., 2017) being implemented as a way to engage students in learning science to promote social justice and as a means to address the under representation of women, working-class children and some ethnic groups in the physical sciences.

The skills and knowledge required to teach ethics is one concern regarding the teaching of ethics in science education. Science teachers are not educated in moral philosophy or social sciences but educated in science. Research (Levinson & Turner, 2001; Garrecht et al., 2022) suggests that secondary school science teachers are less confident than humanities teachers or Personal, Social and Health Education (PSHE) facilitators about teaching social and ethical issues expressing concerns about a lack of expertise. There are also concerns regarding the accessibility of teaching materials, that such lessons could give rise to issues with behaviour management. This point could also be applied to primary school teaching. Even though they teach all areas of the curriculum, this does not mean that they have received much, if any, education in moral philosophy.

Research into this issue has, in the main, been in post-primary science education although more is being published now in the primary sector (Dolan et al., 2009; Evagorou, 2009; Gormley et al., 2019). One criticism regarding the teaching of socio-scientific issues in school science is embedded in the debate about the nature of science. Some argue that science and ethics are completely separate disciplines, maintaining that ethics should not be taught as part of science. Donnelly argued that there is no place for

> ethical categories in the conceptionalization of the world offered by science. This is not to say that science does not stand in a relationship with ethical issues.... But the relationship is of a very special kind. *(Donnelly, 2002, p. 137)*

A scientist is a person who proposes, develops, tests, defends and criticizes proposals for understanding and dealing with the natural order, whereas the nature of ethics is concerned with how we should decide what is morally right and what is morally wrong. Schurr argued that:

> science describes what happens. Ethics describes what we should do. Science is expressed in detailed descriptions and testable theories. Ethics is lived out in actions and passions, which constitute a way of life. *(Schurr, 1977, p. 13)*

Thus, it is claimed by some that science has nothing to say about the way we should act and behave and by the same reasoning ethics has nothing to say about science. For example, Hall (1999) protested about the widening of the science curriculum to include moral and ethical considerations because of the view that science should be value-free. However, science is not, and cannot be, value-free; values relevant to science are both cognitive and moral. Science relies on epistemic values and scientists use their judgement when they seek to predict and explain the world. This means that science generates (and builds on) knowledge via robust methods but is also a creative activity which is collaborative and underpinned by cultural diversity; thus, the conduct of science has values associated with it (Ratcliffe, 2007). The persistent inculcation of science as 'value-free' knowledge is in itself a value position (Layton, 1986).

Students of all ages are aware of local and global controversial issues in the news and care deeply about them (Claire & Holden, 2007). Furthermore, the purpose of teaching socio-scientific issues should not be only to enhance students' decision-making skills. Rather, it is important for children to understand the nature of controversial issues and for teachers to develop students' open mindedness, thirst for knowledge and ability to identify bias and reflect critically (Oulton, Dillon & Grace, 2004) as many young people are interested in political and controversial issues. In addition to this, several authors (Kolsto, 2001; Ratcliffe & Grace, 2003; Sadler, 2011) suggest that socio-scientific issues should be used to promote responsible citizenship in a world which is increasingly becoming more dependent on science and technology.

Research produced by Claire and Holden (2007) and Woolley (2010) focused on the teaching of controversial issues in primary school. Claire and Holden (2007) interviewed over 500 children aged from 9 to 11 to find out what young people have to say about the world and their concerns about the future. They found that children were not only interested in controversial issues but talked with considerable knowledge and insight about a variety of issues that concerned them, such as racism, drug abuse, alcoholism, crime, pollution and child abuse. They further concluded that children 'wished to learn about these issues at school so that they could understand them better and be proactive in working for change' (Claire & Holden, 2007, p. 4).

Woolley's book *Tackling Controversial Issues in the Primary School* (2010) sagely states that children are not simply members of society of the future but are members of society now, living in society amongst the rest of us. Woolley reminds us that although we need to prepare children for adult life, it is imperative to support them in the present; children are undoubtedly, as members of the community, 'affected by and concerned with political issues ... they need to be enabled to take on increasing responsibility for their own ideas, actions, attitudes and values' (2010, p. 135).

Recommendations from the school inspectorate in England almost thirty years ago (1995) on the teaching of controversial issues in schools included that 'controversial issues cannot, and should not, be excluded from the curriculum in schools: they will rise spontaneously from pupils' interest, experience and questions' (HMI, 1995, p. 6). Changes to curricula across many countries, such as England, the United States and Finland, as well as data gathered through research, evidences how the teaching of controversial issues in schools is now becoming generally more accepted, although there will always be some who object to certain controversial issues being taught.

The turn to socio-scientific issues and rise of ethics in school science

The Education Reform Act in England (1988) requires that 'The curriculum for a maintained school ... promotes the spiritual, moral, cultural, mental and physical development of pupils of the school' (Great Britain, 1988, p. 1). This means that science teachers in England are now expected to address matters which have previously been the province of teachers of history, PSHE and even Religious Education. In addition to this, inspection requirements by the Office for Standards in Education in England stipulate that a school's intent to provide for the personal development of all pupils must be a whole school issue. Schools are required to demonstrate how their programmes of personal development aim to develop their pupils into responsible, respectful and active citizens who are able to play their part and become actively involved in public life as adults. This should be achieved by developing pupils' character, dispositions and virtues – which Ofsted defines as a set of positive personal values – that inform pupils' motivation and guide their conduct so that they reflect wisely, learn eagerly, *behave with integrity* and cooperate consistently well with others arguing. *All subjects* need to play a part in inviting pupils to reflect on the purpose and meaning of life (Ofsted, 2019).

Therefore, there has been a gradual turn in England and Wales especially in secondary school science, to include socio-scientific issues and ethics. Changes to the KS3 (for 11- to 14-year-olds) and KS4 (for 14- to 16-year-olds) science curriculum for England and Wales in 2008 encouraged the recognition of the role of controversy in science. More recent changes in 2015 to the National Curriculum for science at KS4 required students to learn about the practical and ethical considerations of modern biotechnology (DfE, 2015, p. 10). Aims for KS1-4 also include ensuring that students are 'equipped with the scientific knowledge required to understand the uses and implications of science, today and for the future' (2015, p. 2). These developments are not restricted to England and Wales: the inclusion of ethical reasoning in relation to socio-scientific issues in a number of countries including Australia, New Zealand, Sweden and the United States is also increasingly a focus.

Specific references to socio-scientific issues and scientific debate are lacking from the KS1 and KS2 science curriculum (2015), with guidance stating that the 'social and economic implications of science are important but, generally, they are taught more appropriately within the wider school curriculum' (2015, p. 2). However, topics such as adaptation, evolution, deforestation, diet, drugs and nutrition, exploring human impact on ecology, materials, micro-organisms and studying naturalists such as Sir David Attenborough (who raises ethical questions about the natural world in every television programme he makes) have been included. Clearly, there is some room for debate here about the primary science curriculum, which also states that teachers will 'wish to use different contexts to maximise their pupils' engagement with and motivation to study science' (2015, p. 3). Therefore, it is reasonable to teach such topics in a way that includes ethical aspects. The curriculum does not prevent primary school teachers from doing so, but it may very well be the case that because teachers are not required to do so, they do not feel they should include ethical aspects. We take the view that schools have the freedom and agency to deliver the curriculum in ways that they see best, as long as statutory requirements are adhered to.

Teaching in primary schools is simply not compartmentalized by subject, even though primary schools have been heavily criticized for their focus on mathematics and English to the detriment of other subjects such as science (even though it is one of the four core subjects – English, ICT, mathematics and science). Early years and primary students simply do not compartmentalize their thinking: does anyone? Primary students will not wait to ask an ethical question about a science topic because someone deems it more suited to asking in PSHE (personal, social, health and economic education). Take, for example, the suggestion by the science programme of study (DfE, 2015) that when learning about materials students might wish to learn about people who have developed useful materials, for example, John Dunlop and the invention of pneumatic tyres. Using scientific research skills, it will not take long for a student to raise the ethical issue of the impact of rubber plantations on endangered species in south-east Asia. And perhaps closer to home, when considering the topic of inheritance and cross breeding, ethical questions regarding intentionally breeding animals for their facial features – in the case of a pug (see Figure 7.1) for example – and the impact on their physical health (brachycephalic syndrome affects short-nosed dog breeds, meaning they can suffer from severe respiratory distress amongst other issues) will be raised. Fortunately, whole school approaches to cross curricular teaching in primary schools enable students to make links between subjects and for teachers to deliver a curriculum that is enriched.

In certain areas of the curriculum, e.g. PSHE education and citizenship, teachers are encouraged to undertake activities such as 'circle time' to discuss various issues such as bullying, and at KS2, drugs and sex education are typically on the agenda.

Figure 7.1  An image of a pug.
Source: https://en.wikipedia.org/wiki/Pug.

However, these areas of the curriculum are non-statutory in primary schools in England; therefore, schools can opt out of teaching these issues if they wish. To our mind, the fact that PSHE and citizenship are non-statutory means that teachers do have the opportunity to have some input into the curriculum and introduce socio-scientific issues alongside science, rather than merely opting out from teaching controversial or challenging issues. Furthermore, citizenship, which advocates the teaching of controversial issues, can provide approaches and strategies for teachers when planning to teach socio-scientific issues since engaging in citizenship lessons involves clarifying values, evaluating information and viewpoints, discussion and decision making (Claire & Holden, 2007; Woolley, 2010).

It is obvious that not all science content can be appropriately evaluated by younger children or even adolescents, and we are certainly not proposing that primary school children could debate every ethical scenario, as some issues are simply not suitable, but does that mean that teachers of primary science should not approach any socio-scientific issues at all? Effective teaching takes into account cognitive capacity and child development; therefore, primary school teachers should draw on appropriate topics and teaching strategies with these in mind. In addition, arguing that children are simply too young to engage in ethical thinking about socio-scientific issues does not stop children being affected and concerned by socio-scientific issues relevant to them or this having a negative impact on their mental health as discussed above. Take, for example, climate change and sustainability – a socio-scientific issue that can be argued as a 'wicked problem' and involve complex science. And yet, research has shown that by teaching young children about these issues in an age-appropriate manner, anxiety about these issues is reduced and that this has the potential to lead to a reduction in future carbon emissions (OECD, 2021).

We therefore propose that ethical considerations and demanding scientific content should not overly limit teachers in their classroom ambitions. It has been suggested that it is 'problematic to limit the science curriculum because of the limitations children may have in thinking in abstract ways' (Metz, 1998, p. 23). Jerome Bruner (1960) believed that many complex ideas could be introduced to young children. He argued that any subject could be taught effectively, in some intellectually honest form, at any stage of development. Research by Venville and Donovan (2007) into Year 2 children's understandings of inheritance found that it is possible for children as young as six to associate new ideas about genes and DNA with their own understanding of inheritance. These researchers argue that at least half of the pupils in the class experienced meaningful learning, creating a strong cognitive foundation for their future biological education. Inheritance is now included in the KS2 National Curriculum for science in England (2015).

Perhaps one of the most important aspects of teaching is student motivation and engagement in contemporary issues is what stimulates most interest from students (Sadler, 2011). Reiss (2009) agrees that relevance is key to student motivation, noting that 'it is perhaps unsurprising that for many young people it is the ethical issues raised by science that too often seem to be lacking from their science lessons' (p. 137). If the social, cultural and ethical aspects of science were included more fully in school science then many students might be encouraged to study science longer, as the humanistic side of science appeals to many pupils, particularly girls. Therefore, in a bid to engage more students in enjoying and studying science at higher levels (A level for example) as well as helping students to become more ethically sensitive (Sadler, 2011) some schools have been focusing more on including socio-scientific issues to teach the science curriculum (Hancock et al., 2019).

Strong arguments have also emerged that school science bears only a partial resemblance to real science, with too much emphasis being placed on the learning of individual facts, especially those that emerge from observations. If teaching is fact-dominated, it leads to the view that science is capable of yielding ultimate truths, being value-free and simply 'proving' things. However, if science is seen as exploring ideas, the teaching will involve learners in the process of developing understanding from evidence: 'Ideas will be explored rather than accepted and committed to memory. Alternative views will be examined in terms of supporting evidence' (Harlen, 2010, p. 28). Science will thus be portrayed as constrained by values and as a social enterprise and by engaging in such science, students will develop their moral thinking skills. Thus, a school education in these issues is crucial in order to develop decision-making skills because there is no doubt that the 'ethical implications of biological advances reside in both the public and private domain' (Levinson, 2003, p. 31). As Shakespeare (2003) remarks:

> structured arguments in science lessons can stimulate pupils' thinking, raise motivation and deepen understanding ... they can reveal misconceptions quickly, include all pupils, encourage a learning together atmosphere and produce surprising results! *(2003, p. 108)*

How can schools teach socio-scientific issues?

If we accept that social and ethical issues should be part of teaching science, how can science teachers incorporate these issues in their teaching? Sometimes, controversial issues are dealt with as part of a planned programme within a school, a whole school approach. Such programmes are frequently found in PSHE; issues are selected because they are seen as topical or relevant to the pupils' lives and tend to reflect the major social, political, economic and moral problems of our times. Without these programmes, it is argued, there would be a gap in a child's education (Claire & Holden, 2007; Woolley, 2010). In taking a whole-school approach, teachers should provide opportunities for students to consider the local, national or global scientific and ethical implications of the issue and, where appropriate, build on their own interests which provides students with the opportunity to consolidate or improve their understanding of science concepts (Sadler et al., 2016; McCrory, 2018).

We must remember that students in secondary schools will not be encountering ethical issues only within science but also within many other areas of their studies, and thus science teachers should play the important role of harnessing the skills needed to debate socio-scientific issues alongside their colleagues. It can be argued that departments within secondary schools work in silos: however, schools which take whole school approaches and promote interdepartmental collaboration are effectively building a cultural professional climate of shared pedagogies and continued professional development. If more widespread scientific literacy is to be achieved, policymakers and others responsible for developing the curriculum need to explore ways of bringing humanities and science teachers together: 'Whole school approaches will support the teaching of bioethics in three ways: ethos, interdepartmental collaboration and policies related to sex and drugs education' (Reiss and Levinson, 2003, p. 35). When teaching any subject, first and foremost should be the aims of the teaching. Thus, if aims in science teaching are to promote critical thinking, science teaching for social justice (e.g. in relation to genetics or animal testing), science to promote one's health or the environment or even to develop problem-solving skills and argumentation, then including social and ethical debates is essential. At the very least 'sensible decision-making will include an awareness of the values base and the factors that constitute a good argument. When complex decisions are looked at from personal perspectives, the ethical issues become clearer even if not easy to resolve' (Lewis & Lindsay, 1999, p. 17). There are an increasing number of resources available to aid teachers to teach their students about ethics in school science. The following section highlights ethical decision-making frameworks, authentic real-life scenarios and web-based models. We also recognize that argumentation is one of the most important pedagogical approaches to engaging with the ethical and scientific dimensions of socio-scientific issues, and as such Chapter 8 is dedicated to discussing this.

Ethical decision-making frameworks and authentic scenarios

A common approach to teaching socio-scientific issues in schools is to use one or more frameworks which incorporate ethical decision-making and authentic scenarios. For example, one framework for SSI-based instruction comprises three core aspects (design elements, learner experiences and teacher attributes) which together are shaped by various contexts, such as the classroom, the school/district, the community and state policy (Presley et al., 2013). In addition, when discussing how to construct a socio-scientific classroom, Zeidler et al. (2009) found that real-world relevance (when socio-scientific issues are used as a context to teach scientific content as in the case of Terri Schiavo – the issue being whether or not to terminate the life-support of a brain-dead person) enabled 16- to 18-year-old students to construct meaningful discussions about what they were learning. As a result, these students demonstrated improved understanding of scientific concepts when they were able to attach the concepts to relevant real-life socio-scientific issues.

The PARRISE (Promoting Attainment of Responsible Research and Innovation in Science Education) project (Levinson, 2018) centres on the theme of 'Socio-scientific Inquiry-based Learning'(see Figure 7.2) connecting Inquiry-based Science Education, Socio-scientific Issues and Citizenship Education. This project worked with students and teachers in both primary and secondary schools in the UK and mainland Europe. Its framework examines *authentic* (real-life) socio-scientific scenarios which provide a background for *enaction* (seeking evidence by integrating social and scientific enquiry) by raising research questions to investigate via enquiry-based learning. The solutions to authentic questions must involve a form of *action*, outcomes which address the original question and result in some kind of change. Topics addressed at primary level include infectious diseases, sustainable development in urban ecosystems, heredity and genetics disorders and science and space. At lower secondary level pollution and environmentally friendly policies, genomics, waste and epigenetics were included. And at upper secondary level, solar energy and green supplies, temperature control and regulation, the health effects of statins, nanotechnology and bioinformatics were successfully trialled.

One example of how taking a Socio-scientific Inquiry-based Learning (SSIBL) approach can be conceptualized and operationalized was a project undertaken by school students (aged 7–16) during the development of the London 2012 Olympic Park. This offered local students the opportunity to consider some of the socio-scientific issues involved in the construction of the Olympic stadium. This was achieved via the View Tube – a specially constructed classroom on the Olympic site

Figure 7.2 PARRISE model depicting the relationship between civic involvement in scientific research and innovation through activities in schools. This process is called Socio-Scientific Inquiry Based Learning (SSIBL).
Source: https://www.parrise.eu.

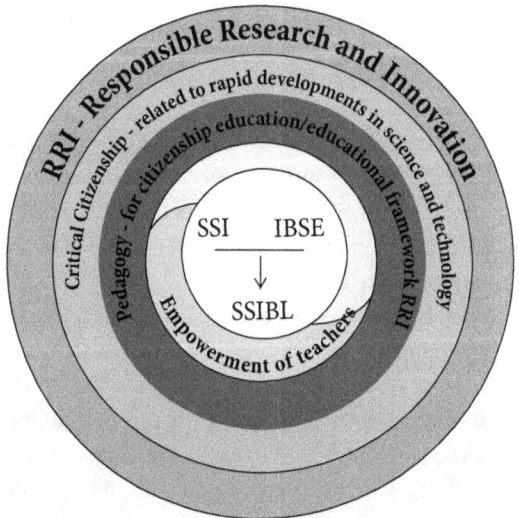

which allowed students to monitor the development of the stadium whilst considering any socio-scientific issues which arose in real time. Two issues of focus were what to do with the colonies of frogs and newts (as well as snakes) living in the area, as well as the discovery of radioactive materials from old industrial workshops. Via the support of their teachers and Field Studies Council staff, students considered the costs and benefits of various solutions. Their enquiries derived from links to and effects on their own environments and communities so that they were able to explore different ways of storing radioactive material safely as well as consider appropriate places to relocate the frogs, newts and snakes. These explorations were supported via discussions with experts and their peers.

This project was realized via the following stages which drew on the SSIBL framework:

- Authenticity – Teachers used the context to develop questions with their students which raised their awareness of the immediacy of the issue in terms of their own and communal well-being. Teachers drew on crucial pedagogic skills such as foregrounding the power of representation, e.g. through the media and jogging student beliefs through encouraging them to present new and diverse points of view. Professional development for teachers focused on any pedagogic challenges as well as national and cultural priorities and opportunities that needed to be considered.

- Enaction – Students were encouraged to define the problem that needed to be investigated; this was achieved once they understood that this was a genuine problem. For example, the students' research helped them understand that populations of these species (frogs, newts and snakes) have been decreasing nationally since the start of the 1900s when there was an intensification of agriculture and an increased use of pesticides. Breeding places have also reduced and the fact that these species are sensitive to changes in the environment as well as having thin skin means they are vulnerable to absorbing lethal toxins was identified. Thus, students needed to consider the ethics of disturbing these species whilst considering critically the views of all young people engaged in the project as well as the rights and responsibilities of all stakeholders. Collaborations between citizenship and science educators were encouraged at this point.

- Action – Once the students defined the problem and the research question for the investigation (enquiry-based scientific education), they then formulated ways of collecting appropriate evidence (socio-scientific issues), and identifying how a research project involving diverse and conflicting parties could be negotiated, considering the pertinent ethical implications. At this point teachers needed support in recognizing the barriers to progress and formulating strategies to overcome these. Teachers then continued to work with students to enable them to decide on the appropriate courses of action which then operationalized and acted upon. How voices are heard is a vital part of the democratic participation, the agency of those involved being promoted (citizenship education). In this example, the colonies of frogs and newts as well as snakes were collected by hand and transported from the site to new habitats specially created for them at the Waterworks Nature Reserve (E10, London), while radioactive materials were left at the site within sealed containers rather than transported.

Teaching materials for both primary and secondary students and the in-depth framework which underpins the PARRISE project can be found at https://www.parrise.eu.

Web-based models

Web-based Inquiry Science Environment (WISE) is another interesting teaching method which can be utilized to promote the process of negotiation and enquiry of socio-scientific issues, in particular, developing critical thinking skills such as asking questions, making arguments and forming hypotheses. WISE modules (Slotta, 2002) were designed by teams of researchers and teachers, in various fields of science, for secondary school-aged students in the United States with the aim of making science accessible to all. The modules highlight thinking skills via student modelling, and subsequent evaluation, of ideas. They encourage students to learn from each other by building on the ideas of others, and to engage in science thus promoting life-long learning (Slotta & Linn, 2009). WISE consists of several dozen modules, each approximately two weeks in length on a variety of topics. The modules serve to introduce science content within health, environmental and social contexts, for example, the Simple Inheritance and Global Warming modules.

Research by Tal et al. (2011) utilized and modified the Simple Inheritance module to teach genetics in an everyday context. Students from the eighth (13–14 years old) to tenth (15–16 years old) grades who took part in the study were required to make decisions about social action, in particular fundraising, and to act as genetic counsellors (deciding whether or not to try to prevent the birth of babies affected by genetic defects). This research intended to give the students opportunities to deal with real and relevant dilemmas by highlighting the complex relationships between science and society, in particular enhancing the understanding of the scientific content involved in cystic fibrosis. The researchers also incorporated a field trip to complement their use of a web-based model to teach inheritance to 15- to 16-year-olds. They found that the field trips enhanced group discourse, eliciting a high degree of interest and engagement in genetics among the students. It also provided the students with an opportunity for meaningful learning; for example, it enabled the students to gain a greater appreciation of the challenges cystic fibrosis sufferers face as well as furthering their understanding of the scientific concepts of inheritance by asking questions of those with the disease and the professional team available. The researchers found that the majority of the students who took part thought that the modified WISE Simple Inheritance module was engaging, enjoyable and interesting to read and more importantly involving students in ethical decision-making, albeit fictitious, was crucial to promoting the students' understanding of genetics. Evagarou (2011) also found that a field trip – in this case a visit to a local pig farm by children aged 10–11 – had a positive impact on children's motivation to engaging with socio-scientific issues, and furthered their understanding of the underlying scientific concepts.

Assessment

Ethical debates can be introduced to children as young as five or six as long as the debates are well planned and executed. The most important thing when implementing an SSI approach is to ensure that the issue can be explored by children in a meaningful way (Gormley et al., 2019). If we do include social and ethical issues when teaching science then naturally this leads to the issue of assessment. Assessment, both formative and summative (Bell, 2001), is integral to the seriousness and depth of teaching a topic. However, there has been little research undertaken on the assessment of students' abilities to deal with ethical issues in science (Reiss, 2009) and therefore little is known about what assessment procedures teachers are using and which are more effective.

Ratcliffe's (1997) work, which built on earlier work by Thier and Hill (1988), is one approach for the assessment of students' abilities to deal with both social and ethical aspects of science (Reiss, 2009). Ratcliffe's work allowed her to assess the reasoning used by students by utilizing (a) the SOLO (Structure of Observed Learning Outcome) taxonomy developed by Biggs and Collis (1982) which is based on Piagetian stages, and (b) her own taxonomy based on both descriptive and normative theories of decision-making. Findings indicated that both instruments correlated better than expected with student outcomes and thus proved of value.

Subsequent research by Ratcliffe and Grace (2003) suggests that it is important to distinguish between what is desirable and what is possible when evaluating learning of socio-scientific issues. They argue that obtaining authentic evaluation is difficult to achieve due to the relationship between 'education and behavioural outcomes … and the practicality of authentic assessment' (p. 41). Changing established behavioural routines is extremely difficult to achieve; therefore, it may be more realistic to 'expect development of opinions and attitude' (p. 42) rather than distinct changes in behaviour. It is important to examine the process of a student's reasoning when arguing their viewpoint rather than the researcher or teacher giving a value judgement about a student's point of view, as this would be inappropriate.

Reiss (2009) notes that, despite much debate, the introduction of ethics in the science curriculum has been hindered because there has been a great deal of disagreement amongst educators and researchers about how best to assess students' knowledge and understanding of ethical issues in science. More generally, assessing students' attitudes, opinions and reasoning in relation to socio-scientific issues is problematic. Multiple learning goals require multiple forms of assessment, encouraging students to show what they have learnt in a variety of formats 'including student-generated projects and oral assessment' (Ratcliffe & Grace, 2003, p. 43). This is time-consuming, requiring careful and skilful planning; however, when done produces authentic assessment which is high in validity.

Research by McCrory (2014) explored the capabilities of 7-8-year-olds, in relation to their perceptions, knowledge and understanding of socio-scientific issues in tandem with their ability to think morally and scientifically. Three schemes of work – 'Morals', 'Energy' and 'Genetics' – were taught to twenty-one Year 3 students, one topic per term, across one academic year. Lessons were carefully planned to take into account the students' cognitive capabilities, especially important when considering topics such as genetics (Vennville & Dawson, 2007). Lessons were not centred around field trips or authentic socio-scientific issues affecting the local community as suggested above; instead, socio-scientific issues were used that were raised by the children themselves which either affected them or their families or arose from their engagement with film and media.

For example, topics such as cloning and genetic inheritance arose due to watching *Star Wars*, reading newspaper reports about Dolly the Sheep and talking about inherited genetic diseases, e.g. sickle-cell anaemia which one of the children in the class had and openly shared. A discussion of the merits of luminous zebra fish which glow green when put in polluted water was a focus after being reported via Children's BBC Newsround. The effects of climate change (e.g. flooding) on countries such as Bangladesh (a country where many children of the class had relatives) were also a focus. In with thinking about pedagogical content knowledge (Pollard et al., 2023) and relevant research on teaching socio-scientific issues (which was at the time, and still is to an extent, is an under-researched area of science education), lessons incorporated a variety of pedagogies including argumentation, role-play, pictorial representations, mind-maps, concept cartoons, dialogic talk and reporting.

Outcomes indicated that students' moral thinking when considering socio-scientific issues was underpinned by their belief in the following values:

- *Being fair* – For example, when discussing renewable energy, students commented that: 'It's very unfair when we [humans] pollute habitats, like when there was that ship that spilt loads of oil into the sea. The birds were covered in oil and they couldn't fly and the fish died, lots were washed up on the beach. It made me feel really angry and upset, the poor birds and fish were suffering. If we used more renewable energy, like wind turbines, then that probably wouldn't happen as much because we would be using less oil.' Furthermore, when considering cloning:
  'Only the rich will be able to afford a clone and that's not fair to the poor.'

- *Honesty and truthfulness* – For instance, when considering recycling:
  'Sometimes people don't recycle because they can't be bothered even though they know that they should ... and then some people say that they recycle even when they don't so they lie which is silly. Maybe it's because they are embarrassed?'

Also, when thinking about a dilemma (based on inherited diseases): 'She has to tell her partner [about having the faulty gene] ... the partner will not get angry with her because she has told the truth.'

- *Respect* – For example, when thinking about their local environment:
 'When we throw rubbish on the ground and litter in the parks we are disrespecting it [the environment] and that's wrong.'
 Furthermore, when considering whether or not to use a clone for their own future benefit: 'We are not respecting the clone ... We'd be saying that we're better than the clone and that it is not worth anything which is really terrible because it would be a person just like me.'

- *Being responsible and considering the welfare of others* – For instance, when thinking about the behaviour of the engineers at the Chernobyl plant: 'They didn't think about anyone but themselves. They didn't care that other people might get hurt or die.'

It has been argued by some researchers (e.g. Zeidler & Sadler, 2009) that moral sensitivity should be included in the negotiation of socio-scientific issues, although to what degree would depend on the developmental stage of the child. In specifically focusing on teaching with reference to moral values when considering socio-scientific issues, the aim of the assessment framework in Table 7.1 (McCrory, 2014) is to promote the knowledge and understanding, and skills needed when undertaking moral decision making for children of primary age. The work that led to the framework in Table 7.1 entailed initially presenting the students with moral dilemmas and then presenting them with socio-scientific issues which also demanded the same decision-making skills. The students were given repeated opportunities to become aware of and identify with their own moral values to promote moral awareness and development, as clarification of values is cited as integral to moral education (Layton, 1986). The lessons aimed to help pupils to develop a critical appreciation of issues of right and wrong, fairness, rights and obligations in society, and to promote social awareness and development through helping pupils to begin to acquire the knowledge, understanding and skills needed to for them eventually to become responsible and effective members of society.

Studies suggest that children apply multiple forms of reasoning, namely moral (fairness, justice, rights), conventional (customs, etiquette) and psychological (autonomy, identity), simultaneously when evaluating transgressions or social dilemmas (Tisak & Turiel, 1998; Smetana et al., 2006). Therefore, the framework in Table 7.1 was constructed to analyse the children's statements as a way of assessing them, not to neatly categorize the children's responses into separate, hierarchical sub-levels, as can be the norm in primary school assessment.

What do the children's responses in this study have in common with research pertaining to moral thinking and reasoning? Piaget argued that a child's moral concepts develop in an unvarying sequence and that by the age of nine the morality of reciprocity begins to emerge, with children then able to consider the feelings or viewpoints of others when judging situations rather than relying solely on

Table 7.1 Framework for the determination of Moral Thinking and Perspective Taking (MTPT) when reasoning about socio-scientific issues in the primary school.

Level	Criterion	Examples from the participants' responses
MTPT0	No use of moral thinking or perspective taking	When asked to consider whether anything might be wrong about choosing the hair colour or sex of a child when designing babies, Sh replied, 'If you choose too many boys, then we won't be able to make as many babies (in the future) because you need a boy and a girl to make a baby.'
MTPT1	Some use of moral thinking or perspective taking	When asked, 'Should we clone humans?' V replied, 'There will be a population increase which means that there will not be enough homes. So, poverty will rise and only people who are rich will be able to pay which is unfair to the poor. Also, more food will be needed so species of animals may die out.'
MTPT2	Pupil identifies a moral concern/dimension in a socio-scientific issue but is unable to reason further (for example, to explore intentions and consequences or take more than one perspective)	When thinking about why the two engineers responsible for the Chernobyl disaster carried on with their experiment, R wrote, 'They were selfish, they didn't care'. R was unable to explain this any further.
MTPT3	Pupil analyses the morality of a specific socio-scientific issue using intentions and consequences and/or demonstrating perspective taking	When deciding whether or not Jane (a character who has inherited Huntington's disease) should tell her partner this, M wrote, 'She has to tell her partner (about having the faulty gene) because then her partner will know. And when she says "I might die", the partner will not get angry because she told the truth.'
MTPT4	Pupil analyses the morality of a specific socio-scientific issue using intentions and consequences and/or demonstrating perspective taking and makes a decision about what to do using moral language and thinking	When asked to consider, 'What if, in the future, we could make a clone of ourselves and keep him/her to use in case we became ill?', V noted, 'We are not respecting the clone', followed by Sh adding 'We'd be saying that we're better than the clone, that it's worthless and that it doesn't have any human rights.'

MTPT5	Pupil uses moral language and understanding to ask abstract questions to further his/her knowledge and understanding of socio-scientific issues	When asked, 'What if, in the future, we could make a clone of ourselves and keep him/her to use in case we became ill?', S questioned, 'But what if the clone refuses to give away their heart (if needed) because they know that they won't live? Then, that's not right and I'd feel guilty.'

Source: McCrory, A. (2014). Investigating the moral and scientific thinking of 7–8 year olds when taught socio-scientific issues related to energy and genetics. Unpublished PhD thesis. London: University of London, Institute of Education.

consequences. The evidence from this study concurs with the criticisms of Piaget from Chandler, Greenspan and Barenboim (1973), who argued that he underestimated the cognitive abilities of young children, with the research of Yuill and Perner (1988), who found that even young primary-aged children were able to use intentions as the basis of judgements, and with Turiel (2006), who proposed that moral understanding was present in children as young as four. When considering moral dilemmas and socio-scientific issues, the children in this study were able to take into account intentions, extenuating circumstances and consequences when making a judgement, as well as take on the role of others and consider actions and outcomes from the perspectives of others; and all at a much younger age than Piaget argued was possible.

Kohlberg's theory of moral judgements (1969) used dilemmas that were criticized by Damon (1988) for being highly unrealistic. Damon argued that to promote moral development children needed to evaluate good and bad behaviour during discussions about real life issues and events. He repeatedly found that children were capable of moral decisions and actions at a much earlier age than Kohlberg had concluded because they could relate to the dilemmas provided. The moral dilemmas and issues which the children were exposed to in McCrory (2014) were all designed with this in mind.

More recently, as researchers have moved away from the global stage models of Kohlberg and Piaget towards domain-specific models of moral development, there has been a focus on examining different kinds of reasoning rather than explaining moral judgements via hierarchical stages. Smetana (2006) argued that children apply multiple forms of reasoning – conventional, moral and psychological – when evaluating transgressions or social dilemmas. McCrory (2014) had found that children apply multiple forms of reasoning when considering socio-scientific issues, although the study was limited to examining and promoting only moral and scientific thinking.

In summary, considering the ethical aspects of socio-scientific issues can positively impact both primary and secondary students' engagement with and enjoyment of science, understanding of science knowledge and scientific literacy.

Ethics in school science – the role of argumentation

What is argumentation in science?

Argumentation in science is a discourse process which is a critically important element of how science is undertaken. It is a process of scientific reasoning which scientists utilize to attempt to convince others of the claims that they are making. In doing so, scientists support their claims with evidence that has been collected via established scientific methods. This includes observation, the formation of hypotheses and experimentation, which scientists then rationalize and use to justify why the evidence provided supports their claims. Argumentation is also used to critique the claims of other scientists. This is an important process which underpins the nature of science because scientific ideas and theories are not static; they change over time as new evidence is discovered and new theories are developed; scientific explanations try to be consistent with new empirical evidence as this arises. These ideas therefore need to be shared amongst the scientific community, to be evaluated and subsequently refined before they can become an accepted part of the body of knowledge that scientists use to explain the natural world.

There are many examples of scientific theories or ideas which were at one time accepted by the scientific community but then later refuted by compelling empirical evidence; in other cases, subsequent empirical evidence reinforced the theory or idea. Additionally, theoretical considerations can also lead to the revision or replacement of theories. One example of such refutation was the idea of aether (or ether), a mysterious substance that was at one time thought to transmit gravitational force and electromagnetic radiation throughout the universe. However, experiments on the reflection and refraction of light via the formulation of a wave theory of light (Christiaan Huygens, 1690), and later Albert Einstein's special theory of relativity (1905) discredited this theory. Put bluntly, there was no evidence found for the aether and new theories didn't need to posit its existence.

Another example of a scientific idea being supported by subsequent evidence is the 'equivalence principle' which was first tested by Galileo Galilei more than 400 years ago and is a key tenet of Albert Einstein's general theory of relativity. In its original formulation by Galileo, this principle states that objects with different masses fall at exactly the same rate under gravity. Whether Galileo actually dropped spheres of different masses off the Leaning Tower of Pisa is doubtful (it was probably a thought experiment). However, his principle has been tested many times since. The most recent rigorous evidence to support this theory is provided by a French satellite experiment in space (Cartlidge, 2017). The satellite, named *Microscope*, found no discrepancy in the acceleration of two small test masses to around one part in 100 trillion. This example illustrates the enduring worth of the methods of science. Once data have been collected and analysed, scientists talk about their interpretations and make their conclusions available to other scientists to discuss through such means as conferences and publication. Put simply, argumentation is essential for the advancement of science.

What is argumentation in school science education?

Research trends in science education over the last twenty years reveal a large body of research in argumentation, underpinned by philosophical and cognitive perspectives (Chin & Osborne, 2010; Harlen, 2012; Fraser et al., 2012; Erduran et al., 2015). The impact of argumentation on the development of students' scientific knowledge and understanding across primary and secondary science education has been an increasing focus. In particular, effective teaching techniques to promote students' development in argumentation as well as the continuing professional development needed for teachers to feel confident in taking this approach are of interest.

Argumentation can take many different forms, but all involve discussion (whether spoken or written) that includes the use and evaluation of evidence to support or refute claims. Science attempts to provide explanations for phenomena and in doing so theories are constructed which are subsequently critiqued; 'science proceeds through dispute, conflict and argumentation' (Erduran et al., 2015, p. 2). When students learn how to argue, they can better understand and evaluate scientific claims. We can use argumentation in the classroom to helps students hone scientific enquiry skills and understand key scientific principles. There is also much research to demonstrate that using argumentation in school science can promote students' critical thinking and scientific reasoning skills (Erduran, 2008) as well as it being an effective way to engage students in scientific discussions (Kuhn, 2010).

In particular, argumentation focuses on the interpretation of evidence and the validity of knowledge claims. From a cognitive perspective, argument is an important feature of reasoning and thinking; as students engage in argumentation, they learn to appreciate the connection between evidence and claim and the importance of justification in scientific argument. Another important aspect of argumentation is the ability to assess risk and when it comes to framing, understanding and decision-making in relation to this, there will be both subjective and objective knowledge and values which need to be considered (Schenk et al., 2019).

Taking into account these different perspectives, science education researchers have developed various theoretical and methodological frameworks for examining and analysing argumentation in school science. These can also be used as an assessment tool, to help teachers evaluate students' understanding of scientific concepts (Duschl, 2008; Harlen et al., 2012). It is important to distinguish between argumentation and debate in the science classroom. When developing argumentation skills in the classroom, students learn to conduct research, communicate with their peers, evaluate points of view and make new judgements underpinned by an evaluation of the evidence available, rather than by expressing an opinion. Indeed, an advantage of argumentation over (excessive) use of debate is that while some students find debate to be motivating, they may end up favouring a position simply because they argued for it, even if the scientific consensus is that the position in question is incorrect.

The nature of science, scientific literacy and argumentation

In Chapter 4 we discussed the arguments which favour students learning about the nature of science. A review by Simon (2013) of a number of studies across primary and secondary schools in England found that when it comes to teaching argumentation, teachers need to engage with the nature of science and focus on the evidence base of science in their teaching. Traditionally, focusing on scientific concepts rather than the process by which these become established has dominated curricula and so students' understandings as to the purpose and practice of science have been somewhat limited. The reasons for this are many. Simon argues that some teachers avoid the issue of what science is because school science bears only a partial resemblance to real science and so the nature of science becomes an academic point. In addition to this, studies have shown that there is a widespread weakness of teachers' understanding of the nature of science (Tsai, 2006; Harlow, 2010; Vazquez-Alonso et al., 2013; Zion & Schwartz, 2020). In order to counter this, there has been research into effective teaching approaches to argumentation, but Osborne et al. (2013) note that both primary and secondary teachers still need resources and collaborative reflection to support their learning in understanding this. Students of all ages need to understand that scientists use a variety of methods and different thinking strategies when undertaking scientific endeavours (Sadler, 2011). In the past, too much emphasis has been placed on the learning of individual facts of science, especially those that emerge from observations. Facts are part of science, but they must not be confused with understanding; thus, teaching which goes little beyond these facts will lead only to learning facts rather than learning science (Osborne & Dillon, 2010). Therefore, developing an understanding of the nature of science for teachers is crucial if we wish to develop students' understanding of science in real-life contexts (Sadler et al., 2016).

Public engagement with science is vital to the health of a nation as well as its economic outputs. Being scientifically literate is more important than ever before. In 2002, the then prime minister of the UK, Tony Blair, called for 'a robust and engaging dialogue with the public' (Blair, 2002, p. 2) about matters concerning science and technology in order to address sensitive areas of scientific and technological policy. Indeed, there has been a drive to gauge public reactions to scientific innovations and involve the public more in debates about science and technology in America, Australia and Europe, especially as there is an increasing call for accountability about the impact of science and technology on society (UKRI, 2022). Therefore, there has been significant investment in science and society programmes and initiatives aimed at raising public awareness of science. For example:

- The OST (Office of Science and Technology) funds public dialogue projects through its ScienceWise programme.
- The Royal Institution's 'Young Person's Programme', aimed at 12- to 16-year-olds, is designed to inform how science affects daily lives by providing online webcasts and games as well as lectures and workshops which schools can attend on day trips.
- The Wellcome Trust supports research and activities to promote learning, stimulate informed debate and inform research and policy. Programmes focus on a wide variety of areas including education, science and art, biomedical ethics, exhibitions and public consultation.
- The Economic and Social Research Council's (ESRC) £5.2 million 'Science in Society Programme' aimed to facilitate research into the relations between science and the wider society using practical interventions concerning the public understanding of science and the nature of citizenship and expertise within contemporary society.
- Beacons for Public Engagement (2008), funded with £9.2m over four years by the UK Higher Education Funding Councils and Research Councils (UK), was one of the largest initiates ever launched to support public engagement with science throughout the UK.
- 21st Century Science programme was developed as a national examination for 14- to 16-year-olds, with the aim of improving scientific literacy in the secondary school by examining a variety of issues such as GM crops and cloning (21st Century Science Project Team, 2003), whilst addressing contemporary sociopolitical issues by providing students with the opportunities for critical analysis. One teaching strategy incorporates the critical analysis of media reports in the classroom.
- The Building Awareness programme (2022) provided by the Smithsonian Science Education Centre works collaboratively with communities across the globe to improve teaching and learning as well as engagement with STEM.

This has impacted positively on the public's attitudes towards science and society (Department for Business, Energy & Industrial Strategy, 2019), with attitudes to public engagement changing from a position of seeing the communication of science as a one-way to a two-way process, enabling the public to feel heard and scientists to understand the public's ideas, concerns, needs and interest better, thereby helping scientists to see the societal value of their work. Scientific literacy is a lifelong pursuit; thus, argumentation can be a very powerful tool for promoting scientific literacy in the classroom to develop the skills needed to engage with science long term (Av-Shalom et al., 2019).

The value of talk in school science for both teachers and students

Talking and thinking critically in the classroom have long been recognized as vitally important in developing children's cognition (Smith, 2010). Argumentation can be described as cognitive-linguistic (Kuhn, 2010) as it derives from the field of linguistics; thus, the role of talk in promoting argumentation is important to recognize and understand. Recognizing that talk is crucial to cognitive development, Alexander (2008) argues that talk is particularly important during a child's formative years (birth to around 11 years of age). It is recognized that the overuse of asymmetrical communication (which is characterized by teacher direction) gives students very few opportunities to contribute in class or develop robust critical thinking skills. These exchanges often fall into the pattern of Initiation-Response-Feedback, what Barnes (1976) described as a question-and-answer routine, and although this has its place within a varied classroom discourse, if this is the dominant form of questioning, students will have very few opportunities to develop higher-order thinking skills. Dialogic talk – talking to learn – is based on a more equal dialogue between teachers and students and among students themselves, promoting student agency and voice. First proposed by Robin Alexander (2008), taking a dialogic approach to teaching includes five defining characteristics:

- it is collective – teachers and students address learning tasks together, whether as a group or as a class;
- reciprocal – teachers and students listen to each other, share ideas and consider alternative viewpoints;
- supportive – students articulate their ideas freely, where ideas are 'valued' and there is no fear of embarrassment over wrong answers;
- cumulative – teachers and students build on their own and others' ideas and organize them into coherent lines of thinking;
- purposeful – teachers plan and facilitate dialogic teaching with particular goals in mind.

However, research tells us that 'talk' in the classroom has not always been seen as positive. Levinson and Turner (2001) found that, for some science teachers, informal talk is seen as a diversion from the subject and therefore not worthwhile. Science teachers referred to social and ethical issues only if there was time or if students raised an issue. This was in part a result of time constraints, but mostly because the teaching of 'value-free' (teaching which does not express the values of the class teacher) concepts is the preferred teaching approach for most science teachers. Furthermore, Osborne et al. (2010) found that teachers felt that exposing pupils to a range of alternative views about a scientific topic ran the risk of reinforcing children's misconceptions. Teachers asked, 'How can we be sure that the children have the right answers?' Therefore, in an attempt to conceptualize talk which was more productive in the classroom, Alexander drew on a wide range of research but in particular on the ideas of Mercer (2004) and Vygotsky (1978). The central idea is that thinking and talk is more of a social activity than we might imagine and is one in which students construct their knowledge and understanding through dialogue. As discussed in Chapter 4, changes to school science curricula over the last twenty years have seen the introduction of ethical implications of science; teacher pedagogy therefore has adapted to this. The ability to understand and practise valid ways of arguing in a scientific context is an important aspect of scientific literacy; furthermore, this approach to teaching school science gives students the opportunity to reflect critically on their own values (Oulton et al., 2004).

From a broader sociological perspective, researchers (Erduran et al., 2015; Sadler, 2016, Reiss, 2019) have argued that that there is a need to improve the quality of young people's understanding of the nature of scientific argument within the context of a society where scientific issues are of increasing importance and ethical dimensions need to be considered. Children need to be able to recognize not only the strengths but also the limitations of such arguments and be able to use them effectively. Part of this is helped by the skill of effective questioning, and the importance of students' questions has been emphasized as important to scientific literacy and argumentation: 'Questioning is one of the thinking processing skills which is structurally embedded in the thinking operation of critical thinking, creative thinking, and problem solving' (Cuccio-Schirripa & Steiner, 2000, p. 210). Students' questions therefore play a key role in the learning process and serve as a useful pedagogical tool for the teacher. Good practice must attempt to detect bias, root out prejudice and examine evidence so that young people have the knowledge and skills to choose between alternative interpretations or points of view. Procedures such as these depend upon the values of respect for others, toleration and fairness. Therefore, continuing professional development is key to ensuring that teachers feel confident teaching argumentation and the ethics related to this. Encouragingly, research has focused on how teachers can implement talk to foster rather than hinder students' intellectual contributions to classroom talk (Lee at al., 2012), taking cognitive demand into account to create meaningful learning opportunities for their students.

When it comes to promoting students' argumentation in school science, Archila (2017) claims that small-group and whole-class debates are good opportunities to achieve this. However, Osborne et al. (2013) assert that incorporating these presents challenges for teachers when implementing argumentation in the science classroom because the organization and management of group work so that all students can take an active role to promote inclusion and student agency takes time to develop. Teachers also find that there needs to be a shift in their pedagogy from taking a didactic to a dialogic approach which involves listening to students and encouraging students to take a position, justify an argument and counter an argument, as well as reflect on an argument – all in all, developing active agents who think and reflect. In this way teachers are facilitators and part of a social process of enquiry rather than being seen as the providers of the 'right' answers. Of course, the importance of children understanding knowledge should not be underestimated if we wish them to be able to look at an argument in a balanced way. Science teachers need to be able to help their students to examine the evidence in a scientific manner and evaluate the evidence at hand. This approach can help students distinguish between fact and opinion, to develop respect for evidence and to keep an open mind on the issues, not to mention being able to assess bias.

Puppets

One way in which dialogic talk can be utilized in school science, and thus argumentation skills developed, is via the use of puppets. Puppets have long been part of cultures worldwide and often reflect the historical, cultural and political context of a society at any given time. In primary education, using puppets in drama, languages and PSHE is well established and can help develop students' confidence, communication and understanding of concepts (McCrory & Worthington, 2018). They can also be used to promote personal, social and emotional development in sensitive areas where strong personal feelings may be present (Peterson et al., 2015). Science theatre which incorporates the use of puppets (verbal or non-verbal) has been shown to have the potential to support public health programmes and engage local communities in scientific research (Chaeh et al., 2018). However, in the case of science education, although there have been examples of science theatre being utilized (without the use of puppets) to help teach science to older students (Braund, 2015), generally research involving puppets has taken place with younger children. It has been found that using puppets in science lessons can impact positively on children's understanding of science concepts and argumentation (Naylor et al., 2008). Perhaps most importantly, using puppets can significantly increase the amount of teacher discourse oriented towards reasoning and argument, decreasing the amount of talk that focuses on recall. The development and use of reasoning is critical in the construction of scientific arguments and developing the skills of argumentation are recognized as an important part of children learning about the nature of science (Simon et al., 2008).

Thinking and language are developed via social interaction (Vygotsky, 1978), and as we have already seen, this view has underpinned much empirical research. When students interact in effective talk, voicing their opinions and reasons, this can be an effective catalyst for learning (Dawes, 2004) and for developing argumentation skills. Puppets can resemble real people but also an array of characters which can be seen in popular television shows such as The Muppets. In using puppets, children enter a world of imagination and cognitive development. Egan (1998) proposed a five-stage model of children's cognitive development in which he argued that children make sense of the world via what he refers to as 'forms' or 'kinds' of understanding. For Egan, education is a process where children learn about different kinds of understandings in the following order as they age: somatic, mythic, romantic, philosophic and ironic. Each of these is best developed once a child has developed a variety of cognitive tools which are characteristic of each kind of understanding. These ages at which children become capable of each kind of understanding are not fixed. With the exception of somatic understanding, which refers to knowing through the physical senses, all of the other kinds of understandings are 'language dependent and a connection between cultural development in the past and educational development in the present' (Egan, 1998, p. 27). Young children are drawn to stories of a mythical kind, underpinned by ethical values such as good and evil, bravery and cowardice, fairness and selfishness, and although Egan's work demonstrates how story books can be utilized to engage children with ethical thinking, character education research has focused on how puppets can play an important role in this too (McCrory, 2014).

Puppets therefore represent subjects to whom children can relate and with whom they communicate; although they are not living, for the child, what the puppets do and say is real. Children interact with a puppet and communication, which can be led by the teacher or by the child, takes place *because of* the puppet, and this is particularly powerful with younger children. Puppets can be used to 'mirror' the behaviour and thoughts of children in the class, giving the children the opportunity to act as the expert or helper in advising the puppet what to do – this is empowering for the child. Keough and Naylor (2009) found that puppets were most effective in engaging children in scientific talk when they (the puppets) did not know about the science and were presenting scientific problems, because the children were eager to explore scientific ideas that could assist in problem solving. Their research also found that older children responded as positively to the use of puppets as did younger ones, but they had a preference for human characters rather than animal puppets.

Puppets can also be a vehicle for teachers to model behaviour and learning conversations without their being perceived as an authority figure by the children. In addition, they can be used to demonstrate children's thinking about scientific concepts and scaffold thinking in the dialogic process, with the puppet also acting as the expert or a more knowledgeable other. Through the use of puppets, teachers can create cognitive conflict via the introduction of new ideas and help children to resolve this conflict via dialogic talk. Often, scientific misconceptions or alternative ideas arise during science learning or are already part of children's pre-existing schemas and thus teachers need a way to address these (Allen, 2019). The use of puppets is therefore one vehicle that can support teachers in achieving this (McCrory, 2014). In addition, the puppets should represent a range of cultural backgrounds and genders. In science education this is particularly important given that historically scientists have overwhelmingly been seen as white, middle-class men. If we wish our children to see that science is inclusive, diverse and for them, then visual representations of scientists which reflect what our children see in the mirror is key (McCrory, 2014).

In 2008, Simon and colleagues researched the impact of puppets on primary school children's argumentation in science. The PUPPETS (Puppets Promoting Engagement in Talk in Science Project) project compared the talk in whole-class science lessons taught with and without puppets. Hand-held human puppets were utilized by teachers who made the science problematic by creating a range of scenarios based around the everyday lives and engaged the children. For example, one teacher using a male puppet called Fudge took the class into the playground to observe his shadow. The teacher and class then returned to the same spot in the playground in the afternoon but, much to the alarm of Fudge, his shadow had moved and reduced in size. The children were then invited to discuss with Fudge what had happened, using evidence to underpin their arguments.

Another example reported by Simon et al. (2008) involved the use of two puppets, one named Mark and the other Kay. A scenario was created where Mark was sad because he wanted to float one of his toys on the water but did not have a boat. His friend Kay tired to sympathize with him but could not find a way to solve the problem so she invited the children in the class to explore ways in which objects float and sink, so as to help Mark find a solution. Findings demonstrated that there was an increase in argumentation and reasoning about science by the children because of the inclusion of puppets. Interviews with the children revealed that they found lessons with the puppets easier to understand because the puppets spoke more slowly and explained things in language that the children could relate to and understand.

The researchers concluded that puppets allowed teachers to pose questions and problems which were slightly in advance of the children's reasoning and in doing so provided an opportunity for the children to communicate their thinking. This important research led to further research into the pedagogic use of puppets in primary science, with Carr et al. (2008) investigating the use of puppets for reluctant speakers in early years science lessons, Hackling et al. (2011) examining the quality of student talk in primary science lessons and Burns (2017) investigating young children's perspectives on using puppets in the science classroom.

In 2008, one author of this book, McCrory, was involved as a teacher participant in the PUPPETS project. Drawing on the professional development she had received during the research element of the project, her own existing reflective pedagogical approaches to teaching primary science (Pollard et al., 2023) and the outcomes of the research mentioned above, McCrory designed three schemes of work focusing on morals, climate change and genetics to promote children's moral thinking, decision-making and argumentation when considering controversial issues in science. Taught across one year, teaching approaches utilized a variety of pedagogical tools including puppets, concept cartoons, concept maps, dialogic talk (Alexander, 2008) and moral thinking frameworks to promote argumentation skills with younger children.

The project was designed in part to help young children examine moral dilemmas in everyday (not necessarily scientific) concrete and abstract scenarios, thus developing ethical thinking skills which could then be used to promote argumentation when engaging with issues in science. In her research, McCrory (2014) was interested in discovering whether children aged 7–8 were able to engage in abstract reasoning (think, have ideas or ask questions which aid solving problems on a complex-level through analysis and evaluation) or whether they were only able to reason in a concrete manner (analysing information and solving problems on a literal level) when considering science. Abstract reasoning is essential to entertain alternatives in moral thinking, to identify multiple perspectives when engaging with socio-scientific issues and to order priorities in values. Therefore, she utilized a number of moral thinking frameworks adapted from examples given in the book *Ethics and Citizenship* (Born, Mirk, Mulligan & Price, 2006), which focuses on the character development of older children (11–16 year-olds).

Figure 8.1 is one example in McCrory's (2014) project where children considered a scenario and were asked to make a 'right' moral choice, justifying their reason for doing so. In this case, the children were asked to consider a hypothetical scenario of whether or not one should cheat to pass a maths exam. This scenario was an appropriate one for the children taking part in the project as they were accustomed to undertaking maths tests each term. In this example, a framework utilized four tests – the rule test, the gut-feeling test, the news test and the role-model test. The scenario was designed to help children consider multiple perspectives of a problem and the consequences of the decisions they make and then choose the 'right' choice from their own perspective, justifying their reasoning. The children were asked to apply the four tests when making their choice and helped to understand that if their choice didn't pass any of the tests, then it was most probably the 'wrong choice'. The four tests were as follows:

- The rule test: Does the choice you are about to make go against a rule or a law? If your choice goes against an established rule or law, then clearly it doesn't pass this test.

- The gut-feeling test: Take time to see how you feel about the choice you are about to make. Are there physical indications that your choice does not pass the gut-feeling test? If so, then it's more likely to be the wrong choice.

- The news test: Imagine the choice you are about to make finds it way into the news tomorrow; in this case do you feel comfortable with your choice? If you feel ashamed or embarrassed about your choice, it doesn't pass the news test.

- The role-model test: Think of a person you know well and admire. Would your role-model make the same choice as you? If the person you admire would probably not make this choice, it doesn't pass the role-model test.

In McCrory's project (2014), this maths test scenario was presented to the children via a puppet. The puppet then asked the students what they *should* do in this situation and what they *would* do if they were in this situation. The children then recorded

Figure 8.1 One child's response to a puppet's questions about whether or not she should cheat in a maths exam.
Source: McCrory, A. (2014). *Investigating the moral and scientific thinking of 7–8 year olds when taught socio-scientific issues related to energy and genetics.* Unpublished PhD thesis. London: University of London, Institute of Education.

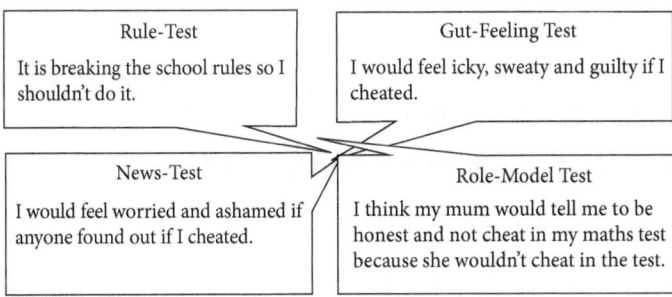

their own thoughts about their responses to these two questions and fed them back to the puppet.

Following on from this, a more complicated scenario was enacted using a puppet. The scenario was entitled 'A Question of Need' and centred on a young teenager called Nina who volunteered at her local library as part of a school community project. She enjoyed this because the work was varied and fun. The library staff valued her assistance because they were understaffed and Nina was well aware that the library was struggling to meet costs. One day, while Nina was in the lavatories, she witnessed a homeless woman taking a box of soap and a large packet of toilet paper. The woman looked like she really needed the supplies so Nina decided not to tell anyone. After all, she was only doing it the one time and was in need. Nina forgot about the incident until she witnessed the same thing happen again the following week. To Nina the issue now posed a worrying dilemma. Should she tell one of the librarians, as the library could not afford for someone to take its supplies, or should she turn a blind eye again, since the woman was so clearly in need? Each of these looks like a right choice; the children were encouraged to see if they could think of a third possibility. Children worked in groups to consider the dilemma; a puppet (operated by the class teacher) was used to represent Nina and it voiced her concerns. Table 8.1 shows the children's responses to the puppet and reasons for their thinking.

All of the children were able to identify the two right choices available to Nina and suggest a third choice that Nina could consider. The children's suggested solutions take into account and reflect their own moral values and the moral code of conduct created by the class. The actions that the children suggest Nina should take show that they have considered the consequences for the homeless lady, the library and for Nina herself, thus demonstrating moral perspective taking. McCrory then went on to promote these moral thinking skills when the children considered the topics of climate change and genetics. In the following scenario, the children and McCrory engaged in a conversation about cloning humans, in particular about cloning themselves. This conversation arose from two of the boys

Table 8.1 Children's responses to the puppet and reasons for their thinking.

What are the two right choices Nina needs to choose from?

Choice one: Nina should tell the librarian about the homeless woman because:
a) the librarian could help her.
b) the woman is stealing and this is wrong.

Choice two: Nina should turn a blind eye again and forget all about it as the woman clearly needs the supplies.

Is there a 'third' choice you that you can think of?

Nina could buy more supplies and replace them for the library so that no-one would know.
Nina could talk directly to the woman and explain that the library cannot afford to lose money and therefore she must stop.
Nina should talk to the woman and find out why she is stealing.
Nina should talk to the homeless lady and warn her that if she comes again [and steals again] then she will report her.
Nina could help the old lady find somewhere to live and even help her get a job.

What do you think Nina should do and why?

I think Nina should tell somebody because they can get the lady some help so that she doesn't have to come back again.
I think Nina should tell the librarian because it is wrong to steal and if you know something and you don't tell anyone, you're being dishonest.
Nina needs to find an adult who can help the woman find a home.
Nina should call the homeless shelter and talk to them about it.
Nina should report the incident as the woman might have been taking the supplies for a long time so the library is suffering and someone might be able to help her.

Source: McCrory, A. (2014). *Investigating the moral and scientific thinking of 7–8 year olds when taught socio-scientific issues related to energy and genetics.* Unpublished PhD thesis. London: University of London, Institute of Education, p. 145.

in the group discussing clones in George Lucas's film *Star Wars: Attack of the Clones* and how they would like a clone of themselves to do 'their homework, tidy their bedroom, go to school so they could stay at home' (McCrory, 2014, p. 168). At this point the children came to realize that if (hypothetically) we were able to clone humans, the process would involve a normal timescale for pregnancy and growth of the child and that their 'clone' would inevitably always be younger than them. The following is an example of two children discussing the possible ethical dimensions of cloning; the children's responses demonstrate perspective taking and justification.

> Child 1: We shouldn't clone humans. It is not up to doctors to make humans, it is up to God so God would be very angry and it would be very wrong to do it.

Child 2: But if you don't believe in God then it doesn't matter. It would be so cool to have a clone. You would always have someone to talk to, who is like you and would listen to you, and you would never be alone. Someone to play with and do stuff with.

Child 1: If you cloned yourself, then you would need to feed your clone, buy them clothes and have somewhere for them to sleep so it would cost a lot of money (smiling and giggling)!

Child 2: (thought for a while and then answered) Yes, but when your clone is old enough then they can go to work to earn money for you and you wouldn't have to work!

Child 1: (replied indignantly) But, that's like having a slave and you know that's morally wrong! *(McCrory, 2014, p. 167)*

McCrory (2014) therefore found that across three schemes of work that focused on morals, climate change and genetics, the children in the study progressively used moral language (when discussing socio-scientific issues and engaging in argumentation). In addition, the use of puppets, concept maps and cartoons as a pedagogical tool contributed to their developing scientific knowledge and understanding.

Concept maps and cartoons

Concept maps are graphical tools for organizing and representing conceptual knowledge and can be used to assess or describe a variety of constructs and outcomes and are thus a useful tool for engaging students in argumentation. For example, they can be used in formative or summative assessment to gauge both declarative knowledge (knowing that something is the case; information that can be conveyed in words) and procedural knowledge (knowing how to do something, which involves making discriminations, understanding concepts and applying rules that govern relationships; often includes the development of motor skills and cognitive strategies).

Concept maps can be represented in many forms; they typically include boxes of some type with the relationships between concepts indicated by a connecting line. In addition, concept maps include words or phrases which specify the relationship between the two concepts. Concept maps are thus a relational device, enabling students to make connections between their ideas and concepts.

Another characteristic of concept maps is that the concepts are typically represented in a hierarchical fashion with the most general concepts at the top of the map. The hierarchical structure depends on the context in which that knowledge is being applied or considered. The concept map may pertain to a question that we seek to answer or some situation or event that we are trying to understand through the organization of knowledge in the form of a concept map, thus providing the context for the concept map.

Cross-links are also an important aspect of concept maps. These are relationships or links between concepts in different parts of the concept map. Cross-links help us to see how a concept in one part of the map is related to a concept in another. In the creation of new knowledge, cross-links often represent creative leaps on the part of the learner when he or she is able to create a well-structured map which makes links between various concepts, thus facilitating argumentation. The use of concept maps is not limited to any particular group of learners, with both primary school children and secondary school children (Edmonson, 2005) demonstrating capability to develop and explain concept maps.

Concept mapping can be both easily taught to children of all abilities and differentiated to meet their varying needs. In addition, once children know how to create concept maps, they can be a powerful instrument for independent learning and thinking. Meaningful learning takes place because students link new concepts to existing knowledge; this allows the element of learning to relate to how cognitive knowledge is developed structurally by the learner, and therefore it is argued that representations of knowledge are stored longer in the memory (Maas & Leauby, 2005). Concept maps allow students to identify the causes and effects of complex issues, but they are limited to being only relational.

Research by McCrory (2014) used concept maps with young children (aged 7–8 years old) in argumentation to gauge children's understanding of different aspects of energy and genetics and as a scaffold to enable children to link and justify their ideas. Typically, the concept maps consisted of at least five boxes, depending on ability (each box contained one word related to the topic studied), and these were linked by

Figure 8.2 A child's concept map linking the words 'cell', 'chromosomes', 'DNA', 'genes' and 'nucleus'.
Source: McCrory, A. (2014). Investigating the moral and scientific thinking of 7–8 year olds when taught socio-scientific issues related to energy and genetics. Unpublished PhD thesis. London: University of London, Institute of Education.

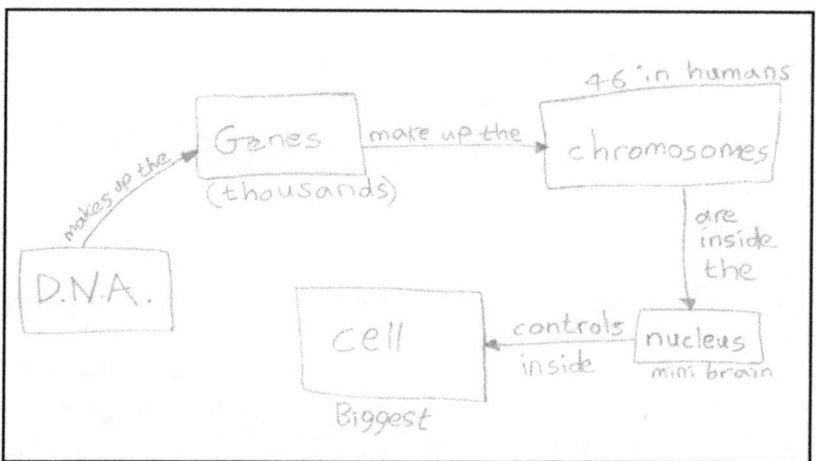

arrows. The task for the child was to write on each arrow how the two words were, in his opinion, linked. There are always a number of ways this can be achieved, thus revealing the child's conceptual, declarative or procedural knowledge. Figure 8.2 provides an example of a child linking the words cell, chromosomes, DNA, genes and nucleus. The child used the arrows to reveal how he understood how each term to be linked.

Concept maps (Figure 8.3) were also used to help the children structure their ideas when considering both the moral and scientific aspects of the Chernobyl disaster. The aim here was for the children to reveal their ideas and thoughts without any guidance from the teacher. Arrows (cross-links) were included to prompt the children to make links between different ideas and concepts in the map. It is clear in Figure 8.3 that the structure of the concept map has helped the child to organize her ideas; she was able to identify multiple consequences of the action and link these consequences using both moral and scientific language.

Concept cartoons were first conceptualized in the 1990s as a pedagogical tool to elicit students' prior knowledge and ideas about science, to challenge their thinking and to support the development of their scientific understanding (Naylor & Keough, 2013). A concept cartoon is a visual representation of science ideas.

Figure 8.3 A child's concept map identifying the consequences of the Chernobyl disaster.
Source: McCrory, A. (2014). Investigating the moral and scientific thinking of 7–8 year olds when taught socio-scientific issues related to energy and genetics. Unpublished PhD thesis. London: University of London, Institute of Education.

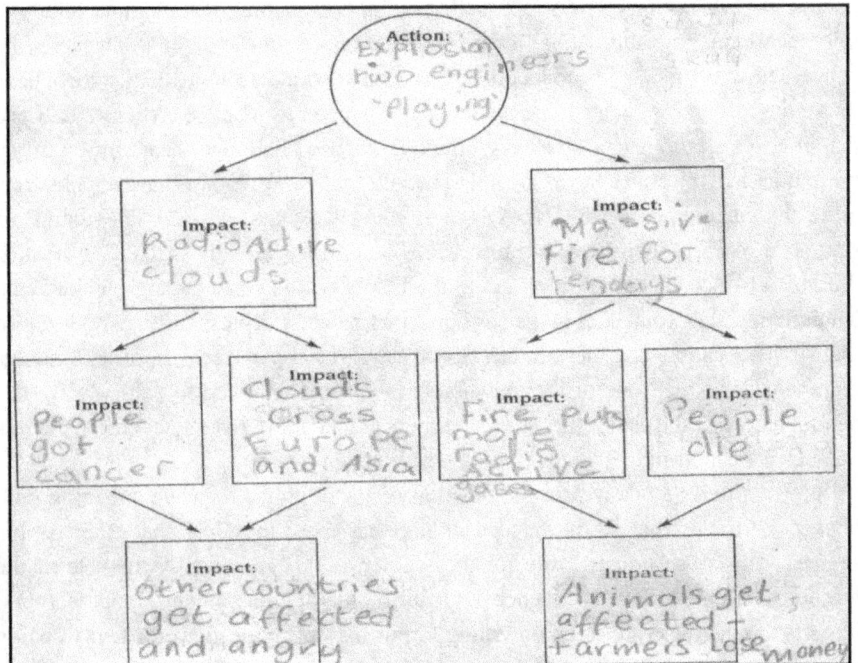

It features a simple cartoon-style drawing which presents a range of viewpoints about science ideas in situations that are designed to motivate and engage students as well as stimulate discussion. Research examining the impact of using concept cartoons in school science has found that they improve reasoning skills and self-confidence (Naylor & Keough, 2013). Concept cartoons promote talk in the classroom, at least in part because the talk is dialogic and focused on developing children's scientific understanding as well as quality of argumentation (Evrekli & Balim, 2015). Via co-constructing arguments, students of all ages are able to restructure their ideas.

Over the years, Keough and Naylor developed their initial idea about concept maps in science teaching. This included a shift from single to multiple statements, from characters making negative to positive comments and to ensuring that the scientifically acceptable viewpoint(s) is always included. Concept cartoons are designed to be visual representations of science ideas. They are based on everyday situations that may not appear to be scientific; this was deliberate. The aim here is to emphasize that science is everywhere and part of our everyday lives, and also to engage students who are disinterested in or intimated by science. In doing this, everyday situations appear to be effective across geographical and cultural boundaries, enabling concept cartoons to be used across a wide range of contexts. Contextual features can influence how the problem in a particular concept cartoon is interpreted and in some cases there can be more than one scientifically acceptable alternative, presenting an additional level of challenge.

Typically, each cartoon includes one science concept and a range of viewpoints about that idea, represented by three or four characters via speech bubbles. Usually, one of the viewpoints is correct with the others containing common scientific misconceptions or alternative ideas. As mentioned earlier, some teachers are concerned that raising misconceptions may make students more likely to believe these, but research indicates that this does not happen in practice (Allen, 2019) and that concept cartoons can be a very effective way to challenge these. In the initial presentation of the concept cartoon, all of the alternative viewpoints have equal status; all of the viewpoints are thus seen as legitimate. This gives less confident students support in voicing their ideas because someone else has already verbalized them. If their idea is incorrect then they can put the blame on the concept cartoon character. Minimizing contextual cues in the cartoon, such as facial expressions, is important so that students cannot use these to attempt to work out the correct response. Students then consider which one of the viewpoints is correct and need to justify why. The neutral nature of the characters allows learners to take more risks since the characters are viewed as non-judgemental.

Students find themselves in the position of the adjudicator when engaging with concept cartoons; that is, they make judgements about the ideas that other people suggest. This is an unusual role for the learner as this is typically the role of the teacher, and one of the consequences of teachers making judgements about learners' ideas is that learners are often unwilling to put forward their ideas for fear of being wrong. Therefore, being the adjudicator can be transformative for learners, especially for those who lack confidence, enabling them to engage in argumentation and put forward their ideas more readily.

A more recent study by Atasoy et al. (2022) used argumentation-based concept cartoons to engage older students in socio-scientific issues. To create the concept cartoons, Atasoy et al. used a framework and a process of review (by teachers and experts in the field) which included informal reasoning modes, argument components (such as claim, evidence, counter argument and rebuttal) and aspects of decision-making. Interestingly, the concept cartoons were displayed in school corridors, and dialogic discussions were then held in class. Outcomes were reviewed as were the concept cartoons, which were then again placed, in their amended forms, in the corridors and used as a prompt for dialogic talk. The researchers then observed the dialogic talk between the students and teachers. It was found that when creating concept cartoons, the process of review by experts and teachers in the field was crucial to creating concept cartoons which were fit for purpose. From observations it was found that discussions were either semi-dialogic or dialogic, enabling the teacher to help students develop their justifications, thereby impacting positively on the development of their argumentation.

Concept cartoons can therefore help students to co-construct arguments and are thus an effective stimulus for argumentation. As they provide a focus, context and purpose for discussion, it is likely that students will question the views of others and construct arguments to justify their own ideas. It is also worth reiterating that concept cartoons have played a valuable role as they enable teachers to see the value of dialogic teaching and help teachers develop their pedagogical subject knowledge as they reconceptualize their own understanding of scientific ideas. If the process of research is made explicit, this can also enable teachers and students to better understand the processes of scientific enquiry and thus value authentic research evidence which is a key aim of argumentation.

Drama and role-play

Drama and role-play can provide effective contexts for argumentation and can also offer opportunities for all students (not only the articulate) to participate in debate and discussion, help students make meaning and contextualize more abstract scientific concepts but this remains an under-researched area in school science education (Braund, 2015). Evidence available from other fields, for example, in the field of conceptual understanding (Wang & Buck, 2015) and the philosophy of science (Archila, 2017) demonstrates how drama can enhance students' argumentation skills. Through drama and role-play, students have the opportunity to take on roles which might express ideas or opinions contrary to their own. For younger students, expressing their ideas via a character in a role in which they feel safe makes it easier for them to 'play in role' and for the teacher or other students in the class or group to question them, where and if necessary. Furthermore, drama and role-play support students in learning how to negotiate with each other, enabling children to explore and understand alternative perspectives. They can also be used to help students develop their thinking about what is ethical in science and why.

Drama in educational settings can be presentational, which involves a small group of students dramatizing features of science in front of an audience (their peers, teachers, parents, wider community, etc.). It can also be experiential, where students adopt an attitude, opinion or motivation (e.g. a role-play with role cards about ethical issues in science). Both categories are suitable to promote argumentation in the classroom.

'Mantle of the expert' is an example of presentational drama, a technique which encourages children to take on the roles of experts and explore a fictional situation that is based (for the purpose of this research) in fact. The 'expert's' information may come from the teacher or from the children who would have researched, in advance, the information required. The responsibility for the activity lies with the children; consequently, children learn to take responsibility for their learning and feel listened to and respected for having an expert status.

Research by McCrory (2014) found this to be an effective way of enabling younger children (aged 7–8 years old) to develop their argumentation skills across a period of time. The children would typically feed back either to their group or the class as a whole once they had researched secondary sources of information. Initially, feedback during a topic on energy was short and concise, focusing on the facts or scientific concepts that were being discussed; for example, when one child reported back on renewable and non-renewable energies, he simply told the class what those energies were. However, as the year progressed the same children began to incorporate more detail in their reporting back, by reflecting what they had been learning and justifying their reasons using evidence from their research. For instance, when looking at the effects of climate change around the world, the same child reported the causes and consequences of this much more specifically to justify their opinion, saying:

> The Eastern Prairie White Orchid is found in prairies in Illinois in America. Numbers of this plant have dropped over the past few years and this now is seen as an endangered plant. Climate change has made the local climate drier and warmer which has threatened the plants survival.

In a study by Archila (2017) in the United States, drama was used as a 'springboard' for promoting argumentation in school science. Ninety-one first-semester undergraduate medical students were asked to express their opinion about a controversial question. This framework is one which could easily be adopted for use with 14- to 19-year-olds. The play *Should've* (written by Nobel laureate Ronald Hoffman in 2006) relates to ethics in science. The play consists of twenty-nine scenes and invites the audience to consider the ethics of decisions made in both science and art through the effect these have on three characters' lives. The researchers aimed to find out if an approach combining drama and argumentation could increase students' awareness of the relevance of ethics in science and whether the pedagogy was effective in engaging students in argumentative. The teaching used four of the twenty-nine scenes (to reflect the ethical question being asked) and was created to combine drama and argumentation. This teaching consisted of five steps and provided students with the opportunity to make decisions about a controversial question. At each step, students were given the opportunity to strengthen the positions they use to argue in favour of the decision that they have made and are arguing for. Students could then, if they so wished, change the decision they had made (at any point). Importantly, each step was designed to engage students in argumentation.

Part 1 of the lesson – initial argumentation

The teaching began by asking all students to consider the ethical question: 'Are scientists responsible for the way their own work is used by others?' Students developed opinions individually but also in groups with the aim to answer the question.

The teacher stressed there was no straightforward yes/no answer. Instead, the teacher highlighted that what was important was the quality of the arguments made by the students and how they critiqued the arguments of others.

Part 2 of the lesson – argumentation before debating

The students read the text individually (a didactic tool for presenting the arguments between the characters) of the four scenes from the play which depict the ethical dimensions of scientific work. These scenes feature three characters. Then three students assume the roles of the three characters and act out the four scenes.

The following is an example of one of the scenes from the play. Two characters are discussing the following scenario:

> In scene 3, Katie discusses with Stefan her idea of studying the genes of a duck killed by the 1918 flu. Her study would help to better understand this flu. In essence, she considers that it is possible to put snippets of that DNA into a bacterium and thus have it make the viral proteins. Nonetheless, Stefan cautions Katie that her work could hurt people if other persons (e.g., terrorists) use her own work. Then, in scene 5, Katie and Stefan discuss Katie's results. She obtained relevant data from the genome of the duck. He continues arguing that other persons could use Katie's work to hurt people. In the same vein, in scene 11, Julia suggests to Katie that she needs to worry about the way others use her own work. In the same scene, Stefan and Julia discuss with Katie about her social responsibility as a scientist. Despite their arguments (e.g., Katie's knowledge can be used to kill people, science can hurt people), Katie maintains her position: scientists are not responsible for the way their own work is used by others. Finally, in scene 12, Katie and Julia continue the discussion. Katie claims that scientists did not create suicide bombers and the concentration camps. Julia reminds Katie that scientists knew how to produce plastic explosives and Zyklon gas for the death camps. After a long discussion, Katie does not change her point of view.

In essence, the discussion recreated in the scenes chosen could be briefly summarized as two positions: (1) Katie argues that knowledge per se is good, and (2) Stefan and Julia suggest that she should worry about the way others use her work (Archila, 2017, p. 353).

Prompt questions then followed to give the students the opportunity to identify the ethical issues and evaluate the arguments put forward by justifying their reasoning:

1. What are the arguments put forth by the three characters?
2. Are their arguments adequate? Explain why or why not.
3. In your opinion, 'Are scientists responsible for the way their own work is used by others?' Explain why or why not.

Following this, each student used the text provided to build and communicate his or her point of view, arguing for or against proposals and arriving at a decision on an individual basis.

Next, the students were organized into groups of four (argumentative interaction via small-group debate) to discuss the views of each student with the intention of making a group decision. Each group then reported its decision to the class (argumentative interaction via whole-class debate) and presented the underlying arguments. Finally, each student reflected and made a final decision about the issue (final argumentation).

Outcomes from this research stressed the importance of using presentational and experiential drama to foster higher-order thinking skills; they also showed that drama can be a powerful resource for enabling students to feel more connected to the core element of the ethical reasoning – in this case an ethical question. The outcomes also highlighted the process of ethical argumentation and the impact this had on the students' argumentation reasoning skills. Researchers found that the initial responses by the students at the start of the process were naïve, which is consistent with the literature that argues that students find it challenging to identify and be aware of the ethical dimensions of scientific work (Bazzul, 2016). However, by the time the students had completed the process, they demonstrated that they were able to use the arguments from the scenes along with their previous knowledge and understanding to enrich their argumentation. Interaction in small groups and then whole class debates promoted student agency and voice, while the role of the teacher as a listener rather than a didactic force was an important factor for the successful implementation of scenarios that enable argumentation.

In conclusion, argumentation in school science is a process of scientific reasoning which can include ethical thinking but differs from debate. Students need to develop their argumentation skills if they are to understand the nature of science and develop their scientific literacy. Dialogic talk, the use of puppets, concept maps and cartoons, as well as drama and role-play, are all pedagogical tools which science educators can successfully utilize to promote argumentation in school science.

Ethics and informal science education

9

What is meant by 'informal science education'?

Education that takes place in a school can be described as 'formal' education. Some people therefore use the term 'informal' education to characterize all out-of-school education, such as the education that takes place on a museum visit. However, many educators have argued that it's not quite as straightforward as that:

> Let's consider for instance a field trip to a science museum. First, it is outside the classroom, so learning in the museum is, according to the above definition, indeed, informal learning. Indeed, the children may more than likely be invited to free, unguided visits, in which they may approach different exhibits as they desire. Yet, in many cases, part of the museum field trip includes a highly structured visit. The children may conduct experiments, fill pre-prepared work files and follow a guide. *(Eshach, 2007, p. 173)*

Eshach suggest that one way forward is to divide out-of-school learning into *informal* learning and *non-formal* learning. Informal learning takes place relatively spontaneously and has no authority figure in charge. It is therefore the sort of learning that takes place in families or when one decides, on one's own, to read a book or search the internet for information (always accepting, of course, that family activities such as a visit to a zoo require a certain amount of planning and tend to have an adult in charge). Non-formal learning takes place in a planned manner but not in school – it therefore includes activities like very structured fieldtrips and carefully planned museum visits dominated by worksheets.

We don't need to get too hung up on this issue, and any attempt at precise categorization runs into problems. Our interest in this chapter, following Eshach (2007), is on learning that takes place in out-of-school settings where learners have considerable autonomy, so that there are open-ended opportunities for learning science.

Learning in informal settings

The days have gone, if ever they existed, when people only learnt their science in schools. Nowadays, people learn about science in hospitals, in science museums, in zoos and botanic gardens and when they read newspapers and magazines, use the internet, listen to radio or watch TV and talk with one another. In all these places where science is communicated, ethics can play and often does play an important role. Should parents get their children vaccinated? How should natural history museums present the theory of evolution? Is there any scientific validity to the concept of race? Can green energy sources provide all our energy needs? Should we eliminate plastics? Is it best to buy Fairtrade products? These are all questions raised in informal science settings.

One advantage of learning in informal settings is that learners are often more motivated than they are in school (Bell et al., 2009; Mujtaba et al., 2018). In addition, they are typically in much smaller groups and may be accompanied by family members. This means that there can be greater opportunity for learning to be personalized and for the subject matter to be an immediate cause of conversation. Furthermore, informal settings may provide rare material (e.g. fossils in a science or natural history museum) of a sort rarely available in schools. Another difference between schools and informal settings such as museums and zoos is that those in informal settings responsible for the provision of teaching and information are generally able to make a commitment of time to the preparation of a single exhibit that is way beyond what a school teacher can manage for a single lesson (Reiss, 2017).

Consider, for example, the exhibit in Figure 9.1. It shows the case on 'Mammals in pouches' (i.e. marsupials) in the Natural History Museum in London in 2013. In all, there are sixteen taxidermic specimens (including a koala, kangaroos and a wombat, as well as a number of less familiar species), each with its own detailed label, as well as distribution maps, a guide to the entire group and lighting. It is clear that a tremendous amount of time, thought and care has gone into the display. One might be tempted to think, 'how can a school compete?' Our focus is not so much on how schools and out-of-school settings can complement one another but the reality, of course, is that they can. A school can do all sorts of things that a museum on its own can't, and *vice versa*. Our focus, rather, is on how informal science education can be enhanced by considering ethical issues.

While, as we shall go on to discuss, we are positive about the potential for informal science education to be enhanced by considering ethical issues, this does need some planning by those responsible for the informal learning opportunities. Take museums, once again. It is hardly surprising that visitors will typically seek out experiences and information sources that complement what they already know: 'Given the free-choice nature of museum experiences, visitors very selectively pick and choose what they want to learn more about, and these decisions are very strongly influenced by what they already know and are interested in' (Falk &

Figure 9.1 The 'Mammals with pouches' cases in the Mammals Gallery at the Natural History Museum, London.
Source: By John Cummings – Own work, CC BY-SA 3.0, https://commons.wikimedia.org/w/index.php?curid=28924338.

Stroksdieck, 2005, p. 119). Both your authors plead guilty when they are visiting museums. Herein lies the huge potential for those in charge of informal science education.

Suppose, to give an example that initially appears to have little to do with science or with ethics, you are interested in old silver and rather like sugar tongs. Consider the ones shown in Figure 9.2. There were made in about 1775 in what is now called the United States. The year 1775 is exactly the year when the thirteen colonies began the American War of Independence. Sugar tongs, of course, are for lifting lumps of sugar. Nowadays, much sugar comes from sugar beet, but in the eighteenth century, virtually all sugar came from sugar cane. Sugar cane at the time was grown in the Americas and on Caribbean islands. Sugar exploded in popularity in the eighteenth century. By 1750 it was the most valuable commodity in Europe (sometimes referred to as 'white gold'), and in the last decades of the eighteenth century, 80 per cent of the sugar came from the British and French colonies in the West Indies (Ponting, 2000). It is clear that sugar could be included as a science topic to do with plant growth, not to mention the properties of silver that make it suitable as a material for making sugar tongs.

But there is another side to sugar. At the time of the sugar tongs in Figure 9.2, and for many decades before and after, sugar production relied wholly on the slave trade (Olusoga, 2016). While slavery has existed in many human cultures, the

Figure 9.2 An innocuous pair of sugar tongs from about 1775 – but intimately connected to the slave trade.
Source: Donated to Wikimedia Commons by the Metropolitan Museum of Art. Bequest of Alphonso T. Clearwater, 1933. https://www.metmuseum.org/art/collection/search/8007 and https://commons.wikimedia.org/wiki/File:Sugar_Tongs_MET_97908.jpg.

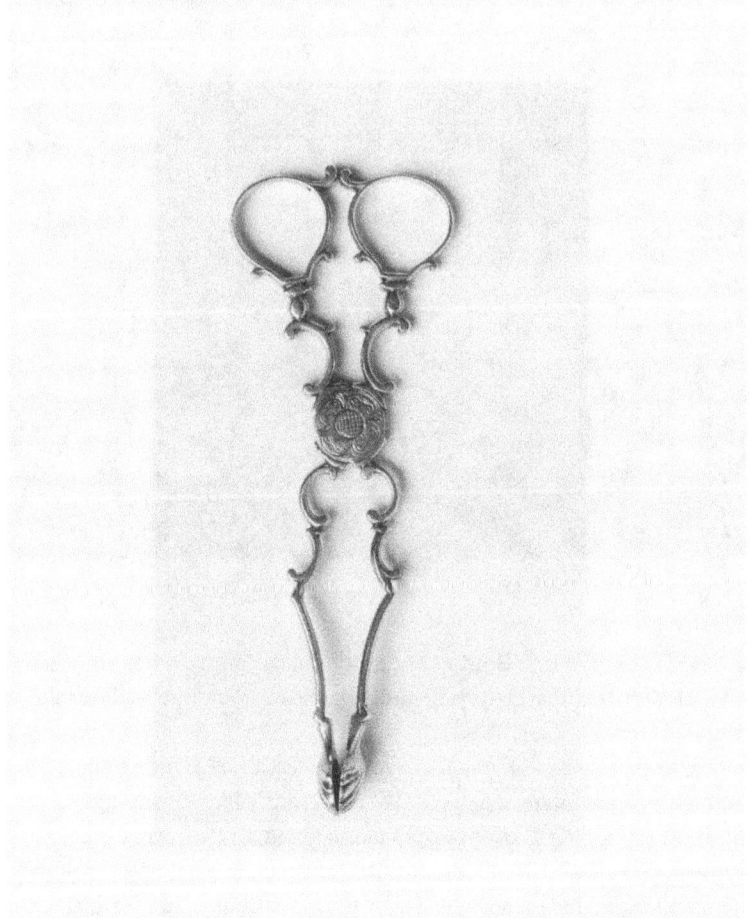

transatlantic slave trade is believed to be the largest long-distance coerced movement of people in history (Eltis, 2007). It was key to the economic growth of England and the colonization and development of what became the United States. The appalling conditions in which slaves were transported from various countries in Africa across the Atlantic (Figure 9.3) have been widely researched, though are still less well known than they should be. Eighteenth- and nineteenth-century sugar tongs and tea spoons are widely available. Those who run museums, whether at national, regional or local level, have the ability to choose what to display from their collections and what stories to tell. It doesn't need a specialist science museum to explore the links between science and everyday objects.

Figure 9.3 The appalling conditions in which slaves were transported across the Atlantic in the eighteenth and nineteenth centuries led to massive loss of life.
Source: By Blake, William O – Internet Archive identifier, Public Domain, https://commons.wikimedia.org/w/index.php?curid=104982444.

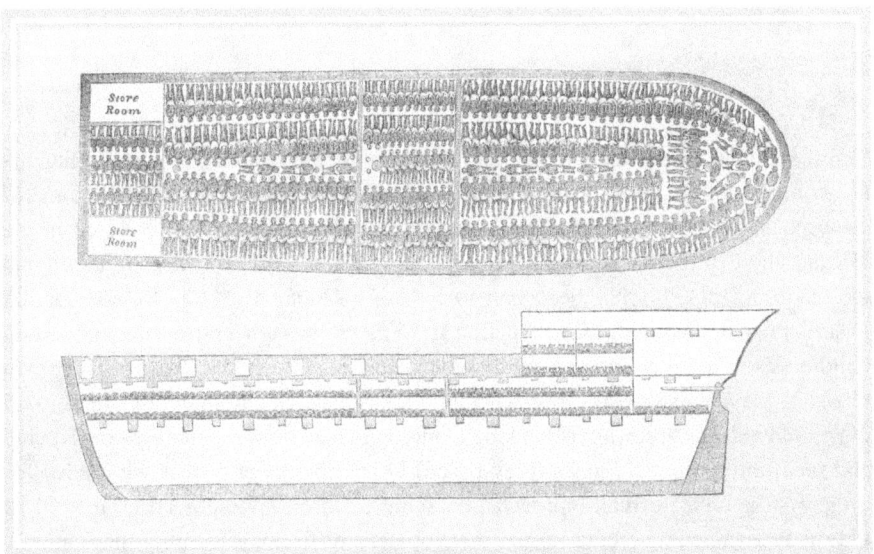

However, museums may need to be explicit if they wish visitors to learn as intended from their exhibits. Monique Scott has written extensively about how evolution is presented in museums and what visitors learn from evolution exhibits (Scott, 2007). Using questionnaires and interviews, Scott gathered the views of nearly 500 visitors at the Natural History and Horniman Museums in London, the National Museum of Kenya in Nairobi and the American Museum of Natural History in New York. Perhaps her key, and disturbing, finding was that many of the visitors interpreted the human evolution exhibitions as providing a linear narrative of progress from African prehistory to a European present. As she put it:

> Progress narratives persist as an interpretive strategy because they still function as a conceptual crutch ... Many museum visitors, particularly Western museum visitors, rely upon cultural progress narratives – particularly the Victorian anthropological notion that human evolution has proceeded linearly from a primitive African prehistory to a civilized Europe – to facilitate their own comprehension and acceptance of African origins. Overwhelmingly, museum visitors relate to origins stories intimately, and in ways that satisfy or redeem the images they already have of themselves. *(Scott, 2007, p. 2)*

As Scott subsequently wrote:

> Even scientifically astute visitors often misunderstand the scale of human evolutionary time and the nature of evolutionary processes; they often find

it more satisfying – indeed, need [–] to imagine a progress-driven Africa-to-Europe evolutionary plan, a Victorian progress motif that fixes Africa in static evolutionary prehistory. *(Scott, 2010, p. 404)*

Young children

Forest School is a perfect example of how we can use informal learning environments to promote children's ethical thinking and increase children's understanding of science via experiential learning. There is a growing concern that children in the UK and the United States are suffering from a lack of engagement with nature and the environment. This has been named by Louv (2005, p. 34) as 'Nature Deficit Disorder', with the claim that alienation from nature has a negative effect on young children's senses, attention and emotions. In societies where there has been a growth in virtual play, reality-based play, whether it takes place in nature or elsewhere, is all the more vital. Also relevant is the long-standing debate between those who advocate child-led, informal approaches (play-based) to learning versus those who argue for a more structured, formal approach for young children (Whitebread et al., 2012). Play is recognized as crucial to the development of lifelong learning dispositions, developing children's self-esteem, imagination, language and the ability to become independent learners (Beeley, 2012). Despite this, the emphasis on play as a rich element of early years pedagogy is not always understood or recognized (Colwell et al., 2015).

Forest School has its origins in Scandinavia, where it was first conceptualized as a way to combat the issue of a lack of funding for childcare and the need for young children to become socialized – to play and learn with their peers. Children were given opportunities to play entirely outside with all that nature provides, all year round, despite the Scandinavian climate! The children flourished and the Scandinavian model was born, to be replicated and adapted around the world. In the UK, however, Forest School was not an entirely new approach; rather, it was a return to a form of nursery care that was widespread in the UK in the twentieth century which recognized the importance of children playing in the natural world, enjoying the benefits of fresh air and developing independent skills in a safe and stimulating environment. Margaret McMillan (1860–1931) was a pioneer of this – driven by the desire to provide a better start for some of London's poorest children and the ethic that children should be taught without the heavy hand of corporal punishment; her nursery provided a healthy, environment for children to play and explore. Children were also encouraged to stay overnight, sleeping outside, in an attempt to counteract the slum conditions that was the reality for many working-class children at the time. Children were also taught to grow their own produce and enjoyed the benefits of these in their diet.

The underlying principles of Forest school are:

- To introduce children to new opportunities and experiences, to foster their curiosity and inspire them;
- To provide regular opportunities for children to explore their own environment independently and/or with their peers if they so choose to;
- To instil a feeling of belonging, respect and understanding of the world around them; to foster a sense of connectedness with nature.

In Chapter 5 we discussed the importance of Piaget's (1951) (little scientist) and Vygotsky's (1978) (guided learning and the more knowledgeable other) ideas on the development of children's minds and conceptions about morality. Experiential learning takes a constructivist approach, giving children the opportunity to learn via the interaction between thinking and learning. For Piaget (1951), the role of the child's direct experience and agency of his/her own learning is critical. It is during this time that the child's imagination plays a crucial part, especially for the development of thinking. Therefore, using informal learning environments such as Forest School gives young children the opportunity to play out their ethical thinking about scientific concepts. Turtle et al. (2015) found that children who engaged with Forest School developed more positive pro-environmental attitudes than children who did not attend Forest School programmes.

The Spiral of Discovery (Brunton & Thornton, 2010) (Figure 9.4) is a useful framework for practitioners to use to support young children's exploration and investigation both in the classroom and informal learning environments. Using this framework enables teachers to provide adult-led, more structured activities which would then lead to child-led exploration. The Spiral of Discovery incorporates some of the processes of science (make predictions and ask questions, observe and

Figure 9.4 The Spiral of Discovery (Brunton and Thornton, 2010).
Source: Brunton, P. & Thornton, L. (2010). Science in the Early Years: Building Firm Foundations from Birth to Five. California: Sage.

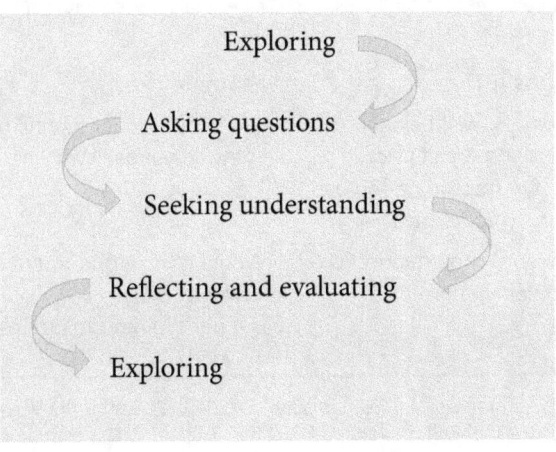

investigate, interpret data, reflect on outcomes), but endeavours to present these in a context which teachers will recognize in relation to children's learning and development (exploring, asking questions, seeking understanding, reflecting and evaluating) (Table 9.1). To help children to think ethically, teachers' questions can be normative. As discussed in Chapter 3, normative questions are questions which ask what ought to be done in a given situation. Teachers can therefore plan 'ethical questions' which they might use during adult-led sessions at Forest School or be responsive to child-led activities. In the latter case, we would suggest that teachers have a list of normative terms to refer to if asking ethical questions is something that is new to a teacher's pedagogy (Table 9.2).

Table 9.1 Using the Spiral of Discovery.

Exploring	Asking questions of child	Seeking understanding	Reflecting and evaluating
Being playful	Non-verbal cues to ask questions	Children make choices	Chance to revisit their ideas
Using all their senses	Posing questions	They look closely, planning what they will do	Reflect on what they have discovered
Displaying curiosity	Shared conversation	Investigate and record what they have discovered	Evaluate their findings
Making connections as they encounter new experiences	Putting forward own ideas	Takes a number of forms – e.g. quiet solitary activities or a shared experience with others	This often leads on to new areas of exploration and the cycle starts again
	Making predictions		

Source: Brunton, P. & Thornton, L. (2010). Science in the Early Years: Building Firm Foundations from Birth to Five. *California: Sage.*

Table 9.2 Normative terms that can be used to elicit ethical thinking with younger children when engaging with Forest School.

Normative terms (ET)	Example
Character: happiness, well-being, thriving, flourishing, virtue, vice, brave, friend, fair (person), good/bad (person), truth, lying, respect	Is it fair not to let Joanna help you count the ladybirds? Why?
Action: right, wrong, consequences, intent, caring, fair (action)	Would it be wrong to put rubbish in our wood? Why? Is it right for you to pick plants in the wood? Why?

Source: Kenyon, E., Terorde-Doyle, D. & Carnahan, S. (2019). Ethics for the Very Young: A Philosophy Curriculum for Early Childhood Education. *Lanham MD: Rowman & Littlefield.*

How might this work in practice?

Explore

A group of children are in the forest looking for invertebrates. They have some collecting trays, magnifiers and clipboards in a role-play area which they have created. They notice some rocks. The teacher advises them, saying, 'Be careful when picking up the rock so that you don't drop it and hurt any woodlice. Why would that be wrong?' They discuss why and then turn over a stone to discover some woodlice and run off to fetch a magnifier and a collecting tray. But by the time they return the woodlice have disappeared.

Asking questions

The children have many suggestions about where the woodlice might have gone: 'Into the ground', 'They flew away', 'They're hiding behind some other rocks'. They discuss where they might look for them and search.

Seeking understanding

The children decide to catch some of the woodlice so that they can track the journeys they make. They discuss this plan with the teacher and negotiate who will do what. But one child is left out and begins to cry. The teacher asks, 'Is it nice not to let Joanna join in? Why?' Once the issue is resolved, it is agreed that the teacher will find a large piece of paper and take photographs whilst the children tip some woodlice onto the paper and use crayons to track their movements. The woodlice moves quite slowly – one child gets very excited and uses her pen to poke the bottom of one woodlouse to make it move. However, she pokes too hard and accidentally squashes the woodlouse. The teacher asks, 'Was that a caring way to treat the woodlouse? Why?'

Reflecting and evaluating

The children recapture a woodlouse. The teacher asks, 'What shall we do with the woodlouse now? Is it right to put it back under its stone? Why?' They talk about the way one woodlouse stopped momentarily inside the circle and then moved on. They discuss different ways they could contain the woodlice – wooden blocks, trays, pencils – then they wonder if they could repeat the same exploration with snails – what might need to be done differently? And so next time, this informs their investigation.

It is important that the teacher ask questions which elicit thinking (and as children grow older, reasoning) in children rather than making statements or value judgements. For example, when the woodlouse was squashed, the teacher could have said, 'That's not nice is it? The poor woodlouse'. Instead, the teacher used ethical terms and questions to help the child to think ethically about what happened. This is an important distinction because as ethics educators we are concerned with the process of ethical thinking and reasoning. What we want to do is help children think about the best way to live (or, in this example, the right course of action to care for woodlice). By doing this, we are therefore guiding the children to develop a moral compass and a moral sense of self.

Learning in gardens

Johnson (2004) describes the range of activities that the Royal Horticultural Society provides at its Wisley Garden for primary-aged visitors. The children can determine soil structure by using sieves of different sizes; they can visit holes dug in different parts of the garden to show a variety of soil profiles with their different horizons; they can measure plant root length to find out which parts of the horizon are reached by different plants or at different stages of a plant's life cycle; they can look at examples of plants that exhibit growth irregularities associated with inadequate supplies of soil nutrients; they can make compost and divide materials into compostable and non-compostable categories; they can identify insects in a compost heap to help them construct a food chain; they can be helped to identify plant species.

All these activities can be used to help children explore ethical issues. Once children have learnt something about soil, they can be introduced to the problem of soil erosion and learn about how certain farming practices can help conserve soil. Looking at plants that have suffered from inadequate supplies of soil nutrients, they can learn about both the benefits of fertilizers (increasing crop yields) and some of the problems associated with them (fertilizer run-off and the consequences for wildlife biodiversity). Plant identification may not be thought immediately to connect with ethical issues but, as Johnson puts it, 'knowing how to identify plants is the first step in conservation of local flora and has implications for local cultural heritage' (2004, p. 71).

In a major report, *Redefining the Role of Botanic Gardens – Towards a New Social Purpose*, Dodd and Jones (2010) note that botanic gardens are well placed to educate the public on conservation issues and the human role in environmental change; they specifically comment that 'by raising awareness of issues of social and environmental justice amongst their audiences, botanic gardens can contribute to wider action upon worldwide moral issues' (p. 2). Research on the actual effects of botanic gardens on visitor behaviour seems somewhat sparse, though it is known that visiting a botanic garden can result in more positive environmental attitudes (Williams et al., 2015).

Of course, gardens exist in many forms. A community garden is a piece of land that is cultivated by a group of people either collectively or individually. They are also known as neighbourhood gardens and allotments. Community gardens have a wide range of benefits; they can encourage residents to walk, be physically engaged in gardening activities, learn about healthy food and consume such healthy food

(Al-Delaimy & Webb, 2017). There are also data that suggest that community gardens can have positive impacts on individuals' mental health and promote biopsychosocial-spiritual well-being (Al-Delaimy & Webb, 2017).

Community gardens can, therefore, be a good thing, but the link with ethics may not yet be evident. Claire Nettle argues that 'Community gardens grow in the fertile intersections between food politics and agrifood studies, environmentalism and urban social movements, policy and planning, social work and social action' (Nettle, 2014, p. 3). In her work on community gardens in Australia, North America and the UK, Nettle sees them as manifestations of social action. This, therefore, is an instance of ethics not only being talked about but enacted. To give one example, Nettle writes about Northey Street City Farm, a community garden of 4 hectares, located 3 kilometres from the centre of Brisbane:

> The Farm has extensive, certified organic demonstration gardens and orchards, a bushfood arboretum, a cabinet timber woodlot and areas of creek-side native revegetation. Northey Street has Queensland's only certified organic retail nursery, community composting facilities and hosts a weekly organic farmers' market. The site also includes an outdoor classroom, numerous sitting and eating areas, art installations, interpretive signage, a performance stage and a community kitchen in which lunch is prepared and served each day. Northey Street functions as a sustainability education centre and is a hub for permaculture, community and sustainability initiatives in Brisbane. *(Nettle, 2014, p. 14)*

Zoos and aquaria

Zoos ('zoological gardens' to give them their formal name) and botanic gardens are often linked together, with aquaria sometimes distinguished from zoos. However, there is one fundamental difference between a zoo/aquarium and a botanic garden – namely, that plants are incapable of experiencing pleasures or pains whereas many animals, specifically sentient animals, can. For all that some children love visiting zoos and aquaria, they should be encouraged to think, perhaps once they are back in school, about whether these institutions should be allowed to exist.

In their article titled 'A Postzoo Future: Why Welfare Fails Animals in Zoos', Pierce and Bekoff conclude:

> Discussions on the welfare of nonhuman animals in zoos tend to focus on incremental improvements without addressing the underlying problem of captivity. But alterations to the conditions of zoo captivity are irrelevant for animals. Real zoo reform will involve working to completely change the landscape. We offer six necessary reforms to bring zoos into a more ethical future: (1) Shut down bad zoos, now; (2) stop exhibiting animals who cannot

and never will do well in captivity; (3) stop killing healthy animals; (4) stop captive breeding; (5) stop moving animals around from one zoo to another; and (6) use the science of animal cognition and emotion on behalf of animals. *(Pierce & Bekoff, 2018, p. 43)*

An example of a species that used to be widely kept in zoos but is now kept less often is the polar bear (*Ursus maritimus*) (Figure 9.5). In the wild, polar bears have huge home ranges (the area over which a single animal roams). A small home range for a polar bear may be 50,000–60,000 km^2 (found near Canadian Arctic islands); a large home range may be in excess of 350,000 km^2 (found in the Bering or Chukchi sea) (SeaWorld Parks & Entertainment, 2022). It is impossible for a zoo to provide anything like this amount of space. The campaigning organization Bear Conservation argues:

> In an ideal world there would be no polar bears in zoos.... Given the appalling conditions in which many of them are kept, it is not surprising that many captive polar bears manifest symptoms of extreme stress, such as continually shaking

Figure 9.5 Polar bear at a zoo sometime between 1909 and 1932.
Source: Library of Congress, Public Domain, https://www.loc.gov/pictures/item/2016820240/ *and* https://commons.wikimedia.org/wiki/File:Polar_bear_at_zoo_LCCN2016820240.tif.

their heads, pacing up and down their enclosures or swimming in a stereotypical fashion.... Captive polar bears, along with orcas and other cetaceans, suffer from more sickness and psychologically related illness than any other animals kept in captivity. *(Bear Conservation, 2022)*

However, while it may be difficult to defend keeping polar bears, orcas (killer whales) and other cetaceans (whales, dolphins and porpoises) in zoos and aquaria, there are many who argue that it is ethically perfectly acceptable to keep many other animals in zoos and aquaria. Such animals can be well fed, receive veterinary attention and may live considerably longer than their counterparts in the wild. Furthermore, if we shift from considering the welfare of individuals to the conservation of species, zoos are playing an increasingly important role in wildlife conservation. Generally, the aim is for captive breeding programmes to lead to successful reintroduction into the wild.

Our aim here is not to come to a decision about whether the arguments in favour of zoos and aquaria outweigh the arguments against them, but rather to point out that these institutions provide a tremendous resource for ethics and science to be discussed together. This chapter is about informal science education but school teachers can use such informal experiences in classroom teaching. Polar bears are an iconic species; in a school setting students could be encouraged to use the ethical tools that we discuss in Chapters 3 and 5 to help answer the question as to whether polar bears should be kept in captivity. Students could then use the same tools to help answer the question as to whether other species, such as giant pandas (*Ailuropoda melanoleuca*) and kākāpōs (*Strigops habroptilus*), should be.

Who gets to go to museums, botanic gardens, zoos and aquaria?

There are inequalities in school systems; both between countries and within them schools differ in the quality of the education they provide, in large measure due to differences in the resources (particularly the teachers) they have. These inequalities are often magnified in countries that have a large private school system and in schools that have little or no mixed-ability teaching. However, inequalities are greater in informal education.

Dawson (2019) reports on a two-year ethnographic study she undertook in central London between the boroughs of Southwark and Lambeth, working in partnership with adults who rarely, if ever, took part in what she refers to as everyday science learning (i.e. informal science education in the language of this chapter). Five community groups took part in the research: an Afro-Caribbean group (n = 7), a Somali group (n = 6), a Sierra Leonean group (n = 16, and five children who came on a visit), a Latin American group (n = 17, and two children who came on a visit) and an Asian group (n = 13). Forty-one of the adult participants were female and 18 were male; ages ranged from 18 to 76.

In Dawson's study, museums were seen by her participants as the most recognized of the places and ways in which everyday science learning could take place. However, this did not mean that they were seen as accessible. As Hawa and Lucille from the Sierra Leonean group put it:

> Hawa: like that those of us from Sierra Leone [...] maybe they need to, like science and the museums, they need to advertise them, more broadly. You see the type of people coming in?
> Lucille: That goes there? It's not us. *(Dawson, 2019, p. 53)*

When the Sierra Leonean group was asked by Dawson if they had ever or would ever consider visiting a science museum, she was told:

> Kadiatu: Not science museums, no (laughs).
> Fatimata: I would go to the cinema, I would never tell anyone I would go to a museum.
> Kadiatu: I would say half of the Sierra Leone community they never just sit down and say, 'let's go to the science museum'. *(Dawson, 2019, p. 53)*

This rejection was because 'Participants recognised traditional everyday science learning practices and institutions, such as museums, as a form of high-brow culture and, as a result, broadly unappealing and inaccessible for people like them' (p. 53). Furthermore:

> while some participants or their children visited science museums on school visits, these were not fondly remembered, nor were these experiences that catalysed further visits. As Fatima from the Somali group argued, 'I probably wouldn't go back to museums any time soon because I was taken there by force [with school]'. *(Dawson, 2019, p. 53)*

One way, which has become increasingly prevalent, of understanding how the access of different individuals and groups to science depends on their circumstances is that of 'science capital'. This term derives from the work of Louise Archer. Archer et al. (2015) begin by noting that the sociologist Pierre Bourdieu 'conceptualizes capital as the legitimate, valuable, and exchangeable resources in a society that can generate forms of social advantage within specific fields (e.g., education) for those who possess it' (p. 923). Bourdieu identified a number of forms of capital – of which 'economic capital' is perhaps the most obvious – and at the end of his life even wrote briefly about 'scientific capital'. Archer extended this to include 'science capital':

> We suggest that science-related resources should be legitimately considered as important contemporary forms of capital, which play a role in the production

of social relations of advantage/disadvantage. This is not least because they command a high symbolic and exchange value within contemporary society. For instance, across numerous international contexts, science is widely framed as a national priority within government policy and rhetoric. *(Archer et al., 2015, p. 926)*

Archer et al. (2015) also point out that 'families and young people may engage with science in a wide range of ways, but, from a dominant perspective, some forms of engagement (e.g., doing experiments, going to a science museum) may be valued as more "scientific" than others (e.g., cooking or "tinkering")' (p. 925).

Nowadays, there is a large literature on science capital. For a nicely designed two-minute video explaining the concept, go to https://www.youtube.com/watch?v=A0t70bwPD6Y (or search for 'Louise Archer science capital' on YouTube). The key point is that science capital can be thought of as the sum of all the science-related knowledge, attitudes, experiences and resources that any of us has. This includes the science we know, what we feel about science (e.g. whether we are attracted or put off by scientific reasoning), the people we know who understand science and the day-to-day engagement we have with science.

Archer et al. (2015) developed an instrument in an attempt to quantify science capital and used it to categorize a large sample of year 7 to year 10 students with whom they were working into three groupings: high science capital (5 per cent), medium science capital (68 per cent) and low science capital (27 per cent). High science capital students were more like to be male, Asian and come from the most socially advantaged homes. They were more likely to be in the top set for science at school and interested in a science-related future career (93 per cent of high science capital students aspired to a science-related job compared to 51 per cent of the whole sample). They were much more likely to be interested in studying science at university (50 per cent of high science capital students vs. 19 per cent of the whole sample).

Applied unthinkingly, the notion of science capital could be taken to mean that the problem resides in those with low science capital. This is not the intention of those who work on science capital. Emily Dawson, whose work on museums we cited above and who is one of Louise Archer's co-authors in the Archer et al. (2015) article that we have just referred to, is explicit about the fact that the problems that those in her sample encountered need to be addressed by changes elsewhere, including in museums and other places where science is presented. Dawson gives an example from the Somali group's visit to a science centre:

The extract that follows is from Hamiido, attempting to use one of the interactive computer exhibits with me. Hamiido was in her mid-30s, had two smart phones and had previously shown me how to use a couple of apps on my phone. She was an adept user of technology in many ways, but that did not help her in the science centre. I joined her at this exhibit, having witnessed her difficult first attempt:

(A voice in an upper class, southern English accent from the machine talks again and says 'Now it's over to you, remember, you need to keep the conditions right, the humidity, the pH ...')

Hamiido: How can I know?
Emily: I think it's going to tell us?
Hamiido: Yeah?
Emily: – Plant cells are growing – so look.
Hamiido: This is coming up.
Emily: Yeah, pH is going down, so, so the temperatures, ok, oh down with the temperature.
Hamiido: This one?
Emily: Yep.
Hamiido: Ok.
Emily: Oh, temperature too low, up a bit, ok, pH low, pH up ...
Hamiido: Oh, confusing.
Emily: I know.
Hamiido: Yes, this is for scientists, yeah?

To use this exhibit Hamiido needed first to understand spoken and written instructions in English at the same time (with no way to slow down or repeat instructions). She then needed to understand several scientific terms and concepts and she needed enough museum literacy to understand how exhibits like this one might work.

Let's break it down. In terms of scientific literacy, the previous extract shows Hamiido needed to know what plant cells were and how they grew, the effect of pH, temperature, water, humidity, waste and nutrients. In terms of museum literacy, she also had a lot to do. This interactive computer exhibit appeared to be designed for multiple users, with a large screen and several moving components of image and text, which proved difficult to use alone or in a pair. To make things worse, a loud siren went off at regular intervals as part of the experience. *(Dawson, 2019, pp. 115–16)*

In a highly cited article, Tara Yosso (2005) asked, 'Whose culture has capital?' Yosso challenged traditional interpretations of Bourdieusian cultural capital theory and introduced an alternative concept that she called 'community cultural wealth'. Yosso's point is that:

Deficit thinking takes the position that minority students and families are at fault for poor academic performance because: (a) students enter school without the normative cultural knowledge and skills; and (b) parents neither value nor support their child's education. *(Yosso, 2005, p. 75)*

Yosso goes on to conceptualize community cultural wealth as being constituted by:

- *Aspirational capital* – the ability to maintain hopes and dreams for the future, even in the face of real and perceived barriers.
- *Linguistic capital* – the intellectual and social skills attained through communication experiences in more than one language and/or style.
- *Familial capital* – those cultural knowledges nurtured in families that carry a sense of community history, memory and cultural intuition.
- *Social capital* – networks of people and community resources that can provide instrumental and emotional support to navigate through society's institutions.
- *Navigational capital* – skills of manoeuvring through social institutions.
- *Resistant capital* – knowledges and skills fostered through oppositional behaviour that challenges inequality.

Habig et al. (2021) use Yosso's notion of community cultural wealth to problematize the prevailing deficit-oriented approach to STEM enrichment programmes for young people underrepresented in STEM. Their research examined a seven-year out-of-school-time programme (the 'Lang program') at the American Museum of Natural History. Children can apply for the programme when they are in Grade 5. After an application and interview process, twenty children are selected annually. Parents must commit to supporting their children to attend all seven years of the programme; this is a major commitment as those on the programme meet on alternate Saturdays during the school year throughout middle and high school and for three weeks during the summer for a minimum of 165 contact hours per year.

One of Habig et al.'s research participants was Cody, an African-American male born and raised in Brooklyn, New York:

> From as far back as Cody remembers, he was always interested in science: In 8th grade, he applied to and was accepted into a very selective public high school in New York City where he joined a program that focuses on preparing students for careers in the medical sciences. Following high school, Cody attended a local private university where he earned a bachelor's degree in chemistry. He is presently working for a city agency where he conducts environmental safety testing on air and water samples. When he is not at work, he spends most of his spare time teaching himself coding as he aspires to be a web developer.
> (Habig et al., 2021, p. 517)

Habig et al. used community cultural wealth theory because it allowed them to recognize the skills, abilities and networks that their participants were able to draw on. Cody exhibited all six forms of cultural wealth that Yosso (2005) identified. From their extensive data, Habig et al. identified four themes in the context of community cultural wealth theory. The first theme was how participation in the programme *expanded the realm of possibilities* for what STEM is and could be, and the options for careers in the STEM disciplines. The second was *creating and sustaining*

STEM social networks. The third was how youth demonstrated *resiliency while facing significant obstacles*. The fourth was the *continuum of STEM experiences* of the research participants during multiple entry and/or re-entry points during their nonlinear STEM trajectories.

To give just one example here, Habig et al. (2021) discuss how Cody used different forms of community cultural wealth to create and sustain social networks:

> Cody's existing social networks expanded beyond his home environment extending to his Brooklyn neighborhood and local school community. He joined a community youth basketball program. He described his coach as being critical and having high expectations. 'What he [my basketball coach] was really trying to do was prepare us for the real world. So, I feel like now that I'm older, I can [take criticism]. I can overlook how it is said … You kind of take that and learn from that, and that's pretty cool.' Cody brought this navigational capital in the form of an awareness of how to negotiate interactions with the world to his school, and to his Lang and college experiences. As a college student, to accomplish his objective of finding a research lab, Cody perused the college Web site and attempted to review each professor's work and to read their research articles. Next, he sent emails summarizing the articles and expressing his interest in joining their labs. However, Cody hit a wall: 'They just weren't getting back to me. I remember I was just like … I don't even understand half of these articles. I can't do this anymore.' However, he did not give up. Instead, he contacted his mentor from the Lang program and together they worked on crafting a cover letter and curriculum vitae. Cody described them as 'going back and forth' until he drafted a polished product. After emailing a number of professors, shortly thereafter, Cody was invited to join a research lab. Cody stated that the PI of the laboratory selected him because of his experience at the museum: 'So, he [the PI] told me that because I see here that you have the experience and you stuck with it [Lang] for 7 years, I trust that when things get sort of slow, that you won't just leave.' Indeed, Cody worked in this laboratory conducting research on a protein that functions in a cancer repair pathway throughout his tenure at the college. As an upperclassman, Cody also joined a bioinformatics laboratory where he was able to carry out research connected to his 'newly found love for computer science'. Thus, the intersection of Cody's aspirational and STEM social capital together with the activation of his navigational capital were collectively important as he navigated through a large research institution in an effort to achieve his educational goals.
> (Habig et al., 2021, p. 530)

Learning about vaccination

Our final example in this chapter of the place of ethics in informal science education is to do with how all of us learn about vaccinations. Clearly, learning about vaccinations, for most of us, has become much more relevant since the onset of the Covid-19 pandemic at the start of 2020. Most of us learn about vaccination in secondary school biology of health classes. We might get a smattering of history based on Edward Jenner's classic 1796 experiment on eight-year-old Edward Phipps, which led to smallpox vaccination – ignoring the long preceding history of treating smallpox by vaccination's predecessor, variolation (Reiss, 2021). (Variolation was practised in China by the tenth century. Material was taken from someone who had smallpox. The material was then dried, mixed with cotton and put up one of the nostrils [the right one for boys, the left one for girls]. It was known that the milder the original case of smallpox and the longer the scabs were left before being used, the milder the disease that resulted from variolation. Variolation was used widely in a number of countries and was brought back to the UK from Turkey by Lady Mary Wortley Montagu in 1721.) We also get taught quite a bit about the biology of the immune system – material about antigens and antibodies and primary and secondary immune responses.

But what doesn't tend to get taught in schools is much if anything about the ethics of vaccination. Indeed, there seems to be a widespread assumption that anyone who doesn't avail themselves or their family of the benefits of vaccination is either stupid or selfish – stupid because vaccination is presumed undoubtedly to be desirable, selfish because a person who refuses vaccination may be relying on the herd immunity that arises when a high proportion of the population has been immunized against a particular disease.

And yet objections to vaccination against smallpox did not take long to arise (Reiss, 2021). Many of the arguments advanced against vaccination then are paralleled today in objections to Covid-19 vaccinations (Figure 9.6). For one thing, there were concerns about safety and efficacy. Of course, it is in the nature of science that nothing can ever be guaranteed to be totally safe or effective, but in the case of smallpox, even in the 1960s, about one in three people given the vaccine took days off work or school because of their reactions to it and about one in a million people died (Belongia & Naleway, 2003).

A different objection to smallpox vaccination resulted from the element of compulsion. The UK 1853 Compulsory Vaccination Act required every child to be vaccinated within three months of its birth (four months for orphans) and parents or guardians who failed to comply, without sufficient reason, were liable to a fine of £1. While the implementation of this policy helped reduce the incidence of smallpox considerably, it was controversial. As the hydropathic practitioner and anti-vaccinationist John Gibbs put it in 1854: 'Are we to be leeched, bled, blistered, burned, douched, frozen, pilled, potioned, lotioned, salivated by Act of Parliament?' (Durbach, 2000, p. 45).

There were violent riots in Ipswich, Henley, Mitford and elsewhere in 1853, and the Anti-Vaccination League was formed in London in the same year and the Anti-Compulsory Anti-Vaccination League in 1867 (Wolfe & Sharp, 2002). Similar movements arose in other countries and the Anti-Vaccination Society of America was founded in 1879. By 1872, vaccination rates in Stockholm had fallen to just over 40 per cent, whereas they approached 90 per cent in the rest of Sweden. A

Figure 9.6 A protest against Covid-19 vaccines, in Islington, London, on 18 September 2021.
Source: By Mx. Granger. https://commons.wikimedia.org/wiki/File:Antivax_protest_in_London_2.jpg.

major smallpox epidemic in Stockholm in 1874 resulted in widespread vaccination and no further epidemics.

One important source of moral objections to certain vaccines has arisen because of the historical use of aborted foetuses in their manufacture. Several live vaccines against rubella (Meruvax, Rudivax, MR-VAX), and vaccines against hepatitis (A-VAQTA and HAVRIX), chickenpox (Varivax) and poliomyelitis (Polivax) fall into this category (Pelčić et al., 2016), and the Roman Catholic Church has suggested that these vaccines should be avoided (Pontifical Academy for Life, 2006). This argument has sprung into prominence again as the recently developed Johnson & Johnson vaccine against Covid-19 similarly uses cell lines from aborted foetuses.

Non-religious objections to vaccines stem from a number of sources. In particular, some communities, particularly Black and minority ethnic communities, have historically had good reasons not to trust what governments, big business or even the medical establishment say to them. There is too much structural inequality in societies around the world for it to be reasonable for those who are advantaged to presume that those who are disadvantaged should simply take official reassurances about medical matters at face value. For example, and specifically in relation to trust around vaccinations, it transpired that in its attempts to locate Osama bin Laden in the wake of the September 11 attacks in the United States in 2001, the Central Intelligence Agency (CIA) used a fake hepatitis B vaccination project to collect DNA in the neighbourhood in Abbottabad, Pakistan, where he was hiding (Martinez-Bravo & Stegmann, 2022). The intention was to obtain DNA from bin Laden's children to confirm bin Laden's presence (bin Laden's sister had died in the United States in 2010, and her DNA was available to the US authorities), thus allowing a mission with the intention of assassinating bin Laden to proceed, as indeed proved to be the case (Reiss, 2022).

News of the CIA initiative led to attacks on polio vaccination workers in Pakistan, with legitimate health care workers targeted as US spies, and some seventy people killed. As a consequence of the fatalities, organizations such as the UN suspended polio vaccination efforts in Pakistan, and parents refused to have their children vaccinated. The Pakistani Taliban launched an anti-vaccine propaganda campaign, maintaining that the polio vaccination campaigns were a conspiracy to sterilize the Muslim population. The result was an upsurge in polio cases in Pakistan.

A final ethical issue to do with vaccinations is to do with health care rationing (Reiss, 2020). Should new vaccinations be given to those most likely to benefit from them (in the case of Covid-19, this means prioritizing the elderly and clinically vulnerable) or those most at risk of infection (those who come into contact with most people) or those who are particularly valuable to society (e.g. health care professionals)? Again, our intention is not to answer such questions but to say that addressing them, using the tools we have discussed in this book, can have a number of benefits to learners, including empowering them and encouraging them to learn more about science.

Conclusion: The only way is ethics! 10

We are living in a time of vast technological advances but also in a time of crisis, one marked by clear advancement in the sciences but also one of extensive human suffering and the destruction of too much of the non-human world. Science educators, as facilitators of knowledge, ought to take this state of affairs and their role in addressing this with their audiences seriously and we are sure many do. There are often concerns surrounding the complexities of incorporating ethical thinking and decision-making within school science and elsewhere where science is communicated and these can act as a barrier for educators incorporating these approaches into their pedagogies. In schools, there is also a very real tension surrounding teacher agency and accountability – teachers may wish to have ownership over their pedagogical practices in their classrooms, but this can be undermined by a culture of directive approaches from senior management in schools, in turn responding to pressures from parents, governors, inspection agencies, national government and others. The question we therefore find ourselves asking is, how can science educators, particularly classroom teachers, incorporate ethics in their science teaching in an educational climate of accountability, lack of teacher agency, curriculum overload and resources which are often lacking?

We have given this chapter title the sub-heading, 'The only way is ethics'. If you are in touch with popular television programmes in the UK, you might very well recognize that this is a slightly tongue-in-cheek play on words inspired by the series that has been running since 2010, 'The Only Way Is Essex'. For those of you in the know, and perhaps more importantly for those who are not, this is reality TV at its questionable 'best', fraught with ethical issues embedded in everyday lives. Originally, we suggested to our publisher that the book be titled *The Only Way Is Ethics? The Place of Ethics in Science Education*. We considered that this might 'hook' people into picking up a book about, and engaging with, a discipline that can be seen as 'heavy going', 'challenging to understand' or dare we say it 'uninteresting' – though we hope that we have been able to demonstrate that this is far from the case.

Does the title of this chapter therefore suggest that the *only* way forward is to include ethics in science education? Quite frankly, yes. We accept that there are aspects of science that are best taught in schools or communicated elsewhere without necessarily including an ethical dimension. However, as we hope we have demonstrated, ethics connects with science more than is sometimes supposed and is crucial for children to really understand the nature of science and what scientists do in the real world. It is also critical if we wish to develop scientifically literate children.

Bearing all this in mind, we eventually decided that we did not want the title of this book to question whether or not ethics should be a part of science education, although we do attend to the debates surrounding this in Chapter 6. Instead, by providing a typology of ways teachers can introduce ethics in their teaching and by drawing on our own research and that of science educators globally, we hope to have convinced the reader of the important 'place' of ethics in science education. We are clear that not only should ethics be an integral part of science education but that this should be a focus of school science education from a young age.

One of the reasons why we wanted to write this book is to empower science educators to understand and see the connections between ethics and science as well as share these with their students. These are not always easy to see, especially in formal science curricula where this link is not explicit and in informal science situations where educators may have not have been introduced to a range of ways of including ethics within their practice. We have organized this book to interweave case studies from the early years of learning through to adulthood, and we have also referred to all teachers and communicators of science as science educators. We see the development of children's moral sensitivity to science issues as the responsibility of all science educators and we do not take the view that this is a process which only starts to take shape when children begin their formal education in school. We have therefore chosen not to organize this book by learner age, although we accept that there are moments in a child's development when learning about ethics will be critical; age is neither a measure nor a benchmark for the development of ethical thinking.

We hope that by presenting the book in the way we have we have persuaded science educators why teaching ethics in school science is so important and how this can be incorporated within overburdened curricula. We also hope that we have helped science educators see how feasible it is to successfully incorporate the pedagogies we have presented across all ages of learners in both formal and informal settings.

If we put to one side the argument about whether or not ethics should be a part of science education and accept that it ought to be, another reason for writing this book is to draw on robust research-informed evidence of what can actually work in and out of the learning situation, for all ages of learners, and those who are responsible for their learning, regardless of where they are in their career. Therefore, as science educators and researchers ourselves, in the arguments presented in this book, we wanted to take an additive rather than a deficit approach. It is our view that teachers and those responsible for learning in informal settings are professionals

Chapter 10 Conclusion: The only way is ethics! 151

who are creative and resourceful, more than able to draw together knowledge to promote children's ethical and scientific thinking. We hope what we have presented here inspires science educators to do so and we look forward to receiving any communication from science educators who might try what we have presented in this book or indeed share alternative approaches that have worked for them. We also hope to inspire researchers to see the merit of researching approaches to including ethics in science education, especially for younger children as this is an under-researched area and yet is crucial to developing children's ongoing moral sensitivity to science.

We also wanted to bring attention to the fact that at a time when there continues to be international concern about the relatively low numbers of students wishing to study STEM subjects beyond statutory requirements, there is also a climate in which there seems to be an increase in young people engaging in socio-scientific issues via social media and activism. These should not be at odds with each other; thus, the place of ethics in science education is very much relevant and timely. Accessing knowledge and being able to critique, analyse and evaluate knowledge are two very different things, and this is where the role of the science educator is so crucial. Teaching our youth the critical thinking and reasoning skills to analyse, evaluate and reason both ethically and scientifically will go a long way to countering dangerous ideologies that can be harmful and divisive. Our view, as set out in Chapter 1 of this book, is that engaging students in ethical thinking in school science might very well go a long way to countering this issue. Research has suggested there is certainly potential for this and we argue that decision-making skills are crucial to the development of moral sensitivity in science education. We posit that as science educators we can either choose to be a part of or apart from this. In order to be the former, marrying school science with the science that our youth are interested and actively engaging in is a positive starting point.

In this book we have therefore considered what the 'place' of ethics is in science education. In answering this, we have kept in mind the following questions: 'What role can formal and informal science education play in the development of students' moral sensitivity to science and understanding of the ethical issues it raises?' and 'What tools and pedagogical approaches do teachers need to effect this?' As discussed in Chapter 9, school is no longer perceived, to the extent that perhaps it once was, as the font of all knowledge; the informal sector has grown in importance for science communication and learning. Nevertheless, school remains a central role in every child's education. Having reflected on the arguments we have put forward in this book, we ask the reader to consider whether the conversations students have in the classroom, in the playground, on field trips, in the corridors, etc., about issues in society related to science are so very different from the conversations they are having on social media and in their communities. What we are questioning here is whether children are being given the opportunity to discuss the same socio-scientific issues in school that they are interested in and pursue in their own time. In contemplating these questions, we remind readers that a classroom is a microcosm of wider society and should reflect this. This should therefore give science educators reason to reflect on the pivotal role they might play in the moral development of children of all ages, if they are to impact on the scientific literacy of the children they serve.

We started this book by conceptualizing for the reader what science is (Chapter 2) and what ethics is (Chapter 3). Here we explored two very different disciplines. It can be broadly argued that science claims to be universalist and open-minded, producing knowledge which should be objective, whereas ethics is a branch of philosophy concerning matters of value that are culturally specific and in that sense more subjective. We suggested, in Chapter 2, how the arrival and subsequent expansion of the internet and social media have had a significant impact on people's understanding of what science is and their involvement in science, although we fully acknowledge that there are stark inequalities in access to this as seen particularly during the Covid-19 pandemic with some children's access to online learning impossible or severely compromised in countries across the globe.

We recognize that the young people today are a generation very able to research and access diverse knowledge, who believe in the power of their own agency and voice and because of social media can now often quickly mobilize themselves to be effective activists in their own right, as we highlight in Chapter 7. However, we also note in Chapter 2 that arriving at an understanding of truth in the social sciences is more complex and more subject to value judgements than in the natural sciences. Social scientists are more interested in how truth arises out of human relationships and in understanding how knowledge is constructed in the light of historical and cultural factors.

In Chapter 3, we discuss how, regardless of whether morality is culturally specific or universal, the ethical principles that guide our society impact on our sense of self, our morality and the values we hold. We therefore argue that science is not separate from society and ethics very much arises from society. In Chapters 4 and 5, we discuss what is meant by science education and by ethics education. We consider whether or not ethics has a role to play in science education and argue that perspectives on this will differ depending on the position one gives to the overall aims of education and the weight science and ethics play within this. We also examine science education and ethics education through historical, philosophical, contextual and pedagogical lenses, discussing the merits and complexities of these in order to provide an in-depth understanding of what underpins ethics education and science education.

In considering the value of working towards a unified theory of morality, we discuss in Chapter 5 why shared ethical frameworks for morality are key to understanding and promoting the role of culture in morality as well as to our understanding of what ethics is and the role it plays in science. We present relevant ethical frameworks and examine theories of justice, considering those who have suffered from oppression and the role power dynamics have played in this, in a bid to highlight the very real consequences to human life. We also expand on these to consider the importance of intergenerational, environmental and animal rights in research and the ethical implications of these. These arguments then underpin the case studies we present in Chapters 7–9, supporting our view that when teachers undertake pedagogical approaches to engage students in thinking ethically about science, they are giving their students opportunities to develop into critical consumers of scientific information and to learn to make reasoned judgements between what is ethical and what is unethical in science.

In Chapters 7–9 we also present strong evidence that when students fail to engage with science, this is often because of the perception that school science can be inauthentic and does not address real-life issues. We also present evidence that engaging in ethical thinking via socio-scientific issues, argumentation and informal learning environments can have a positive impact on student understanding of science knowledge and on their attitudes to science as well as on their ethical and scientific decision-making skills. It is clear that students want to learn about the science that interests and matters to them. This is contrasted with sociological arguments centring on students' negative perceptions of their own ability in science, and that the learning of science can be linked to the passing of examinations rather than an intrinsic enjoyment of the subject, as well as a lack of understanding of career aspirations in STEM. If we view this via one of the main aims of science education, which is to develop students' scientific literacy, then it is crucial for students not only to learn about the regulatory ethical frameworks within which scientists operate (Chapter 8) but also to understand that ethics is frequently an integral part of science, and that scientists are human and must be guided by what society agrees is right or wrong.

Out-of-school scientific institutions and centres of communication, such as natural history museums, botanic gardens, zoos, science centres and learned organizations, are increasingly starting to recognize this too, although we argue in Chapter 9 that ethical aspects of science are under-explored in informal settings, as they are in schools. But for those that are now beginning to focus on this, there is often a shift in the way collections are presented and science is communicated. Collections, of course, provide the evidence from which scientists derive scientific knowledge, but now this is more likely to include knowledge that is directly applied to critical issues facing society. For example, in a time of unprecedented environmental destruction, natural history and other science museums are not only documenting the impact on biological and cultural diversity but increasingly prompting our ethical thinking on this. As discussed in Chapters 7–9, young people today are more likely to ask challenging ethical questions about the collection practices of the past than the generations that preceded them; today's collections are all too often the result of exploitative collection practices, rooted in power imbalances and racism and carried out in the name of exploration and scientific enquiry. We also recognize that there is not a level-playing field here; there are serious inequalities for students accessing science in informal settings which can be a barrier to their engagement with and understanding of science. There is still therefore much to be done in science education to readdress this balance.

Children in the early years of their science education can begin from an egocentric position to consider the rights and wrongs of their own and then that of others' behaviour in relation to science, for they are confronted with ethical issues all the time when attempting to understand the world around them. Curricula in the early years often do not separate subjects, giving science educators of young children the license to take a broader view of science education, starting from either an adult or a child-led perspective. Ethical discussions about science can therefore be raised by the child or the teacher, providing a context in which to understand the science being learned as well as an opportunity for children to discuss important issues with their peers in an open way which allows for the possibility of disagreement. Using frameworks such as the Spiral of Discovery (Brunton & Thornton, 2010), and approaches which incorporate art, games and experiential learning underpinned by normative terms and questions, allows younger children to demonstrate their thinking in both verbal and non-verbal ways and engage with ethical ideas of what makes something in a scientific context just or fair, right or wrong.

As children progress through the primary years, we have shown how ethical frameworks, dialogic talk and multi-model approaches to science, such as using concept cartoons, drama and puppets, can develop children's argumentation skills and enable them to engage in thinking ethically about socio-scientific issues in both formal and informal learning environments. We note in Chapter 8 Egan's (1993) proposed stage model of children's cognitive development – the Mythic and Romantic understanding of children's minds – which stresses children's imaginative development. It argues that young children are drawn to stories of a mythical kind, underpinned by ethical values such as good and evil, bravery and cowardice, fairness and selfishness, and demonstrates how story books can be utilized to engage younger pupils with ethical thinking in science. We also note how authentic informal learning environments, such as Forest School, can develop skills of argumentation by giving children opportunities to assess and analyse risk and judge the best course of action to be taken by evaluating the evidence at hand as well as the impact this might have on various stakeholders. This can all be achieved whilst children learn to justify their thinking, ideally, as they get older, within an established ethical framework, with a view to taking action and evaluating the impact of this.

We have shown that these approaches can also be extended to deepen the ethical decision-making skills of older learners when negotiating controversial issues in science. A number of projects provide an in-depth framework for teachers to take an integrated approach to enquiry-based learning via engagement with authentic socio-scientific issues. The use of drama as a pedagogical approach to enable older students to contextualize the ethical dimensions of science, stressing the importance of using presentational and experiential drama to foster higher-order thinking skills, can be highly effective. Drama can be a powerful resource for enabling students to feel more connected to the core element of ethical reasoning, moving students from initial naïve responses to using knowledge, argument and evidence to justify their decision. With regard to informal learning environments, we have argued that there can be a number of benefits to students, including motivation to learn science.

In presenting these arguments and case studies we assert that science educators, whatever the age of their learners, do not need to have had prior training in ethics education in order to include ethics in science education. It is encouraging that school science curricula across the world are slowly incorporating the engagement of critical ethical thinking as an approach for students to better understand the nature of science and argumentation, as well as negotiating socio-scientific issues in both formal and non-formal learning environments.

References

Chapter 1

Bazzul, J. (2016). *Ethics and Science Education: How Subjectivity Matters*. Dordrecht: Springer.
Bryant, J. A. & La Velle, L. (2019). *Introduction to Bioethics*, 2nd edn. Hoboken NJ: Wiley.
Food and Agriculture Organization of the United Nations (2021). *Sustainable food and agriculture*. https://www.fao.org/sustainability/news/detail/en/c/1274219/.
Jones, A., McKim, A. & Reiss, M. (Eds.) (2010). *Ethics in the Science and Technology Classroom: A New Approach to Teaching and Learning*. Rotterdam: Sense.
Levinson, R. & Reiss, M. J. (Eds.) (2003). *Key Issues in Bioethics: A Guide for Teachers*. London: RoutledgeFalmer.
Rudolph, J. L. (2023). *Why We Teach Science (and Why We Should)*. Oxford: Oxford University Press.
Saxena, A. (2019). *Ethics in Science: Pedagogic Issues and Concerns*. Singapore: Springer Nature.
Turvey, S. T. & Crees, J. J. (2019). Extinction in the Anthropocene. *Current Biology*, 29(19), R982–R986.
Wageningen University (2020). *Oil palm*. https://perennialcrops.wur.nl/oil-palm.
Wilmott, C. & Macip, S. (2016) *Where Science and Ethics Meet: Dilemmas at the Frontiers of Medicine and Biology*. Santa Barbara CA: Praeger.
World Wide Fund for Nature (2020). *How many species are we losing?* https://wwf.panda.org/discover/our_focus/biodiversity/biodiversity/.

Chapter 2

Akmal, M., Zulkifle, M. & Ansari, A. (2010). Ibn Nafis – a forgotten genius in the discovery of pulmonary blood circulation. *Heart Views*, 11(1), 26–30.
Albertr, L. H. (1986). 'Scientific' Creationism as a pseudoscience. *Creation/Evolution Journal*, 6(2), 26–35. https://ncse.ngo/scientific-creationism-pseudoscience.
Anon (2007). Neolithic Vinca was a metallurgical culture. *Archaeo News*, 17 November. https://www.stonepages.com/news/archives/002605.html.
Bates, C. & Rowell, A. (2004). *Tobacco Explained … The Truth about the Tobacco Industry … in Its Own Words*. San Francisco: University of California Center for Tobacco Control Research and Education. https://escholarship.org/uc/item/9fp6566b.

Bazerman, C. (Ed.) (2008). *Handbook of Research on Writing: History, Society, School, Individual, Text*. New York: Lawrence Erlbaum.

Boudry, M. & Pigliucci, M. (Eds.) (2018). *Science Unlimited? The Challenges of Scientism*. Chicago: University of Chicago Press.

Briggs, A. & Reiss, M. J. (2021). *Human Flourishing: Scientific Insight and Spiritual Wisdom in Uncertain Times*. Oxford: Oxford University Press.

Brown, P. (1991). Science: Controversy over origin of AIDS. *New Scientist, 1797* (30 November). https://www.newscientist.com/article/mg13217973-200-science-controversy-over-origin-of-aids/.

CNN (2021). *Overview*. http://cdn.cnn.com/cnn/2021/images/09/15/rel5e.-.elections.pdf.

Efron, B. (1998). R. A. Fisher in the 21st century (Invited paper presented at the 1996 R. A. Fisher Lecture). *Statistical Science, 13*(2), 95–122.

Enders, A. M., Uscinski, J. E., Seelig, M. I. Klofstad, C. A., Wuchty, S., Funchion, J. R., Murthi, M. N., Premaratne, K. & Stoler, J. (2021). The relationship between social media use and beliefs in conspiracy theories and misinformation. *Political Behavior*. https://doi.org/10.1007/s11109-021-09734-6.

Erduran, S. & Dagher, Z. R. (2014). *Reconceptualizing the Nature of Science for Science Education: Scientific Knowledge, Practices and Other Family Categories*. Dordrecht: Springer.

Feyerabend, P. (1993). *Against Method, 3rd edn*. London: Verso.

Fisher, R. (1958). Cigarettes, cancer, and statistics. *The Centennial Review of Arts & Science, 2*, 151–66.

Fisher R. A. (1959). *Smoking – The Cancer Controversy; Some Attempts to Assess the Evidence*. Edinburgh: Oliver and Boyd.

Flood, A. (2017). Fake news is 'very real' word of the year for 2017. *The Guardian, 2 November*. https://www.theguardian.com/books/2017/nov/02/fake-news-is-very-real-word-of-the-year-for-2017.

Hansson, S. O. (2021). Science and pseudo-science. In: Zalta, E. N. (Ed.), *The Stanford Encyclopedia of Philosophy*, https://plato.stanford.edu/archives/fall2021/entries/pseudo-science/.

Hecker, S., Haklay, M., Bowser, A., Makuch, Z., Vogel, J. & Bonn, A. (2018). *Citizen Science: Innovation in Open Science, Society and Policy*. London: UCL Press.

Horton, R. (2021). The origin story – division deepens. *The Lancet, 18–25 December*, 2221.

Huber, B., Barnidge, M., Gil de Zúñiga, H. & Liu, J. (2019). Fostering public trust in science: The role of social media. *Public Understanding of Science, 28*(7), 759–77.

Hur, J. (2019). *The history of gold*. https://bebusinessed.com/history/the-history-of-gold/.

Irzik, G. & Nola, R. (2011). A family resemblance approach to the Nature of Science for science education. *Science & Education, 20*, 591–607.

Kampourakis, K. (2016). The 'general aspects' conceptualization as a pragmatic and effective means of introducing students to the nature of science. *Journal of Research in Science Teaching, 53*, 667–82.

Keyes R. (2004). *The Post-truth Era: Dishonesty and Deception in Contemporary Life*. New York, NY: St Martin's Press.

Khanijahani, A., Calhoun, B. & Kiel, J. (2021). Internet use habits and influenza vaccine uptake among US adults: Results from seven years (2012–2018) of the National Health Interview Survey. *Public Health, 195*, 76–82.

Kuhn, T. S. (1970). *The Structure of Scientific Revolutions, 2nd edn*. Chicago: University of Chicago Press.

Lederman, N. G. (1992). Students' and teachers' conceptions of the nature of science: A review of the research. *Journal of Research in Science Teaching, 29*(4), 331–59.

Lederman, N. G. (2007). Nature of science: Past, present and future. In: Abell, S. K. & Lederman, N. G. (Eds.), *Handbook of Research on Science Education*, 831–79. Mahwah, NJ: Lawrence Erlbaum.

Liberatore, A., Bowkett, E., MacLeod, C.J., Spurr, E. & Longnecker, N. (2018). Social media as a platform for a citizen science community of practice. *Citizen Science. Theory and Practice*, *3*(1), 3, 1–14.

Marinković, S., Lazić, D., Kanjuh, V., Valjarević, S., Tomić, I., Aksić, M. & Starčević, A. (2014). Heart in anatomy history, radiology, anthropology and art. *Folia Morphologica*, *73*(2), 103–12.

Matthews, M. R. (2012). Changing the focus: From Nature of Science (NOS) to Features of Science (FOS). In: Khine, M. (Ed.), *Advances in Nature of Science Research*, 3–26. Dordrecht: Springer.

McComas, W. F. (2020). Considering a consensus view of Nature of Science content for school science purposes. In: McComas, W. F. (Ed.), *Nature of Science in Science Instruction*, 23–34. Cham: Springer.

Merton, R. K. (1973). *The Sociology of Science: Theoretical and Empirical Investigations*. Chicago: University of Chicago Press.

Pedersen, E. A., Loft, L. H., Jacobsen, S. U., Søborg, B. & Bigaard, J. (2020). Strategic health communication on social media: Insights from a Danish social media campaign to address HPV vaccination hesitancy. *Vaccine*, *38*(31), 4909–15.

Popper, K. R. (1934/1972). *The Logic of Scientific Discovery*. London: Hutchinson.

Putnam, R. D. (1995). Bowling alone: America's declining social capital. *Journal of Democracy*, *6*(1), 65–78.

Regulski, I. (2016). The origins and early development of writing in Egypt. *Oxford Handbooks Online*. https://www.oxfordhandbooks.com/view/10.1093/oxfordhb/9780199935413.001.0001/oxfordhb-9780199935413-e-61.

Reiss, M. J. (1993). *Science Education for a Pluralist Society*. Milton Keynes: Open University Press.

Reiss, M. J. (2018). Creationism and Intelligent Design. In: Smeyers, P. (Ed.), *International Handbook of Philosophy of Education*, 1247–59. Dordrecht: Springer.

Reiss, M. J. (in press). The Nature of Science. In: Hetherington, L., Luke, G. & Moore, D. (Eds.), *Learning to Teach Science in the Secondary School: A Companion to School Experience*, 5th edn, Abingdon: Routledge.

Sharp, P. M. & Hahn, B. H. (2011). Origins of HIV and the AIDS pandemic. *Cold Spring Harbor Perspectives in Medicine*, *1*(1): a006841.

Silvertown, J. (2009). A new dawn for citizen science. *Trends in Ecology & Evolution*, *24*(9), 467–71.

Stolley, P. D. (1991). When genius errs: R. A. Fisher and the lung cancer controversy. *American Journal of Epidemiology*, *133*(5), 416–25.

Temple, R. (1991). *The Genius of China: 3000 Years of Science, Discovery, and Invention*. London: Prion/Multimedia.

Thielking, M. (2015). How Linus Pauling duped America into believing vitamin C cures colds. *Vox*, *27 February*. https://www.vox.com/2015/1/15/7547741/vitamin-c-myth-pauling.

Wittgenstein, L. (1958). *Philosophical Investigations*. Blackwell: Oxford.

Chapter 3

Aristotle (1925). Nicomachean Ethics, in *The Works of Aristotle* Translated into English, Vol. 9, translated by W. D. Ross. Oxford: Oxford Trinity Press.

Audi, R. (2007). *Moral Value and Human Diversity*. New York: Oxford University Press.

Barrett, M. (2014). *Women's Oppression Today: The Marxist/feminist Encounter*. London: Verso Books.

Bartal, I. B. A., Decety, J. & Mason, P. (2011). Empathy and pro-social behaviour in rats. *Science*, *334*(6061), 1427–30.

Bartky, S. L. (2015). *Femininity and Domination: Studies in the Phenomenology of Oppression*. New York: Routledge.
Bentham, J. (1789). *An Introduction to the Principles of Morals and Legislation*. Buffalo, NY: Prometheus Books.
Bhabha, H. K. (2012). *The Location of Culture*. London and New York: Routledge.
Blackburn, S. (2001). *Ethics: A Very Short Introduction*. Oxford: Oxford University Press.
Bradley, S. T. (2021). The ethics and politics of addressing health Inequalities. *Clinical Medicine* (21), 2, 147–9.
Briggs, A. & Reiss, M. J. (2021). *Human Flourishing: Scientific Insight and Spiritual Wisdom in Uncertain Times*. Oxford: Oxford University Press.
Cudd, A. E. (2006). *Analyzing Oppression*. Oxford: Oxford University Press.
Curry, O. S., Mullins, D. A. & Whitehouse, H. (2019). Is it good to cooperate? Testing the theory of morality-as-cooperation in 60 societies. *Current Anthropology, 60*(1), 47–69.
Dahlsgaard, K., Peterson, C. & Seligman, M. E. P. (2005). Shared virtue: The convergence of valued human strengths across culture and history. *Review of General Psychology, 9*(3), 203–13.
Das Neves, J. C., & Melé, D. (2013). Managing ethically cultural diversity: learning from Thomas Aquinas. *Journal of Business Ethics* 116(4), 769–780.
Dreiser, J. (Ed.) (2006). *Contemporary Debates in Moral Theory*. Oxford: Blackwell.
Friere, P. (1970). *Pedagogy of the Oppressed*. New York: Continuum.
Gardiner, S. M. (2006). A perfect moral storm: Climate change, intergenerational ethics and the problem of moral corruption. *Environmental Values, 15*(3), 397–413.
Gowans, C. (2012). Moral relativism. In E. N. Zalta (Eds.) *The Stanford encyclopedia of philosophy* (http://plato.stanford.edu/archives/spr2012/entries/moralrelativism/.
Groves, C. (2014). *Care, uncertainty and intergenerational ethics*. London: Palgrave Macmillan.
Haidt, J. (2008). Morality. *Perspectives on Psychological Science, 3*(1), 65–72.
Jia, F. & Krettenauer, T. (2017). Recognizing moral identity as a cultural construct. *Frontiers in Psychology, 8*, 412.
Jones, A., McKim, A. & Reiss, M. J. (2010). *Ethics in the Science and Technology Classroom: A New Approach to Teaching and Learning*. Rotterdam: Sense.
Kant, I. (1797) *The Metaphysics of Morals*. Die Metaphysik der Sitten by Friedrich Ricolovius in Konigsberg.
Knowles, G. & Lander, V. (2012). *Thinking through Ethics and Values in Primary Education*. London: Sage Learning Matters.
Krausz, M. (Ed.) (1989). *Relativism. Interpretation and Confrontation*. Notre Dame, IN: Notre Dame University Press.
Leopold, A. (2017). The land ethic. In: Brennan, A. (Ed.), *The Ethics of the Environment*, 99–113. Aldershot: Dartmouth.
Marino, L. (2017). Thinking chickens: a review of cognition, emotion, and behavior in the domestic chicken. *Animal cognition, 20*(2), 127–47.
Naess, A. (1973). The shallow and the deep, long-range ecology movement. *Inquiry, 16*(1), 95–100.
Palmer, G. L., Fernandez, J. S., Lee, G., Masud, H., Hilson, S., Tang, C., Thomas, D., Clark, L., Guzman, B., & Bernai, I. (2019). Oppression and power. In Jason, L. A., Glantsman, O., O'Brien, J. F., & Ramian, K. N. *Introduction to Community Psychology*. Montreal: Rebus Community.
Shafer-Landau R (Ed) 2013. *Ethical theory: An Anthology* (2nd edn). Malden, MA: Wiley-Blackwell.
Shweder, R. A. (2000). Moral maps, 'first world' conceits, and the New Evangelists. In: *Culture Matters, How Values Shape Human Progress*. New York: Basic Books.
Taylor, P. W. (2011). *Respect for Nature: A Theory of Environmental Ethics*. Princeton: Princeton University Press.

Whitehouse, H. (2004). *Modes of Religiosity: A Cognitive Theory of Religious Transmission*. Lanham MD: AltaMira.

Yang, T. (2006). Towards an egalitarian global environmental ethics. *Environmental Ethics and International Policy*, 8, 23–45.

Chapter 4

Abrahams, I. & Millar, R. (2008). Does practical work really work? A study of the effectiveness of practical work as a teaching and learning method in school science. *International Journal of Science Education*, 30(14), 1945–69.

Abrahams, I. & Reiss, M. J. (2012). Practical work: Its effectiveness in primary and secondary schools in England. *Journal of Research in Science Teaching*, 49, 1035–55.

Aikenhead, G. S. (2007). Expanding the research agenda for scientific literacy. In: Linder, C. et al. (Eds.), *Promoting Scientific Literacy: Science Education Research in Transaction*, 64–71. Uppsala: Geotryckeriet.

AQA (2008a). *AQA Advanced Level Religious Studies Unit 4: An Introduction to Religion and Ethics*. Manchester: AQA.

AQA (2008b). *AQA Advanced Level Religious Studies Unit 4: An Introduction to Religion and Ethics – Mark Scheme*. Manchester: AQA.

Beck, U. (1986/1992). *Risk Society: Towards a New Modernity*, translated by Mark Ritter. London: SAGE.

Bennett, J. (2003). *Teaching and Learning Science: A Guide to Recent Research and Its Applications*. London: Continuum.

Bennett, J., Lubben, F. & Hogarth, S. (2007). Bringing science to life: A synthesis of the research evidence on the effects of context-based and STS approaches to science teaching. *Science Education*, 91(3), 347–70.

Carpendale, J. I. M. (2009). Piaget's theory of moral development. In: Müller, U., Carpendale, J. I. M. & Smith, L. (Eds.), *The Cambridge Companion to Piaget*, 270–86. Cambridge: Cambridge University Press.

Davis, N. R. & Schaeffer, J. (2019). Troubling troubled waters in elementary science education: Politics, ethics & Black children's conceptions of water [justice] in the era of Flint. *Cognition and Instruction*, 37(3), 367–89.

Department for Education (2015). *Statutory Guidance – National Curriculum in England: Science Programmes of Study*. https://www.gov.uk/government/publications/national-curriculum-in-england-science-programmes-of-study/national-curriculum-in-england-science-programmes-of-study.

Gibbs, J. C. (2019). *Moral Development and Reality: Beyond the Theories of Kohlberg, Hoffman, and Haidt*. Oxford: Oxford University Press.

Gilligan, C. (1982). *In a Different Voice*. Cambridge, MA: Harvard University Press.

Guerrero, G. R. & Torres-Olave, B. (2021). Scientific literacy and agency within the Chilean science curriculum: A critical discourse analysis. *The Curriculum Journal*. https://doi.org/10.1002/curj.141.

Haraway, D. J. (2016). *Staying with the Trouble: Making Kin in the Chthulucene*. Durham NC: Duke University Press.

Hodson, D. (1990). A critical look at practical work in school science. *School Science Review*, 70(256), 33–40.

Hodson, D. (1994). Seeking directions for change: The personalisation and politicisation of science education. *Curriculum Studies*, 2(1), 71–98.

Kohlberg, L. (1958). *The Development of Modes of Thinking and Choices in Years 10 to 16*, PhD Dissertation. Chicago: University of Chicago.

Liverpool Life Sciences UTC (2021). *Plastic Lunch: Can Mealworms Digest Plastic Waste?* https://researchinschools.org/case-studies/young-researchers-investigate-if-mealworms-can-digest-plastic/.

Mansfield, J. & Reiss, M. J. (2020). The place of values in the aims of school science education. In: Corrigan, D., Buntting, C., Fitzgerald, A. & Jones, A. (Eds.), *Values in Science Education*, 191–209. Cham: Springer.

National Geographic (2019). *Water Inequality*. https://www.nationalgeographic.org/article/water-inequality/.

Nuffield Foundation (2009). *Assessing Ethics in Secondary Science: A Report of a Seminar Held at the Nuffield Foundation*. London: Nuffield Foundation. Available at https://www.nuffieldfoundation.org/sites/default/files/files/Assessing_Ethics_in_Secondary_Science(1).pdf.

Ofsted (2021). *Research Review Series: Science*. https://www.gov.uk/government/publications/research-review-series-science/research-review-series-science#fnref: 6.

Pearson Edexcel (2018). *Pearson Edexcel Level 3 Advanced GCE in Biology* A *(Salters-Nuffield) Specification – Issue 4*. https://qualifications.pearson.com/content/dam/pdf/A%20Level/biology-a/2015/specification-and-sample-assessment-materials/9781446930885_GCE2015_A_BioA_spec.pdf.

Piaget, J. (1932). *The Moral Judgment of the Child*. London: Kegan Paul, Trench, Trubner and Co.

Reiss, M. J. (2010). Ethical thinking. In: Jones, A., McKim, A. & Reiss, M. (Eds.), *Ethics in the Science and Technology Classroom: A New Approach to Teaching and Learning*, 7–17. Rotterdam: Sense.

Reiss, M. J. (2018). The curriculum arguments of Michael Young and John White. In: *Sociology, Curriculum Studies and Professional Knowledge: New Perspectives on the Work of Michael Young*, Guile, D., Lambert & Reiss, M. J. (Eds.), 121–31. Abingdon: Routledge.

Reiss, M. J. & White, J. (2013). *An Aims-Based Curriculum: The Significance of Human Flourishing for Schools*. London: IOE Press.

Reiss, M. J. & White, J. (2014). An aims-based curriculum illustrated by the teaching of science in schools. *The Curriculum Journal*, 25, 76–89.

Roberts, D. A. (2007). Scientific literacy/science literacy. In: Abell, S. K. & Lederman, N. G. (Eds.), *Handbook of Research on Science Education*, 729–80. Mahwah, NJ: Lawrence Erlbaum.

Roberts, D. A. & Bybee, R. W. (2014). Scientific literacy, science literacy, and science education. In: Lederman, N. G. & Abell, S. K. (Eds.), *Handbook of Research on Science Education, Volume II*, 559–72. New York: Routledge.

Roth, W. M. & Barton, A. C. (2004). *Rethinking Scientific Literacy*. New York: RoutledgeFalmer.

Sjöström, J. & Eilks, I. (2018). Reconsidering different visions of scientific literacy and science education based on the concept of *Bildung*. In: Dori, Y. J., Mevarech, Z. R. & Baker, D. R. (Eds.), *Cognition, Metacognition, and Culture in STEM Education*, 65–88. Cham: Springer.

Tolppanen, S., Jäppinen, I., Kärkkäinen, S., Salonen, A. & Keinonen, T. (2019). Relevance of life-cycle assessment in context-based science education: A case study in lower secondary school. *Sustainability*, *11*(21), 5877.

Valladares, L. (2021). Scientific literacy and social transformation. *Science & Education*, 30, 557–87.

Young, M. F. D. (2008). *Bringing Knowledge Back in: From Social Constructivism to Social Realism in the Sociology of Knowledge*. London: Routledge.

Young, M. (2014). Knowledge, curriculum and the future school. In: Young, M. & Lambert, D. with Roberts, C. & Roberts, M. (Eds.), *Knowledge and the Future School: Curriculum and Social Justice*, 9–40. London: Bloomsbury.

Chapter 5

Aronfreed, J. (1976). Moral development from the standpoint of a general psychological theory. In Lickona, T. (Ed.), *Moral Development and Behavior*, 54–69. New York: Holt, Rinehart & Wilson.

Bandura, A. (1977). *Social Learning Theory*. Englewood Cliffs, NJ: Prentice-Hall.

Beck, C. (1990). *Better Schools: A Values Perspective*. Falmer Press, Taylor & Francis.

Chandler, M. J., Greenspan, S. & Barenboim, C. (1973). Judgments of intentionality in response to videotaped and verbally presented moral dilemmas: The medium is the message. *Child Development* (44), 315–20.

Clifford, M. (2009). The psychoanalytic view of teaching and learning. *Journal of Curriculum Studies*, 41(4), 539–67.

Damon, W. (1977). *The Social World of the Child*. San Francisco: Jossey-Bass.

Damon, W. (1988). *The Moral Child: Nurturing Children's Natural Moral Growth*. New York: Free Press.

Doise, W. (1990). Social representations. In: Bonnet, C., Ghiglione, R., & Richard, T. F. (Eds.), *Treatise on Cognitive Psychology*, 3, 111–74. Paris: Dunod.

Dunn, J. (2013). Moral development in early childhood and social interaction in the family. In: Killen, M. & Smetana, J. G. (Eds.), *Handbook of Moral Development*, 135–59. New York, NY: Psychology Press.

Edwards, C. P. (1987). Culture and the construction of moral values: A comparative ethnology of moral encounters in two cultural settings. In: J. Kagan & S. Lamb (Eds.), *The Emergence of Morality in Young Children*, 123–50. Chicago: University of Chicago Press.

Edwards, D. (1997). Supervision today: the psychoanalytic legacy. In: Shipton, G. (Ed.), *Supervision of Psychotherapy and Counselling: Making a Place to Think*, 11–23. Milton Keynes: Open University Press.

Ferguson, T. J. & Rule, B. G. (1982). Influence of inferential set, outcome intent, and outcome severity on children's moral judgments. *Developmental Psychology*, 18(6), 843.

Freud, S. (1938). *An Outline of Psycho-Analysis*. (SE 23), 141–207.

Garbarino, J. & Bronfenbrenner, U. (1976). The socialization of moral judgment and behavior in cross-cultural perspective. In: Lickona, T. (Ed.), *Moral Development and Behaviour*, 70–83. New York: Holt, Rinehart & Winston.

Gibson, J. J. (1979). *The Ecological Approach to Visual Perception*. Boston: Houghton Mifflin.

Gilligan, C. (1982). New maps of development: new visions of maturity. *American Journal of Orthopsychiatry*, 52(2), 199–212.

Halstead, J. M. & Taylor, M. J. (2000). Learning and teaching about values: A review of recent research. *Cambridge Journal of Education*, 30(2), 169–202.

Havighurst, R. J. & Neugarten, B. L. (1955). *American Indian and White Children: A Sociopsychological Investigation*. Chicago: University of Chicago Press.

Hoffman, M. L. (1976). Empathy, role-taking, guilt, and development of altruistic motives. In: Lickona, T. (Ed.), *Moral Development of Behaviour: Theory, Research and Social Issues*, 124–43. New York: Holt, Rinehart and Winston.

Hoffman, M.I. (1979) Development of moral thought, feeling, and behaviour. *American Psychologist*, 34(10), 958.

Hoffman, M. L. (1991). Empathy, social cognition and moral action. In: Kurtines, W. M. & Gewirtz, J. L. (Eds.), *Handbook of Moral Behaviour and Development*, 275–301. London: Taylor & Francis.

Howes, C. (2009). Friendship in early childhood. In: Rubin, K. H., Bukowski, W. M. & Laursen, B. (Eds.), *Handbook of Peer Interactions, Relationships and Groups*, 180–94. New York, NY: Guilford Press.

Kim, M. & Sankey, D. (2009). Towards a dynamic systems approach to moral development and moral education: a response to the JME Special Issue, September 2008. *Journal of Moral Education*, *38*(3), 283–98.

Kohlberg, L. (1958). *The Development of Modes of Moral Thinking and Choice in the Years 10 to 16*. Unpublished doctoral dissertation, University of Chicago.

Kohlberg, L. (1963). Moral development and identification. In: H. W. Stevenson, N. B. Henry, & H. G. Richey (Eds.), *Child Psychology: The Sixty-Second Yearbook of the National Society for the Study of Education*, Part 1, 277–332. Chicago, IL: National Society for the Study of Education.

Kohlberg, L. (1976). Moral stages and moralisation: The cognitive development approach. In: Lickona, T. (Ed.), *Moral Development and Behaviour: Theory, Research, and Social Issues*, 31–53. New York: Holt, Rinehart and Winston.

Kohlberg, L. (1978). Revisions in the theory and practice of moral development. *New Directions for Child and Adolescent Development*, *1978*(2), 83–87.

Kruger, A. C. (1992). The effect of peer and adult-child transactive discussions on moral reasoning. *Merrill-Palmer Quarterly* (38), 191–2.

Langford, P. E. (1995). *Approaches to the Development of Moral Reasoning*. New York: Psychology Press.

Lei, T. & Cheng, S. W. (1984). An empirical study of Kohlberg's theory and scoring system of moral judgment in Chinese society. *Unpublished manuscript, Harvard University, Cambridge, MA*.

Maccoby, E. E. (1980). *Social Development: Psychological Growth and the Parent-Child Relationship*. New York: Harcourt Brace Jovanovich.

Mammen, M., Köymen, B. & Tomasello, M. (2021). Young children's moral judgments depend on the social relationship between agents. *Cognitive Development*, *57*, 100973.

Matthews, G. (1980). *Philosophy and the Young Child*. Cambridge, MA: Harvard University Press.

Nucci, L. P., Narvaez, D. & Krettenauer, T. (Eds.) (2014). *Handbook of Moral and Character Education*. New York: Routledge.

Núñez, M. & Harris, P. L. 1998). Psychological and Deontic Concepts: Separate Domains or Intimate Connection? *Mind & Language*, *13*(2), 153–70.

Nunner-Winkler, G. (2007). Development of moral motivation from childhood to early adulthood. *Journal of Moral Education*, *36*(4), 399–414.

Piaget, J. (1965). *The Moral Judgement of the Child*, translated by M. Gabain. New York: Free Press.

Pritchard, M. (2022). Philosophy for Children. In *Stanford Encyclopedia of Philosophy*. https://plato.stanford.edu/entries/children/.

Rest, J. R. (1979). *Development in Judging Moral Issues*. Minneapolis: University of Minneapolis Press.

Rest, J. R. (1985). An interdisciplinary approach to moral education. In: Berkowitz, M. W. & Oser, F. (Eds.), *Moral Education: Theory and Application*, 9–27. Hillsdale, NJ: L. Erlbaum.

Rest, J. R. (1986). *Moral Development: Advances in Research and Theory*. New York: Praeger Press.

Sankey, D. & Kim, M. (2009). Cultivating Moral Values in an Age of Neuroscience. In: Joldersama, C. W. (Ed.), *Neuroscience and Education: A Philosophical Appraisal*, 111–27. New York: Routledge.

Shweder, R. A. & Much, N. C. (1987). *Determinations of Meaning: Discourse and Moral Socialization*. Hoboken NJ: John Wiley & Sons.

Smetana, J. G. (2006). Social–cognitive domain theory: Consistencies and variations in children's moral and social judgments. In: Killen, M (Ed.), *Handbook of Moral Development*, 137–72. New York, NY: Psychology Press.

Snarey, J., Reimer, J. & Kohlberg, L. (1985). The kibbutz as a model for moral education: A longitudinal cross-cultural study. *Journal of Applied Developmental Psychology*, 6(2–3), 151–72.

Turiel, E. (1998). The development of morality. In: Damon, W. (Series Ed.) & N. Eisenberg (Vol. Ed.), *Handbook of Child Psychology*, Vol. 3: Social, emotional, and personality development (5th ed., 863–932). New York: Wiley.

Turiel, E. (2006). Thought, emotions, and social interactional processes in moral development. In: Killen, M. & Smetana, J. G. (Eds.), *Handbook of Moral Development*, 7–35. Mahwah, NJ: Lawrence Erlbaum.

Walker, L.J. (1989). A longitudinal study of moral reasoning. *Child Development*, 157–66.

Walker, L. J. (2006). Gender and morality. In Killen, M. & Smetana, J. G. (Eds.), *Handbook of Moral Development*, 111–34. New York, NY: Psychology Press.

Walker, L. J., de Vries, B. & Trevethan, S. D. (1987). Moral stages and moral orientations in real-life and hypothetical dilemmas. *Child Development* (58), 842–58.

Watson, J. B. (1919). A schematic outline of the emotions. *Psychological Review*, 26(3), 165.

Whiting, B. B., & Whiting, J. W. M. (1975). *Children of Six Cultures: A Psycho-Cultural Analysis*. Cambridge, MA: Harvard University Press.

Wolff, S. & Smith, R. A. A. M. (2000). Child homicide and the law: implications of the judgements of the European Court of Human Rights in the case of the children who killed James Bulger. *Child Psychology and Psychiatry Review*, 5(3), 133–8.

Wright, D. (1992) Towards an adequate conception of early moral development." In Rogers, C and Kutnick, P. (eds) *The Social Psychology of the Primary School*, 143–155. New York: Routledge.

Youniss, J. (1988). *Mutuality in Parent-Adolescent Relationships: Social Capital for Impending Adulthood*. Washington DC: William T. Grant Foundation Commission on Work, Family and Citizenship.

Youniss, J. (1999). Children's friendships and peer culture. *Making Sense of Social Development* (38), 13–26.

Yuill, N. & Perner, J. (1988). Intentionality and knowledge in children's judgments of actor's responsibility and recipient's emotional reaction. *Developmental Psychology*, 24(3), 358.

Chapter 6

Abrahams, I. & Reiss, M. (2012). Evolution. In: *The Routledge International Handbook of Learning*, Jarvis, P. with Watts, M. (Eds.), 411–18. Abingdon: Routledge.

BIO (2010). *All about Animal Cloning*. https://www.bio.org/sites/default/files/legacy/bioorg/docs/files/Cloning_onepager.pdf.

Bryant, J. A. & La Velle, L. (2019). *Introduction to Bioethics*, 2nd edn. Hoboken, NJ: Wiley Blackwell.

Carlsson, L., Williams, P. L., Hayes-Conroy, J. S., Lordly, D. & Callaghan, E. (2016). School gardens: Cultivating food security in Nova Scotia public schools? *Canadian Journal of Dietetic Practice and Research*, 77(3), 119–24.

Cerini, B., Murray, I. & Reiss, M. (2003). *Student Review of the Science Curriculum: Major Findings*. London: Planet Science. Available at https://www.academia.edu/40836145/Student_Review_of_the_Science_Curriculum_Major_Findings.

Chowdhury, M. (2018). Emphasizing morals, values, ethics, and character education in science education and science teaching. *MOJES: Malaysian Online Journal of Educational Sciences*, 4(2), 1–16.

Chowning, J. T., Griswold, J. C., Kovarik, D. N. & Collins, L. J. (2012). Fostering critical thinking, reasoning, and argumentation skills through bioethics education. *PloS ONE*, 7(5), e36791.

CIWF (2022). *Cloning = Cruelty*. https://www.ciwf.org.uk/our-campaigns/other-campaigns/cloning/.
DCSF (2007). *Guidance on Creationism and Intelligent Design*. Available at https://humanists.uk/wp-content/uploads/1sja-creationism-guidance-180907-final.pdf.
Deane-Drummond, C. (2008). *The Ethics of Nature*. New York: John Wiley & Sons.
Donnelly, J. (2002). Instrumentality, hermeneutics and the place of science in the school curriculum. *Science & Education*, *11*(2), 135–53.
Gola, B. (2017). Is formal environmental education friendly to nature? Environmental ethics in science textbooks for primary school pupils in Poland. *Ethics and Education*, *12*(3), 320–36.
Gopnik, A., Meltzoff, A. N. & Kuhl, P. K. (1999). *The Scientist in the Crib: Minds, Brains, and How Children Learn*. New York: William Morrow & Co.
Goswami, U. (2008). *Cognitive Development: The Learning Brain*. Hove: Psychology Press.
Goswami, U. (2015). *Children's Cognitive Development and Learning*. Cambridge: Cambridge Primary Review Trust.
Hume, D. (1739). *A Treatise of Human Nature*. London: John Noon.
Levinson, R. & Turner, S. (2001). *Valuable Lessons: Engaging with the Social Context of Science in Schools*. London: Wellcome Trust. Available at https://wellcome.org/sites/default/files/wtd003446_0.pdf.
Ozer, E. J. (2007). The effects of school gardens on students and schools: Conceptualization and considerations for maximizing healthy development. *Health Education & Behavior*, *34*(6), 846–63.
Pennock, R. T. (2019). *An Instinct for Truth: Curiosity and the Moral Character of Science*. Cambridge, MA: MIT Press.
QCA (2006). *How Can We Answer Questions about Creation and Origins? Learning from Religion and Science: Christianity, Hinduism, Islam and Humanism – Year 9*. York: Qualifications and Curriculum Authority. Available at https://www.natre.org.uk/resources/qca-unit-of-work-for-key-stage-3-year-9/.
Reiss, M. J. (1997). Seeking values in science. *Questions of Maths and Science*, *4*, 28–30.
Reiss, M. J. (1999). Teaching ethics in science. *Studies in Science Education*, *34*, 115–40.
Reiss, M. J. (2022). Learning to teach controversial topics. In: Luft, J. A. & Jones, M. G. (Eds.), *Handbook of Research on Science Teacher Education*, 393–403. New York: Routledge.
Ryder, J. & Banner, I. (2013). School teachers' experiences of science curriculum reform. *International Journal of Science Education*, *35*(3), 490–514.
Saxena, A. (2019). *Ethics in Science: Pedagogic Issues and Concerns*. Singapore: Springer.
Schwartz, B. (2022). Science, scholarship, and intellectual virtues: A guide to what higher education should be like. *Journal of Moral Education*, *51*(1), 61–72.
Teke, H. (2021). Making ethics teaching more effective with a three step model. *International Journal of Ethics Education*, *6*, 149–62.
The P4C Co-operative (2022). https://p4c.com.
Willmott, C. & Macip, S. (2016). *Where Science and Ethics Meet: Dilemmas at the Frontiers of Medicine and Biology*. Santa Barbara, CA: Praeger.

Chapter 7

Archer, L., Dawson, E., DeWitt, J., Seakins, A. & Wong, B. (2015). 'Science capital': A conceptual, methodological, and empirical argument for extending Bourdieusian notions of capital beyond the arts. *Journal of Research in Science Teaching*, *52*(7), 922–48.
Bell, B. (2001). *Formative Assessment and Science Education*. Netherlands: Kluwer.

Biggs, J. & Collis, K. (1982). *Evaluating the Quality of Learning: The SOLO Taxonomy*. New York: Academic Press.

Briggs, L. (2007). *Tacking Wicked Problems: A Public Policy Perspective*. Australian Government, Commonwealth of Australia.

Bruner, J. (1960). *The Process of Education*. Cambridge, MA: Harvard University Press.

Bullock, J., Lane, J. E. & Shults, F. L. (2022). What causes COVID-19 vaccine hesitancy? Ignorance and the lack of bliss in the United Kingdom. *Humanities and Social Sciences Communications*, 9(1), 1–7.

Chandler, M. J., Greenspan, S. & Barenboim, C. (1973). Judgments of intentionality in response to videotaped and verbally presented moral dilemmas: The medium is the message. *Child Development*, 44(2), 315–20.

Chapman, A. & Wilschut, A. (Eds.) (2015). *Joined-Up History: New Directions in History of Education Research*. Charlotte NC: Information Age Publishing.

Claire, H. & Holden, C. (2007). *The Challenge of Teaching Controversial Issues*. Stoke-on-Trent: Trentham Books.

Damon, W. (1988). *The Moral Child: Nurturing Children's Moral Growth*. London: MacMillan.

Darwin, C. (1859). *On the Origin of Species by Means of Natural Selection, or the Preservation Favoured Races in the Struggle for Life*. London: John Murray.

Department for Education (2015). *National Curriculum in England: Science Programmes of Study*. Department for Education. https://www.gov.uk/government/publications/national-curriculum-in-england-science-programmes-of-study/national-curriculum-in-england-science-programmes-of-study.

Department of Health and Social Care & The Department of Education (2017). *Transforming Children and Young People's Mental Health Provision: A Green Paper:* https://www.gov.uk/government/consultations/transforming-children-and-young-peoples-mental-health-provision-a-green-paper

Dillion, J., Stevenson, R. B. & Wals, A. E. (2016). Introduction to the special section: Moving from citizen to civic science to address wicked conservation problems. *Conservation Biology*, 30(3), 450–5.

Dolan, T. J., Nichols, B. H. & Zeidler, D. L. (2009). Using socioscientific issues in primary classrooms. *Journal of Elementary Science Education*, 21(3), 1–12.

Donnelly, J. (2002). Instrumentality, hermeneutics and the place of science in the school curriculum. *Science & Education*, 11(2), 135–53.

Evagorou, M. (2011). Discussing a socioscientific issue in a primary school classroom: The case of using a technology-supported environment in formal and nonformal settings. In: *Socio-Scientific Issues in the Classroom*, 133–59. Dordrecht: Springer.

Fullam, J. (2017). Becoming a youth activist in the internet age: a case study on social media activism and identity development. *International Journal of Qualitative Studies in Education*, 30(4), 406–22.

Garrecht, C., Czinczel, B., Kretschmann, M. & Reiss, M. J. (2022). Should we be doing it, should we not be doing it, who could be harmed? *Science & Education*, 1–33.

Glazzard, J. (2018). The role of schools in supporting children and young people's mental health. *Education and Health*, 36(3), 83–8.

Godec, S., King, H. & Archer, L. (2017). *The Science Capital Teaching Approach: Engaging Students with Science, Promoting Social Justice*. UCL Institute of Education. London: UK.

Gormley, K., Birdsall, S. & France, B. (2019). Socio-scientific issues in primary schools. *Teaching and Learning*. 2019, DOI:10.18296/set.0139.

Great Britain (1988). *Education Reform Act*, 1988. London: HMSO.

Guile, D., Reiss, M. & Lambert, D. (2018). *Sociology, Curriculum Studies and Professional Knowledge*. Abingdon: Routledge.

Hall, E. (1999). Science Education and Social Responsibility. *School Science Review*, *81*(295), 14–16.

Hancock, T. S., Friedrichsen, P. J., Kinslow, A. T. & Sadler, T. D. (2019). Selecting socio-scientific issues for teaching. *Science & Education*, *28*(6), 639–67.

Harlen, W. (Ed.) (2010). *Principles and Big Ideas of Science Education*. Association for Science Education.

Harlen, W. (2009). *The Teaching of Science in Primary Schools*. London: David Fulton Publishers.

Hickman, C., Marks, E., Pihkala, P., Clayton, S., Lewandowski, R. E., Mayall, E. E., Wray, B., Mellor, C. & van Susteren, L. (2021). Climate anxiety in children and young people and their beliefs about government responses to climate change: a global survey. *The Lancet Planetary Health*, *5*(12), 863–73.

HMI (1995). *The Teaching of Controversial Issues in Schools*. London: Inner London Education Authority.

Hodson, D. (1999). Going beyond cultural pluralism: Science education for sociopolitical action. *Science education*, *83*(6), 775–96.

Kahn, S. & Zeidler, D. L. (2019). A conceptual analysis of perspective taking in support of socio-scientific reasoning. *Science & Education*, *28*(6), 605–38.

Kawa, N. C., Arceño, M. A., Goeckner, R., Hunter, C. E., Rhue, S. J., Scaggs, S. A., Biwer, M. E., Downey, S. S., Field, J. S., Gremillion, K. & McCorriston, J. (2021). Training wicked scientists for a world of wicked problems. *Humanities and Social Sciences Communications*, *8*(1), 1–4.

Killen, M., Smetana, J. G. & Smetana, J. (2006). Social–cognitive domain theory: Consistencies and variations in children's moral and social judgments. In *Handbook of Moral Development*. New York: Psychology Press.

Kohlberg, L. (1969). *Stage and Sequence: The Cognitive-Developmental Approach to Socialisation*, 347–480. New York: Rand McNally.

Kolstø, S. D. (2001). Scientific literacy for citizenship: Tools for dealing with the science dimension of controversial socioscientific issues. *Science Education*, *85*(3), 291–310.

Lambert, D. (2011). Reviewing the case for geography, and the 'knowledge turn' in the English National Curriculum. *The Curriculum Journal*, *22*(2), 243–64.

Layton, D. (1986). *Innovations in Science and Technology Education. Vol. I*. UNIPUB, 4611-F Assembly Drive, Lanham, MD 20706-4391.

Layton, D. (1986). *Science Education and Values Education – an Essential Tension*. In: Brown, J., Cooper, A., Horton, T., Tortes, F. & Zeldin, D. (Eds.), *Science in Schools*, 110–20. Milton Keynes, UK: Open University Press.

Levinson, R. (2003). *Teaching Bioethics in Science: Crossing a Bridge Too Far?* Paper presented at the Annual Meeting of the National Association of Research in Science Teaching. Philadelphia: PA.

Levinson, R. (2006). Towards a theoretical framework for teaching controversial socio-scientific issues. *International Journal of Science Education*, *28*(10), 1201–24.

Levinson, R. (2013). Practice and theory of socio-scientific issues: an authentic model?, *Studies in Science Education*, *49*(1), 99–116.

Levinson, R. (2018). Introducing socio-scientific inquiry-based learning (SSIBL). *School Science Review*, *100*(371), 31–5.

Levinson, R., Douglas, A., Evans, J. E., Kirton, A., Koulouris, P., Turner, S. & Finegold, P. (2001). *Valuable lessons: Engaging with the social context of science in schools*. The Wellcome Trust: https://wellcome.org/sites/default/files/wtd003446_0.pdf.

Levinson, R. & Reiss, M. J. (Eds.) (2003). *Key Issues in Bioethics: A Guide for Teachers*. Psychology Press.

References

Lewis, A. & Lindsay, G. (Eds.) (1999). *Researching Children's Perspectives.* Buckingham: Open University Press.

Lin, F. & Chan, C. K. (2018). Promoting elementary students' epistemology of science through computer-supported knowledge-building discourse and epistemic reflection. *International Journal of Science Education, 40*(6), 668–87.

Macafee, T. & De Simone, J. J. (2012). Killing the bill online? Pathways to young people's protest engagement via social media. *Cyberpsychology, Behavior, and Social Networking, 15*(11), 579–84.

McCrory, A. (2014). Investigating the moral and scientific thinking of 7–8 year olds when taught socio-scientific issues related to energy and genetics. Unpublished PhD thesis. London: University of London, Institute of Education.

McCrory, A. (2018). Scientific enquiry and engaging primary-aged children in science lessons (part 2): why teach science via enquiry? *Journal of Emergent Science, 14*, 28–39.

Metz, K. E. (1998). Scientific inquiry within reach of young children. In: Fraser, B., Tobin, K. (Eds.), *International Handbook of Science Education* (2), 81–96. London: Kluwer.

Millar, R., Bell, D. & Perks, D. (2007). Science education for the 21st century. *Science in Parliament – Harlow then London, 64*(3), 25.

OECD (2021). 'Think green: Education and climate change', *Trends Shaping Education Spotlights*, No. 24, OECD Publishing, Paris, https://doi.org/10.1787/2a9a1cdd-enOfsted. (2019). *Education Inspection Framework.* OFSTED. https://www.gov.uk/government/publications/education-inspection-framework.

Ofsted (2019). *School Inspections Handbook.* London, UK: Office of Standards in Education. https://www.gov.uk/government/publications/school-inspection-handbook-eif/school-inspection-handbook.

Osborne, J. (1995). Recovering reality. *Studies in Science Education, 25*, 3–38.

Oulton, C., Dillon, J. & Grace, M. M. (2004). Reconceptualizing the teaching of controversial issues, *International Journal of Science Education, 26*(4), 411–23.

Owens, D. C., Sadler, T. D. & Zeidler, D. L. (2017). Controversial issues in the science classroom. *Phi Delta Kappan, 99*(4), 45–9.

Piaget, J. (1932). *The Moral Judgement of the Child.* London: Kegan, Paul, Trench, Trubner and Co.

Pollard, A., Wyse, D., Craig, A., Daly, C., Seleznyov, S., Harley, S., Hayward, L., Higgins, S. & McCrory, A. (2023). *Reflective Teaching in Primary Schools.* London: Bloomsbury.

Pope, T. C. (2017). Socioscientific Issues: A framework for teaching ethics through controversial issues in science. *Teach Journal of Christian Education, 11*(2), 8.

Presley, M. L., Sickel, A. J., Muslu, N., Merle-Johnson, D., Witzig, S. B., Izci, K. & Sadler, T. D. (2013). A framework for socio-scientific issues based education. *Science Educator, 22*(1), 26–32.

Ratcliffe, M. (1997). Pupil decision-making about socio-scientific issues within the science curriculum. *International Journal of Science Education, 19*(2), 167–82.

Ratcliffe, M. (2007). Values in the science classroom-the'enacted'curriculum. In *The Re-emergence of Values in Science Education*, 119–32. Leiden: Brill.

Ratcliffe, M. and Grace, M. (2003). *Science Education for Citizenship: Teaching Socio-Scientific Issues.* McGraw-Hill Education (UK).

Reiss, J. (2019). Expertise, agreement, and the nature of social scientific facts or: Against epistocracy. *Social Epistemology, 33*(2), 183–92.

Reiss, M. J. (2009). Ethical reasoning and action in STSE education. In: *International Handbook of Research and Development in Technology Education*, 307–18. Leiden: Brill.

Reiss, M. J. & White, J. (2014). An aims-based curriculum illustrated by the teaching of science in schools. *Curriculum Journal, 25*(1), 76–89.

Ritter, H. W. & Webber, M. M. (1973). Dilemmas in a general theory of planning. *Policy Sciences, 4*(2), 155–69.

Sadler, T. D. (2004). Informal reasoning regarding socioscientific issues: A critical review of research. *Journal of Research in Science Teaching: The Official Journal of the National Association for Research in Science Teaching*, 41(5), 513–36.

Sadler, T. D. (2011). Socio-scientific issues-based education: What we know about science education in the context of SSI. In: *Socio-scientific Issues in the Classroom*, 355–69. Springer: Dordrecht.

Sadler, T. D. & Donnelly, L. A. (2006). Socioscientific argumentation: The effects of content knowledge and morality. *International Journal of Science Education*, 28(12), 1463–88.

Sadler, T. D., Romine, W. L. & Topçu, M. S. (2016). Learning science content through socio-scientific issues-based instruction: A multi-level assessment study. *International Journal of Science Education*, 38(10), 1622–35.

Santos, W. L. D. (2009). Scientific literacy: A Freirean perspective as a radical view of humanistic science education. *Science Education*, 93(2), 361–82.

Scherman, A. & Rivera, S. (2021). Social media use and pathways to protest participation: Evidence from the 2019 Chilean social outburst. *Social Media+ Society*, 7(4), 205.

Schurr, G. (1977). *Science and Ethics*. London: Open University Press.

Shakespeare, D. (2003). Starting an argument in science lessons. *School Science Review*, 85, 103–8.

Slotta, J. D. (2002). Partnerships in the web-based inquiry science environments (WISE). *Cognitive Studies*, 9(3), 351–61.

Slotta, J. D. & Linn, M. C. (2009). *WISE Science: Web-Based Inquiry in the Classroom*. Technology Education: Connections.

Standish, A. & Sehgal-Cuthbert, A. (2017). *Disciplinary Knowledge and School Subjects*. London: UCL IOE Press.

Tal, T., Kali, Y., Magid, S. & Madhok, J. J. (2011). Enhancing the authenticity of a web-based module for teaching simple inheritance. In: *Socio-Scientific Issues in the Classroom*, 11–38. Springer: Dordrecht.

Technology and the Wellcome Trust, O.O.S.A. (2001). Science and the public: A review of science communication and public attitudes toward science in Britain. *Public Understanding of Science*, 10(3), 315–30.

Thier, H. D. & Hill, T. (1988). Chemical Education in schools and the community: the CEPUP project. *International Journal of Science Education*, 10(4), 421–30.

Tisak, M. S. & Turiel, E. (1988). Variation in seriousness of transgressions and children's moral and conventional concepts. *Developmental Psychology*, 24(3), 352.

Turiel, E. (2006). The Development of Morality. In: Eisenberg, N., Damon, W. & Lerner, R. M. (Eds.), *Handbook of Child Psychology: Social, Emotional, and Personality Development*, 789–857. Hoboken NJ: John Wiley & Sons, Inc.

Venville, G. & Donovan, J. (2007). Developing year 2 students' theory of biology with concepts of the gene and DNA. *International Journal of Science Education*, 29(9), 1111–31.

Wellington, J. & Ireson, G. (2013). *Science Learning, Science Teaching*. London: Routledge.

Wintersgill, B. (Ed.) (2017). *Big Ideas for Religious Education*. Exeter: University of Exeter.

Woolley, R. (2010). *Tackling Controversial Issues in the Primary School: Facing Life's Challenges with Your Learners*. London: Routledge.

Wu, J., Snell, G. & Samji, H. (2020). Climate anxiety in young people: a call to action. *The Lancet Planetary Health*, 4(10), 435–6.

Young, M. (2018). Can 'powerful knowledge' be the basis of a school curriculum for all pupils? *The Japanese Journal of Curriculum Studies*, 27, 71–6.

Yuill, N. & Perner, J. (1988). Intentionality and knowledge in children's judgments of actor's responsibility and recipient's emotional reaction. *Developmental Psychology*, 24(3), 358.

Zeidler, D. L. & Zeidler, L. (Eds.) (2003). *The Role of Moral Reasoning on Socio-scientific Issues and Discourse in Science Education* (Vol. 19). Springer Science & Business Media.

Zeidler, D. L., Sadler, T. D., Simmons, M. L. & Howes, E. V. (2005). Beyond STS: A research-based framework for socioscientific issues education. *Science Education*, 89(3), 357–77.

Zeidler, D. L., Sadler, T. D., Applebaum, S. & Callahan, B. E. (2009). Advancing reflective judgment through socioscientific issues. *Journal of Research in Science Teaching: The Official Journal of the National Association for Research in Science Teaching*, 46(1), 74–101.

Chapter 8

Alexander, R. J. (2008). *Towards Dialogic Teaching, 4th edn.* York: Dialogos.

Allen, M. (2019). *Misconceptions in Primary Science, 3rd edn.* McGraw-Hill Education (UK).

Archila, P. A. (2017). Using drama to promote argumentation in science education. *Science & Education*, 26(3), 345–75.

Atasoy, S. & Calik, M. (2022). Development of argumentation based concept cartoons for socioscientific issues: A case of science and art centres. *Education and Science*, 47(211), 323–67.

Av-Shalom, N. A. Y., Zimmerman, R. M., Chinn, C. A. & Duncan, R. G. (2019). Analysis of different categories of epistemic and metacognitive discourse in argumentation. *Studia Paedagogia*, 24(4), 101–18.

Barnes, D. (1976). *From Communication to Curriculum*. Harmondsworth: Penguin.

Bazzul, J. (2016). *Ethics and Science Education: How Subjectivity Matters*. New York: Springer International Publishing.

Blair, T. (2002). PM Speech: 'Science Matters'. *IUBMB Life*, 54(4), 155–9.

Blok, H. P., Ferwerda, H. A., & Kuiken, H. K. editors Huygens' principle, 1690–1990: Theory and applications: proceedings of an international symposium, the Hague/Scheveningen, 10. November 19–22, 1990. (Amsterdam: Elsevier Science Publishers B. V., 1992.)

Born, P., Mirk, P., Mulligan, J. & Price, E. (2006). *Ethics in Citizenship: Tools for Moral Decision–Making*. Middleton WI: Institute for Global Ethics.

Braund, M. (2015). Drama and learning science: an empty space? *British Educational Research Journal*, 41(1), 102–21.

Burns, R. (2017). Using puppets to encourage dialogue in the primary classroom: a study of pupils' perspectives on the use of puppets in their lessons. *Journal of Trainee Teacher Education Research* (8), 127–52.

Carr, S., Rix, C. & Burton, N. (2008). Encouraging reluctant speakers: do puppets have a place in primary science discussions? *Science Teacher Education*, 52, 22–27.

Cartridge, E. (2017). Galileo's 400 year-old theory of free falling objects passes space test, *Science*: https://www.science.org/content/article/galileos-400-year-old-theory-free-falling-objects-passes-space-test.

Cheah, P. Y., Jatupornpimol, N., Suarez-Idueta, L., Hawryszkiewycz, A., Charoenboon, N., Khirikoekkong, N., Wismol, P., Htee Khu, N. & Richardson, E. (2018). Understanding a science-themed puppet theatre performance for public engagement in Thailand. *Wellcome Open Research* (3), 217–31.

Chin, C. & Osborne, J. (2010). Supporting argumentation through students' questions: Case studies in science classrooms. *The Journal of the Learning Sciences*, 19(2), 230–84.

Cuccio-Schirripa, S. & Steiner, H. E. (2000). Enhancement and analysis of science question level for middle school students. *Journal of Research in Science Teaching: The Official Journal of the National Association for Research in Science Teaching*, 37(2), 210–24.

Dawes, L. (2004). Talk and learning in classroom science. *International Journal of Science Education*, 26(6), 677–95.
Department for Business, Energy & Industrial Strategy (2019). Public Attitudes to Science. Available at: https://www.gov.uk/government/publications/public-attitudes-to-science-2019.
Dijksterhuis, J. F. (2004). *Lenses and Waves: Christiaan Huygens and the Mathematical Science of Optics in the Seventeenth Century*. Dordrecht: Springer Science.
Duit, R. (1991). Argumentation in Science Education. *Science Education*, 75(1), 33–42.
Duit, R. & Law, M. (Eds.) (2008). *Argumentation in Science Education*. Dordrecht: Springer.
Duschl, R. (2008). Science education in three-part harmony: Balancing conceptual, epistemic, and social learning goals. *Review of Research in Education*, 32(1), 268–91.
Edmonson, K. (2005). Assessing science understanding through concept maps. In: J. Mintzes, J. Wandersee & J. Novak (Eds.), *Assesing Science Understanding: A Human Contructivist View*, 19–40. Estados Unidos: Elsevier Academic Press.
Egan, K. (1998). The Educated Mind: How Cognitive Tools Shape Our Understanding, *Canadian Journal of Education*, 68(2), 21–38.
Einstein, A. (1905). On the special theory of relativity. *Annals of Physics*, 17, 891–921.
Erduran, S. & Jiménez-Aleixandre, M. P. (2008). *Argumentation in Science Education. Perspectives from Classroom-Based Research*. Dordre-cht: Springer.
Erduran, S., Ozdem, Y. & Park, J. Y. (2015). Research trends on argumentation in science education: A journal content analysis from 1998–2014. *International Journal of STEM Education*, 2(1), 1–12.
Evrekli, E. & Balım, A. G. (2015). The effects of concept cartoons assisted animations on 6th grade students' inquiry learning skills perceptions. *Western Anatolian Journal of Educational Sciences*, 6(11), 109–36.
Fraser, B. J., Tobin, K. G. & McRobbie, C. J. (Eds.) (2012). *Second International Handbook of Science Education* (Vol. 1). Dordrecht: Springer.
Gopnik, A. (2009). *The Philosophical Baby. What Children's Minds Tell us about Truth, Love & Meaning*. London: Bodley Head.
Hackling, M., Smith, P. & Murcia, K. (2011). Enhancing classroom discourse in primary science: The Puppets Project. *Teaching Science*, 57(2), 18–25.
Harlen, W. (Eds.) (2012). Developing Policy, Principles and Practice in Primary School Science Assessment, Nuffield Foundation, London. Available at https://www.nuffieldfoundation.org/wpcontent/uploads/2019/11/Developing_policy_principles_and_practice_in_primary_school_science_assessment_Nuffield_Foundation_v_FINAL.pdf.
Harlow, D. B. (2010). Structures and improvisation for inquiry-based science instruction: A teacher's adaptation of a model of magnetism activity. *Science Education*, 94(1), 142–63.
Keogh, B. & Naylor, S. (2007). Talking and thinking in science. *School Science Review* 88(324), 85–90.
Keogh, B. & Naylor, S. (2009). Puppets count. *Mathematics Teaching*, 213, 32–4.
Kuhn, D. (2010). Teaching and learning science as argument. *Science Education*, 94(5), 810–24.
Lee, Y., Kinzie, M. B. & Whittaker, J. V. (2012). Impact of online support for teachers' open-ended questioning in pre-k science activities. *Teaching & Teacher Education*, 28, 568–77.
Maas, D. & Leauby, B. A. (2005). Concept Mapping – exploring its value as a meaningful learning tool in accounting education. *Perceptions on Accounting Education* (2), 75–98.
McCrory, A & Worthington, K. (2018). *Mastering Primary Science*. London: Bloomsbury.
Mercer, N., Dawes, L., Wegerif, R. & Sams, C. (2004). Reasoning as a scientist: ways of helping children to use language to learn science. *British Educational Research Journal* 30(3), 359–77.
Miller, A. I. (1981). *Albert Einstein's Special Theory of Relativity: Emergence (1905) and Early Interpretation (1905–1911)* (Vol. 4679). Reading, MA: Addison-Wesley.

References

Naylor, S. & Keogh, B. (2013). Concept cartoons: what have we learnt? *Journal of Turkish Science Education, 10*(1).

Naylor, S., Keogh, B. & Downing, B. (2007). Argumentation and primary science. *Research in Science Education, 37*(1), 17–39.

Osborne, J. (2010). Arguing to learn in science: The role of argumentation in the learning process. *International Journal of Science Education, 32*(7), 933–49.

Osborne, J. & Dillon, J. (2010). *Good Practice in Science Teaching: What Research Has to Say*. McGraw-Hill Education (UK).

Osborne, J., Erduran, S. & Simon, S. (2004). Enhancing the quality of argumentation in school science, *Journal of Research in Science Teaching 41*(10), 994–1020.

Osborne, J., Simon, S., Christodoulou, A., Howell-Richardson, C. & Richardson, K. (2013). Learning to argue: A study of four schools and their attempt to develop the use of argumentation as a common instructional practice and its impact on students. *Journal of Research in Science Teaching, 50*(3), 315–47.

Peterson, A., Durrant, I. & Bentley, B. (2015). Student teachers' perceptions of their role as civic educators: evidence from a large higher education institution in England. *British Educational Research Journal, 41*(2), 343–64.

Pollard, A., Wyse, D., Craig, A., Daly, C., Seleznyov, S., Harley, S., Hayward, L., Higgins, S. & McCrory, A. (2023). *Reflective Teaching in Primary Schools*. London: Bloomsbury.

Reiss, J. (2019). Expertise, agreement, and the nature of social scientific facts or: Against epistocracy. *Social Epistemology, 33*(2), 183–92.

Sadler, T. D. (2011). Socio-scientific issues-based education: What we know about science education in the context of SSI. In *Socio-scientific Issues in the Classroom*, 355–69. Dordrecht: Springer.

Sadler, T. D., Romine, W. L. & Topçu, M. S. (2016). Learning science content through socio-scientific issues-based instruction: A multi-level assessment study. *International Journal of Science Education, 38*(10), 1622–35.

Schenk, L., Hamza, K. M., Enghag, M., Lundegård, I., Arvanitis, L., Haglund, K. & Wojcik, A. (2019). Teaching and discussing about risk: Seven elements of potential significance for science education. *International Journal of Science Education, 41*(9), 1271–86.

Sharma, A. & Chunawala, S. (2011). Teachers' understanding of the nature of science, and their views about the primary school environment studies curriculum. In: *Proceedings epiSTEME 4: International Conference to Review Research on Science, Technology and Mathematics Education, Macmillan: Homi Bhabha Centre for Science Education, TIFR*, 75–80.

Simon, S., Naylor, S., Keogh, B., Maloney, J. & Downing, B. (2008). Puppets promoting engagement and talk in science. *International Journal of Science Education, 30*(9), 1229–48.

Smith, J. (2010). *Talk, Thinking and Philosophy in the Primary Classroom*. Exeter: Learning Matters.

Smithsonian Science Education Centre (2022). https://ssec.si.edu/building-awareness-science-education.

Toulmin, S., Rieke, R., & Janik, A. (1984). *An Introduction to Reasoning*. New York: MacMillan.

Tsai, C. C. (2006). Reinterpreting and reconstructing science: Teachers' view changes toward the nature of science by courses of science education. *Teaching and Teacher Education, 22*(3), 363–75.

UK Research and Innovation (2022). Research and Innovation Strategy. Available at: https://www.ukri.org/publications/ukri-strategy-2022-to-2027/ukri-strategy-2022-to-2027/.

Vázquez-Alonso, Á., García-Carmona, A., Manassero-Mas, M. A. & Bennàssar-Roig, A. (2013). Science teachers' thinking about the nature of science: A new methodological approach to its assessment. *Research in Science Education, 43*(2), 781–808.

Vygotsky, L. S. (1978). *Mind in Society: The Development of Higher Psychological Processes*. Cambridge, MA: Harvard University Press.

Wang, J. & Buck, G. (2015). The relationship between Chinese students' subject matter knowledge and argumentation pedagogy. *International Journal of Science Education*, 37(2), 340–66.

Zion, M., Schwartz, R.S., Rimerman-Shmueli, E. & Adler, I. (2020). Supporting teachers' understanding of nature of science and inquiry through personal experience and perception of inquiry as a dynamic process. *Research in Science Education*, 50(4), 1281–304.

Chapter 9

Al-Delaimy, W. K. & Webb, M. (2017). Community gardens as environmental health interventions: Benefits versus potential risks. *Current Environmental Health Reports*, 4(2), 252–65.

Archer, L., Dawson, E., DeWitt, J., Seakins, A. & Wong, B. (2015). 'Science capital': A conceptual, methodological, and empirical argument for extending Bourdieusian notions of capital beyond the arts. *Journal of Research in Science Teaching*, 52(7), 922–48.

Bear Conservation (2022). *Captive Polar Bears*. http://www.bearconservation.org.uk/polar-bears-in-zoos/.

Beeley, K. (2012). *Science in the Early Years. Understanding the World through Play-Based Learning*. London: Featherstone Education.

Bell, P., Lewenstein, B., Shouse, A. & Feder, M. A. (2009). *Learning Science in Informal Environments: People, Places and Pursuits*. Washington, DC: National Academies Press.

Belongia, E. A. & Naleway, A. L. (2003). Smallpox vaccine: The good, the bad, and the ugly. *Clinical Medicine & Research*, 1(2), 87–92.

Brunton, P. & Thornton, L. (2010). *Science in the Early Years: Building Firm Foundations from Birth to Five*. California: Sage.

Colwell, J., Pollard, A. & Pollard, A. (Eds.) (2015). *Readings for Reflective Teaching in Early Education*. London: Bloomsbury.

Dawson, E. (2019). *Equity, Exclusion and Everyday Science Learning: The Experiences of Minoritised Groups*. Abingdon: Routledge.

Dodd, J. & Jones, C. (2010). *Redefining the Role of Botanic Gardens: Towards a New Social Purpose*. Leicester: Research Centre for Museums and Galleries.

Durbach, N. (2000). They might as well brand us: Working class resistance to compulsory vaccination in Victorian England. *The Society for the Social History of Medicine*, 13(1), 45–62.

Eltis, D. (2007). A brief overview of the Trans-Atlantic Slave Trade. Voyages: *The Trans-Atlantic Slave Trade Database*, 1700–810. https://resources.saylor.org/wwwresources/archived/site/wp-content/uploads/2013/05/HIST211-1.3.3-TransAtlanticSlaveTrade.pdf.

Eshach, H. (2007). Bridging in-school and out-of-school learning: Formal, non-formal, and informal education. *Journal of Science Education and Technology*, 16(2), 171–90.

Falk, J. & Storksdieck, M. (2005). Learning science from museums. *Historia, Ciencias, Saude – Maguinhos, Rio de Janeiro*, 12(Suplemento), 117–43.

Habig, B., Gupta, P. & Adams, J. D. (2021). Disrupting deficit narratives in informal science education: Applying community cultural wealth theory to youth learning and engagement. *Cultural Studies of Science Education*, 16(2), 509–48.

Johnson, S. (2004). Learning science in a botanic garden. In: Braund, M. & Reiss, M. J. (Eds.), *Learning Science outside the Classroom*, 63–79. London: RoutledgeFalmer.

Kenyon, E., Terorde-Doyle, D. & Carnahan, S. (2019). *Ethics for the Very Young: A Philosophy Curriculum for Early Childhood Education*. Lanham MD: Rowman & Littlefield.

Louv, R. (2005). *Last Child in the Woods*. London: Atlantic Books.

Martinez-Bravo, M. & Stegmann, A. (2022). In vaccines we trust? The effects of the CIA's vaccine ruse on immunization in Pakistan. *Journal of the European Economic Association*, 20(1), 150–86.

Mujtaba, T., Lawrence, M., Oliver, M. & Reiss, M. J. (2018). Learning and engagement through Natural History Museums. *Studies in Science Education*, 54(1), 41–67.

Nettle, C. (2014). *Community Gardening as Social Action*. Farnham: Ashgate.

Olusoga, D. (2016) *Black and British: A Forgotten History*. London: MacMillan.

Pelčić, G., Karačić, S., Mikirtichan, G. L., Kubar, O. I., Leavitt, F. J., Cheng-Tek Tai, M., Morishita, N., Vuletić, S. & Tomašević, L. (2016). Religious exception for vaccination or religious excuses for avoiding vaccination. *Croatian Medical Journal*, 57(5), 516–21.

Piaget, J. (1951). *Play, Dreams and Imitation in Childhood*. London: Routledge & Kegan Paul.

Pierce, J. & Bekoff, M. (2018). A postzoo future: Why welfare fails animals in zoos. *Journal of Applied Animal Welfare Science*, 21(sup1), 43–8.

Pontifical Academy for Life (2006). Moral reflections on vaccines prepared from cells derived from aborted human fetuses. *The National Catholic Bioethics Quarterly*, 6(3), 541–537.

Ponting, C. (2000). *World History: A New Perspective*. London: Chatto & Windus.

Reiss, M. J. (2017). Teaching the theory of evolution in informal settings to those who are uncomfortable with it. In: Patrick, P. G. (Ed.), *Preparing Informal Science Educators: Perspectives from Science Communication and Education*, 495–507. Cham: Springer.

Reiss, M. J. (2020). Science education in the light of COVID-19: The contribution of History, Philosophy and Sociology of Science. *Science & Education*, 29(4), 1079–92.

Reiss, M. J. (2021). Vaccine hesitancy: Why trust science and science education? In: McCloughlin, T. J. J. (Ed.), *The Nature of Science in Biology: A Source for Educators*, 83–98. Dublin: Graphikon Teo.

Reiss, M. J. (2022). Trust, science education and vaccines. *Science & Education*. DOI: 10.1007/s11191-022-00339-x.

Scott, M. (2007). *Rethinking Evolution in the Museum: Envisioning African Origins*. London: Routledge.

Scott, M. (2010). The pleasures and pitfalls of teaching human evolution in the museum. *Evolution: Education and Outreach*, 3(3), 403–9.

SeaWorld Parks & Entertainment (2022). *Polar Bears: Habitat and Distribution*. https://seaworld.org/animals/all-about/polar-bear/habitat/.

Smith, K. (2016). *Working Scientifically: A Guide for Primary Science Teachers*. London: Routledge.

Turtle, C., Convery, I. & Convery, K. (2015). Forest schools and environmental attitudes: A case study of children aged 8–11 years. *Cogent Education*, 2(1), 1100103.

Vygotsky, L. S. (1978). *Mind in Society: The Development of Higher Psychological Processes*. Cambridge, MA: Harvard University Press.

Whitebread, D., Basilio, M., Kuvalja, M. & Verma, M. (2012). *The Importance of Play*. Cambridge: University of Cambridge, Toy Industries of Europe.

Williams, S. J., Jones, J. P., Gibbons, J. M. & Clubbe, C. (2015). Botanic gardens can positively influence visitors' environmental attitudes. *Biodiversity and Conservation*, 24(7), 1609–20.

Wolfe, R. M. & Sharp, L. K. (2002). Anti-vaccinationists past and present. *British Medical Journal*, 325(7361), 430–2.

Yosso, T. J. (2005). Whose culture has capital? A critical race theory discussion of community cultural wealth. *Race Ethnicity and Education*, 8(1), 69–91.

Chapter 10

Thornton, L. and Brunton, P. (2010). *Science in the Early Years: Building Firm Foundations from Birth to Five*. London: Sage.

Egan, K. (1993). Narrative and learning: A voyage of implications. *Linguistics and Education*, 5(2), 119–26.

Index

Abrahams, I. 47
abstract reasoning 63, 116
advocacy (controversial issues) 83
affirmative neutrality (controversial issues) 83–4
Aikenhead, G. S. 44
Ala ad-Din Abu al-Hasan Ali Ibn Abi-Hazm-al-Qarshi (Ibn Nafis) 10
Albert, L. H. 17
Alderman, N., *The Power* 41
Alexander, R. J. 111–12
Altatawi, Dr 10
Alzheimer's disease 46
American Museum of Natural History (New York) 143
animal rights 4, 32, 39, 152
Anthropocene 46
anthropogenic climate change 37
Anti-Compulsory Vaccination League 145
Anti-Vaccination Society of America 145
appalling conditions (Africa across the Atlantic) 130–1
aquaria, zoos and 137–44
Aquinas, T. 29
Archer, L. 140–1
Archila, P. A. 112, 124
argumentation 6–7, 46, 70, 97, 107, 153–5
  concept maps and cartoons 119–23
  before debating 125–6
  drama and role-play 123–5
  initial 125
  NOS, scientific literacy and 109–11
  in school science education 108–9
  value of talk (*see* talk (argumentation))
Aristotle 32, 35
  Nicomachean Ethics 32
Aronfreed, J. 61
aspirational capital 143–4
assessment 5, 51, 74
  mark scheme 53–4

Religious Studies 53
Salters-Nuffield Advanced level biology course 52
socio-scientific issues 101–5
Atasoy, S. 123
Attenborough, D. 93
Atwood, M. 41
Audi, R. 31
authentic teaching/learning 61
autonomous morality 54, 62

Bandura, A. 61
Banner, I. 73–4
Barenboim, C. 65, 105
Barnes, D. 111
Bartal, I. B. A. 39
Barton, A. C. 44
Bazzul, J., *Ethics and Science Education: How Subjectivity Matters* 3
Beacons for Public Engagement 110
Bear Conservation 138–9
Bekoff, M., 'A Postzoo Future: Why Welfare Fails Animals in Zoos' 137–8
Bentham, J. 31
Bhabha, H. K. 28
Biggs, J. 101
bin Laden, O. 146–7
biodiversity 38
  and conservation 82–3
bioethics education 55, 75, 97
Black Widow 42
Blade Runner 2049 41
Bourdieu, P. 140, 142. *See also* cultural capital theory
breeding animals for facial features 94
British Medical Journal 19
Bronfenbrenner, U. 62
Bruner, J. 95
Bryant, J. A., *Introduction to Bioethics* 3
The Building Awareness program 110

Burns, R. 115
Bybee, R. W. 43–4

caregivers 68
Carr, S. 115
categorical imperative, theory 53
Central Intelligence Agency (CIA) 146–7
Chandler, M. J. 65, 105
character education movement 5, 69
child development 61–2, 95
China 9–10
    Covid-19 controversy in food markets 12–13
    variolation 145
Claire, H. 92
climate change 4, 6, 37–8, 85, 87–9, 102, 124
    and genetics 115, 117, 119
    and sustainability 95
cloning
    animals 81
    ethical dimensions of 118
    and genetic inheritance 102
    humans 117–18
    of non-human animals 81
cognitive development 111
    five-stage model 114, 154
    theories 62–7
cognitive-epistemic system 16–17
cognitive knowledge 120
cognitive-linguistic 111
Collins Dictionary 20
Collis, K. 101
Columbine High School massacre 69
community cultural wealth 7, 142–4
community gardens 136–7
Compulsory Vaccination Act (1853) 145
concept maps and cartoons 119–23, 126
    Chernobyl disaster 121
    cross-links 120–1
    with young children 120–1
conscious realization 69
consequentialism 30–2
controversial issues, teaching 85–6, 92, 95
    advocacy 83
    affirmative neutrality 83–4
    procedural neutrality 84
Copernican model 14
co-teaching 6, 84
Covid-19 pandemic 4, 12, 85, 88, 145, 152
    controversy in food markets 12–13
    origin of 21
    vaccinations 145–7
creationism 17, 80–1
critical scientific literacy 7, 44
cultural capital theory 140, 142
cultural theory 5, 68
Curry, O. S. 29

Dagher, Z. 16
Damon, W. 58, 66–7, 105
Danish Cancer Society 21
Darwin, C., *On the Origin of Species* 86
Davis, N. R. 49
Dawson, E.
    ethnographic study 139
    museums 140–1
deep ecology 38
Defining Issue Test (DIT) 65
deontology 4, 30–2
Department of Children, Schools and Families (DCSF) 80
deVries, B. 66
DeWitt Clinton Park School Garden (New York) 77
divine command system 33
Dodd, J., *Redefining the Role of Botanic Gardens – Towards a New Social Purpose* 136
Doise, W., cognitive coordinations 68
Dolly the sheep (cloned) 81–2, 102
Donnelly, J. 72, 91
Donovan, J. 95
Dunlop, J. 94
Dunn, J. 60

Early Years Foundation Stage (EYFS) 77
Economic and Social Research Council (ESRC) 110
economic capital 140
The Education Reform Act in England (1988) 92
Egan, K. 114, 154
Egypt 9–10
Eilks, I. 44
Einstein, A., theory of relativity 14, 107
Elefante Enamorado ('The Elephant in Love') 11–12
El Pindal, Spain (painting) 11
empathy 29, 39, 60, 68
enquiry-based learning 98, 154
environmental ethics 4, 38, 79, 152
equivalence principle 107
Erduran, S. 16
Eshach, H. 127
ethical issues 1, 29, 50–1, 57, 95, 97, 101, 126, 128, 136, 147, 153
    as food inequalities 77
    inequity 34–5
    lack of expertise 91
    in school science 85
ethics 1–2, 4–5, 7–8, 25, 57, 74, 87, 153. *See also* morality
    consequentialism, utilitarianism and virtue 30–2
    environmental 4, 38, 79, 152
    feminist approaches to 4, 35–6

intergenerational 4, 37–8, 152
  morality and values 25–7
  role of religion in 4, 26, 32–3
  and science 7, 139, 150
Ethics and Citizenship 116
ethics education 5, 46, 57, 71, 152, 155
  moral development and 58–9
  socio-scientific issues and rise of 92–6
euthanasia, ethics of 53–4, 83
Evagorou, M. 101

Facebook 21–2, 89
familial capital 143
family resemblance approach 16–17
Features of Science (FOS) 16, 124
feminist approaches to ethics 4, 35–6
Ferguson, T. J. 65
Feyerabend, P., *Against Method* 14
Fisher, R. A. 18–19
  personality 19
Forest School 132, 154
  ethical questions 134
  normative terms 134
  positive pro-environmental attitudes 133
  principles of 133
formal learning 81, 127, 150, 155
Frank, A. 75
Freud, S. 61
  Psychoanalytical Theory 59
  theory of moral development 59–60
Friere, P. 34

Galilei, G. 107–8
Garbarino, J. 62
gardens, learning 76–7, 136–7, 139–44
gender inequality 35
genetic testing 85
giant pandas (*Ailuropoda melanoleuca*) 139
Gibbs, J. 145
Gilligan, C. 66–7
Gola, B. 79
Golden Rule 28
Grace, M. 101
Greenspan, S. 65, 105
gut-feeling test 116

Habig, B. 143–4
habitat loss 1
Hackling, M. 115
Haidt, J. 28–9
Hall, E. 91
Halstead, J. M. 58, 69
Hansson, S. O. 18
harnessing 21, 97
Harvey, W. 10
Hill, T. 101
history of science 9–12, 15–16, 86

HIV, origins 13
Hodson, D. 44
Holden, C. 92
Howes, C. 60
Human 2.0 42
human papillomavirus (HPV) vaccine 21
Hume, D. 72
The Hunger Games series 41

Ibn Nafis, *Sharah al Tashreeh al Qanoon*
  (*Commentary on anatomy of the Canon
  of Avicenna*) 10
identification 59, 61
inclusion of ethics (science) 3, 83, 93
  arguments against 71–4
  arguments for 74–7
  values, ethics and controversial issues 83–4
individual rights
  and autonomy 28
  and obligations 66
inequalities 4, 7, 34, 38, 45, 47, 77, 139, 146, 153
inequity 34–5, 37
informal sector/science education 3, 6–7, 82–3, 127, 154
  gardens, learning in 136–7
  learning, settings 128–32, 150
  museums and botanic gardens 139–44
  place of ethics in 144
  vaccination 144–7
  young children (*see* young children)
  zoos and aquaria 137–44
inheritance 94–5, 100, 102
Inquiry-based Science Education, Socio-
  scientific Issues and Citizenship
  Education 98
intergenerational ethics 4, 37–8, 152
internalization 58–9, 68
Irzik, G. 15–16
Ishiguro, K., *Klara and the Sun* 41

Jenner, E. 145
Johnson, S. 136
Jones, A.
  *Ethics in the Science and Technology
  Classroom* 3
  *Redefining the Role of Botanic Gardens –
  Towards a New Social Purpose* 136
Joyce, J. 12

kākāpōs (*Strigops habroptilus*) 139
Kampourakis, K. 15
Kant, I. 30, 53. *See also* theory of ethics, Kantian
Keogh, B. 114, 122
knowledge 4, 9, 14, 45–6, 72, 89, 101, 103,
  112–13, 119, 126, 152
Kohlberg, L. 54–5, 62, 65–7, 105
  theory of moral judgements 66–7, 105

Kuhn, T. 14
Kutnick, P. 68

land ethic 38
La Velle, L., *Introduction to Bioethics* 3
Lederman, N. 15
Leopold, A. 38
Levinson, R. 73, 112
    Key Issues in Bioethics: A Guide for Teachers 3
life-cycle assessment (LCA) 50
linguistic capital 143
Liverpool Life Sciences UTC 48–9
Louv, R. 132
Lucas, G., *Star Wars: Attack of the Clones* 118

Macip, S., *Where Science and Ethics Meet: Dilemmas at the Frontiers of Medicine and Biology* 3
The MaddAddam Trilogy 41
'Mammals in pouches' 128–9
Mandela, N. 75
Marxist theory 36
mass media 60, 88
mathematical truth 9, 22–3
The Matrix Resurrections 42
Matthews, G., *Philosophy and the Young Child* 69
Matthews, M. 16
McComas, W. F. 15
McCrory, A. 3, 102, 105, 115–17, 119–20, 124
McMillan, M. 132
mental health and well-being 89
Mercer, N. 112
Merton, R. 12
Mesoamerica 9
Mesopotamia 9–10
Microscope 108
Millar, R. 47
modelling 61
moral development 5, 54–5, 57, 105, 152
    affective component 59
    behavioural component 58
    cognitive component 58
    cognitive developmental theories 62–7
    and education in schools 58–9
    psychoanalytic theories 59–61
    social learning theories 61–2
    subsequent research into moral reasoning 67–9
moral foundations, universal 28–9
morality 4–5, 25, 54, 58, 60, 72, 133, 152
    as absolutes 30
    compassion and empathy 29
    culturally specific/universal 27–9, 152
    culture in 152
    diversity 29
    of reciprocity 62, 103
    and values, ethics 25–7
moral realism 62
moral reasoning 54, 57–8, 62, 64–6
    ethical and 86
    four-component model of 65
    moral motivation 68
    subsequent research into 67–9
moral thinking and perspective taking (MPTP) 104–5
moral values 28, 58, 62, 69, 103, 117
Mullins, D. A. 29
multi-modal approach 7
Musil, R. 12

National Curriculum 42, 52, 80–1, 93, 95
National Geographic 48
nature of science (NOS) 4, 14–17, 74, 89, 91, 107, 109–11, 113, 126, 145, 150, 155
navigational capital 143–4
Naylor, S. 114, 122
Nettle, C. 137
Never Let Me Go 41
New Scientist magazine 21
news test 116
Newton law 11, 14–15
New Zealand Garden Bird Survey 22
Nola, R. 15–16
non-formal learning 127, 155
normal science 14
Northey Street City Farm (community garden) 137
Nunner-Winkler, G. 68

objective morality 25, 27–8, 33
Obsessive Compulsive Disorder 46
Oedipus complex 59
Office for Standards in Education (England) 93
Office of Science and Technology (OST) 88, 110
Ofsted (Office for Standards in Education, Children's Services and Skills) 42, 93
Oil palm (*Elaeis guineensis*), plantations 2
oppression 4, 34, 36–7, 152
Osborne, J. 109, 112–13
out-of-school learning 127–8, 153

Parkland protests 88
PARRISE (Promoting Attainment of Responsible Research and Innovation in Science Education) project 98–100
Pauling, L. 19
pedagogy/pedagogical approaches 7, 18, 89, 97, 102, 124, 134, 149–50, 152–4
    practical work 46–9
    project work 49–51
    puppets 115
Perner, J. 65, 105

Personal, Social and Health Education (PSHE) 73, 91, 93–6
philosophy and sociology 4, 12–14, 25, 38, 91, 123, 152
Philosophy for Children (P4C) movement 69–70, 81
photosynthesis 76–7
Piaget, J. 54–5, 62–3, 66–7, 69, 101, 103, 105, 133
   child, judgements 64–5
   consciousness and practice of rules 63
   Theory of Moral Development 62
Pierce, J., 'A Postzoo Future: Why Welfare Fails Animals in Zoos' 137–8
place of ethics (science education) 7, 150–1
   in informal science education 144
   in socio-scientific issues 86–7
polar bear (*Ursus maritimus*) 138–9
polio vaccination (Pakistan) 147
Popper, K., criterion of falsifiability 13–14, 17
post-primary science education 91
power 37, 88
powerful knowledge 5, 45, 89
pre-school children 78
primary schools 6, 71, 76, 79, 91–5, 115, 120
Pritchard, M. 70
procedural neutrality 84
pseudoscience 4
   multiplicity of criteria 18
   science vs. 17–20
psychoanalytic theories 5, 59–61
Ptolemaic model 14
public awareness of science 110
public engagement with science 110
pug (breeding animals for facial features) 94
PUPPETS (Puppets Promoting Engagement in Talk in Science Project) project 115
Putnam, R. D. 21

Qualifications and Curriculum Authority (QCA) 80
questioning 112

Ratcliffe, M. 101
reason-based ethics 33
reductio ad absurdum (proof by contradiction) 23
Reiss, M. J. 44, 47, 90, 95, 101
   An Aims-based Curriculum 45
   Key Issues in Bioethics: A Guide for Teachers 3
religion in ethics 4, 26, 32–3
Religious Education (RE) 80–1, 89, 93
resistant capital 143
Rest, J. R. 59, 65–6
Ritter, H. W. 86
Roberts, D. A. 43–5
role-model test 116

Roth, W. M. 44
Royal Horticultural Society 136
Royal Institution's 'Young Person's Programme' 110
Rule, B. G. 65
rule test 116
Ryder, J. 73–4

Salters-Nuffield Advanced level biology course 52
Saxena, A., *Ethics in Science: Pedagogic Issues and Concerns* 3
Schaeffer, J. 49
school gardens 76–7
Schurr, G. 91
Schwartz, B. 75
science 4, 9, 45, 152
   capital 7, 140–1
   and ethics 5–7, 139, 150 (*see also* ethics)
   vs. pseudoscience 17–20
   social media and politics 20–2
   and society 86–7, 89
   as value-free knowledge 91
Science Capital Teaching Approach 90
science curriculum for human flourishing 45–6, 71, 86, 91, 95–6, 101
science education 1, 4, 8, 16, 34, 41, 71, 87, 152–3
   aims of 41–3
   argumentation in 108–9
   decision-making within 149
   early years and primary 77–80
   ethical thinking 149
   goal 89
   informal sector 82–3
   national curriculum 42, 52
   practical work 5
   secondary schools 80–2
   teaching and communication 3–4, 6–7, 73–5, 80, 84, 111, 151
   visions 5, 43–6
science educators 4, 7–8, 15–16, 47, 72, 86, 89–90, 99, 126, 149–51, 154–5
scientific creationism 17–18
scientific knowledge 1, 11, 15, 42, 47, 51, 74, 81, 86–7, 93, 105, 108, 119, 153
scientific literacy 5–7, 44, 89, 97, 105, 109–12, 126, 142, 152–3
Scientific Revolution 9, 14
scientism 14
Scott, M. 131
secondary school systems 6, 47, 71, 73, 80–2, 91, 93, 98, 109
self-control, development 61
Shakespeare, D. 96
Shweder, R. 28
Sierra Leonean group 139–40
Simon, S. 109, 115

Simple Inheritance and Global Warming modules 100
Sjöström, J. 44
smelting 12
Smetana, J. G. 105
Snowpiercer 41
social capital 20, 143
social-institutional system 16, 36
social interaction 20–1, 60, 68, 113
social learning theories 61–2, 68
Social Market Foundation 88
social media 4, 60, 88–9, 144
    and activism 88, 151–2
    and politics 4, 20–2
social sciences, truth 9, 22–3, 152
socio-political action 44
Socio-scientific Inquiry-based Learning (SSIBL) 98–9
socio-scientific issues 6, 46, 51, 73–4, 151, 154–5
    assessment 101–5
    ethical decision-making frameworks and authentic scenarios 97–100
    ethical thinking 153
    MPTP 104–5
    place of ethics in 86–7
    real-life engagement with 87–90, 97–8
    and rise of ethics 92–6
    in school science 90–2
    web-based models 97, 100–1
    and wicked problems 85–6, 95
The Spiral of Discovery 133–4, 154
Squid Game 42
STEM enrichment programmes 143
Stolley, P. 19
structural oppression 36
Structure of Observed Learning Outcome (SOLO) 101
sugar tongs (slave trade) 129–30
surplus value 36

talk (argumentation) 111
    dialogic approach to teaching 111
    puppets 113–19
Tal, T. 100
Taylor, P. W. 58
teachers 6–7, 18, 47, 51, 55, 68, 70–4, 80–1, 83–4, 89, 91, 93, 95–7, 99, 122, 149
    initial argumentation 125
    pedagogy 134, 151
    use of puppets 114–15
    value of talk 111–13
Terri Schiavo case 97
theories of justice 4, 36–7, 152
theory of ethics, Kantian 32
    deontological ethics 30
    morality 26
    theory of universal moral law 35

Thier, H. D. 101
Thunberg, G. 6, 89
Tolppanen, S. 49–50
Trevethan, S. D. 66
Turiel, E. 67, 105
Turner, S. 73, 112
Turtle, C. 133
21st Century Science programme 110

Under the Skin 41
United Nations Climate Summit 89
universalism 28–9
utilitarianism 4, 31–2

vaccination 43, 87
    Covid-19 145–6
    HPV 21
    Influenza 20
    learning about 144–7
    objections to several vaccines 146
    smallpox 145
Valuable Lessons 73
value-free knowledge 73, 91, 112
values 58, 69, 91, 96
    ethics and 3–4, 25–7, 29, 33, 83–4, 154
    moral 58–9, 62, 117
    socio-scientific issues 102–3
variolation 145
Venville, G. 95
Virginia Tech massacre 69
virtue ethics 4, 30–2
Vygotsky, L. S. 112, 133

Walker, L. J. 66–7
water inequality 48–9
Watson, J. B. 61
weak anthropocentrism 38
Web-based Inquiry Science Environment (WISE) 100–1
Webber, M. M. 86
Wellcome Trust 88, 110
Westworld 42
Whitehouse, H. 28–9
White, J., *An Aims-based Curriculum* 45
Whiting, B. B. 68
Whiting, J. W. M. 68
whole-school approach 94, 96–7
wicked problem 86, 95
Wilmott, C., *Where Science and Ethics Meet: Dilemmas at the Frontiers of Medicine and Biology* 3
Wittgenstein, L. 16
Woolf, V. 12
Woolley, R., *Tackling Controversial Issues in the Primary School* 92
World Health Organization 20

The Yellow Emperor's Manual of Corporeal Medicine 10
Yosso, T. 142–3
young children 60, 65, 95, 114–15, 151, 154
   asking questions 135
   concept maps with 120
   explore 135
   Forest School (*see* Forest School)
   philosophical puzzlement 70
   reflecting and evaluating 135–6
   seeking understanding 135
Young, M., *Bringing Knowledge Back In* 45
Yuill, N. 65, 105

Zeidler, D. L. 90, 97
zoological gardens 137–44

www.ingramcontent.com/pod-product-compliance
Lightning Source LLC
Chambersburg PA
CBHW080550230426
43663CB00015B/2778